THE COMPLETE
IDIOT'S
GUIDE TO

Low-Fat Vegan Cooking

by Bo Rinaldi

ALPHA

A member of Penguin Group (USA) Inc.

ALPHA BOOKS

Published by Penguin Group (USA) Inc.

Penguin Group (USA) Inc., 375 Hudson Street, New York, New York 10014, USA • Penguin Group (Canada), 90 Eglinton Avenue East, Suite 700, Toronto, Ontario M4P 2Y3, Canada (a division of Pearson Penguin Canada Inc.) • Penguin Books Ltd., 80 Strand, London WC2R 0RL, England • Penguin Ireland, 25 St. Stephen's Green, Dublin 2, Ireland (a division of Penguin Books Ltd.) • Penguin Group (Australia), 250 Camberwell Road, Camberwell, Victoria 3124, Australia (a division of Pearson Australia Group Pty. Ltd.) • Penguin Books India Pvt. Ltd., 11 Community Centre, Panchsheel Park, New Delhi— 110 017, India • Penguin Group (NZ), 67 Apollo Drive, Rosedale, North Shore, Auckland 1311, New Zealand (a division of Pearson New Zealand Ltd.) • Penguin Books (South Africa) (Pty.) Ltd., 24 Sturdee Avenue, Rosebank, Johannesburg 2196, South Africa • Penguin Books Ltd., Registered Offices: 80 Strand, London WC2R 0RL, England

International Standard Book Number: 978-1-61564-187-1
Library of Congress Catalog Card Number: 2012930857

14   13   12   8   7   6   5   4   3   2   1

Interpretation of the printing code: The rightmost number of the first series of numbers is the year of the book's printing; the rightmost number of the second series of numbers is the number of the book's printing. For example, a printing code of 12-1 shows that the first printing occurred in 2012.

Printed in the United States of America

Note: This publication contains the opinions and ideas of its author. It is intended to provide helpful and informative material on the subject matter covered. It is sold with the understanding that the author and publisher are not engaged in rendering professional services in the book. If the reader requires personal assistance or advice, a competent professional should be consulted.

The author and publisher specifically disclaim any responsibility for any liability, loss, or risk, personal or otherwise, which is incurred as a consequence, directly or indirectly, of the use and application of any of the contents of this book.

Most Alpha books are available at special quantity discounts for bulk purchases for sales promotions, premiums, fund-raising, or educational use. Special books, or book excerpts, can also be created to fit specific needs. For details, write: Special Markets, Alpha Books, 375 Hudson Street, New York, NY 10014.

Publisher: *Marie Butler-Knight*	**Copy Editor:** *Christine Hackerd*
Associate Publisher: *Mike Sanders*	**Cover Designer:** *William Thomas*
Executive Managing Editor: *Billy Fields*	**Book Designers:** *William Thomas, Rebecca Batchelor*
Senior Acquisitions Editor: *Brook Farling*	**Indexer:** *Tonya Heard*
Senior Development Editor: *Christy Wagner*	**Layout:** *Brian Massey*
Senior Production Editor: *Kayla Dugger*	**Proofreader:** *John Etchison*

Contents

Introduction

This book is a collective effort from a lifelong journey that has brought me incredible health with many fascinating discoveries along the way. I've been a vegan since 1960, when a doctor gave my mother the book *Back to Eden*. At the time, I had severe, seemingly incurable asthma and allergies. Within 2 weeks of following the concepts outlined in that book, I was cured, and I've followed the path of a plant-based lifestyle ever since—and created and continue to enjoy many of the low-fat dishes I've included in this book.

Low-fat vegan cooking includes popular ingredients and recipes from around the world that are sure to tantalize any palate. Using all-natural ingredients, the incredible tastes and culinary styles of low-fat vegan cooking can satisfy your body while helping maintain optimal heart health, your ideal weight, and low cholesterol.

At the start of this project, I thought the idea of writing a low-fat vegan cookbook was both inspiring and necessary. In this book, I use the 80-10-10 approach made popular by individuals such as Dr. McDougall and Dr. Douglas Graham. Supported as the best low-fat approach, it's defined as the percentage of calories derived from our food: complex carbohydrates (80), protein (10), and fat (10). Using this approach, you'll never feel starved for nutrition or flavor, and your body won't be taxed by unnecessary fats and unwanted calories. A plant-based diet like this is the healthiest way to live a long and productive life.

I grew up in Southern California in the 1950s, and I can tell you we all had our fair share of rich vegetarian food. Ever since I was a teenage vegan in the '60s, I saw many people eating copious amounts of dairy and other fat-filled foods that actually caused more harm than good. This set the stage for my exploration into the vegan food movement, the low-fat approach to recipe creation, and the utilization of the plant kingdom to create what we now call "vegan fusion."

The organic health foods boom of the 1960s ushered in many innovations in natural healing, but it wasn't until we saw the benefits of eating low-fat foods that we began to realize the true benefits such as boosting energy, improving the immune system, and maintaining a perfect weight. Today, anyone can benefit from lowering their fat intake—after all, every gram of fat is 9 empty calories. Compare that with every gram of carbohydrate, which contributes 4 nutrition-filled calories.

In this book, I share the many options of this incredible lifestyle and how you can approach it one meal at a time. I think you'll find the recipes delicious, satisfying, fun to make, and most importantly, extremely healthy. This book is different from many because with every recipe, I've included nutrition and scientific facts, detailed information on the fat and caloric values of the dish, as well as some of the tasty benefits you can expect to experience. In addition, I show you many of the secrets chefs use in natural food creation. I've been consulting in the vegan world for years, creating recipes, menus, and restaurants, and now I share much of that experience with you in this book.

In just a short while, you'll be a master of low-fat vegan cooking, enjoying the tastes and balance only a plant-based diet can deliver. And you'll feel better than ever knowing you've helped your body and health by eliminating the majority of fat from your diet.

Create any of the more than 200 recipes included in this book, and you, your family, and your friends will marvel at just how wonderful low-fat vegan food is.

May this book answer all your questions and serve as a lifelong guide to your optimal health and well-being, all thanks to low-fat vegan cooking.

How This Book Is Organized

I've organized this book to give you the most information about low-fat vegan recipes in a way that's easy to understand and use on a daily basis.

Part 1, Low-Fat Vegan Living, introduces you to the importance of a low-fat vegan way of eating and living. You learn what to eat, how to prepare it, and what to stock in your pantry. This part also explains basic nutrition principles and the ideal dietary guidelines of eating 80 percent carbs, 10 percent fat, and 10 percent protein. After Part 1, you'll understand how to eat to prevent disease, attain your perfect weight, and maintain a happy, healthy body.

Part 2, Great Starts to Good Mornings, covers a variety of dishes to get your day started, including light starters and lots of hearty breakfast meals to fuel your body after an evening of rest.

Part 3, In the Lunchbox, provides a variety of midday meals that will expand your thinking beyond sandwiches. A variety of hot and chilled soup recipes are presented, along with many salads and slaw recipes with options to be accompanied by grains, beans, and fruits—complete with scrumptious dressings and toppings. A chapter of unique wraps and rolls rounds out this part.

Part 4, Sauces, Spreads, Snacks, and More, teaches you how to make flavorful sauces and gravies to enhance dishes and create ethnic flavors. Marinade recipes are available to flavor tofu, vegetables, and seasonal greens. A chapter of dips, spreads, and snacks offers healthy, low-fat treats for between meals as well as entertaining friends and family.

Part 5, Sumptuous Suppertime, offers a host of entrée ideas, from noodle dishes, to healthy versions of comfort foods, to veggie-packed meals. Chilies, hearty stews, tapas, grains, bean- and veggie-based mains, as well as numerous twists on internationally classic recipes, are all here to make low-fat vegan eating delicious and fun!

Part 6, Sweets and Sippers, offers delicious and healthy sweet endings for any meal. A variety of healthy desserts are available to top off any meal or for a midday treat. Tonics, teas, and fabulous fresh fruit drink ideas are also provided for satisfying between-meal options.

At the back of the book, I've included a glossary of terms you need to know, followed by extra resources to guide you in your quest for knowledge about low-fat vegan cooking and nutrition in general.

Extras

Throughout the book, I've included little nuggets of extra information. Here's what to look for:

FRESH FACT

In these sidebars, I've included tons of fun facts and bits of additional information regarding low-fat vegan cooking.

TASTY TIP

For tips and extra bits of useful information, check out these sidebars.

DEFINITION

Turn to these sidebars for definitions of ingredients, cooking terms, and other words you might not be familiar with.

HEADS-UP

These sidebars offer gentle warnings to help keep you on the right track.

But Wait! There's More!

Have you logged on to idiotsguides.com lately? If you haven't, go there now! As a bonus to the book, we've included additional low-fat vegan recipes online you'll want to check out. Point your browser to idiotsguides.com/lowfatvegancooking, and enjoy!

Acknowledgments

As an author, it's invaluable to know and work closely with an agent who gets it. My agent, Marilyn Allen, is one such person who has both a big heart and a savvy eye.

Having worked in many natural food restaurants and health food stores, I always enjoyed creating life-giving recipes and menus. The low-fat vegan recipes included here are the result of these creations. I thank everyone I have ever worked with in these incredible venues.

Big thanks to Beryl Greensea, who worked side by side with me on the recipe creation and nutritional information in this book. A vegan chef who is a true example of the vibrancy a plant-based diet can offer, Beryl adds much personal knowledge to this work.

Major gratitude goes to Tina Leigh, vegan chef extraordinaire. Tina is the founder of Haute Health and is an acclaimed gourmet vegan chef, food writer, and holistic health counselor. Many of the recipes in this book have been created using Tina's genius in the kitchen. Tina is a true leader in the field of plant-based nutrition, is a member of the American Association of Drugless Practitioners, has been featured in *Cooking Light Magazine*, and has appeared on Fox News and Food Network.

Infinite thanks go to the staff at the Blossoming Lotus Restaurant for serving all organic vegan dishes to our customers every day. To General Manager Tim Hitchins, thank you and our team for your untiring commitment to creating our amazing award-winning dishes.

And of course, thanks to one of the best friends anyone could ever have, my co-founder of Vegan Fusion and Blossoming Lotus, Mark Reinfeld. Your deep and wise ways have allowed us all to blossom.

To the love of my life, the brightest light I have ever known, Star Rinaldi. I was blessed the day I met you, and I am forever in your grace as your beauty and wisdom feed me the one ingredient we all need the most, love.

To you, the reader, from my heart to yours, thank you for letting me share this guide with you. May it inspire you and your family to create these fun, natural, and delicious dishes whenever you want to feel your best.

This book would not have been possible without the vision and creative energy of my acquisitions editor, Brook Farling. Thank you for your belief in me and my writings.

Special Thanks to the Technical Reviewer

The Complete Idiot's Guide to Low-Fat Vegan Cooking was reviewed by an expert who double-checked the accuracy of what you'll learn here, to help us ensure that this book gives you everything you need to know about preparing delicious, low-fat vegan meals. Special thanks are extended to Trish Sebben-Krupka.

Trademarks

All terms mentioned in this book that are known to be or are suspected of being trademarks or service marks have been appropriately capitalized. Alpha Books and Penguin Group (USA) Inc. cannot attest to the accuracy of this information. Use of a term in this book should not be regarded as affecting the validity of any trademark or service mark.

Low-Fat Vegan Living

In Part 1, I explain the many health benefits of a low-fat vegan lifestyle. You learn about the relationship between your body and the nutrients it requires—such as enzymes, vitamins, minerals, carbohydrates, protein, and fat—and why those nutrients are important to your overall well-being and heart health.

You also learn some of the important tricks of the trade that help ensure your low-fat vegan food always tastes amazing while offering you the best nutrition.

Finally, Part 1 provides an in-depth overview of the staple ingredients and specific tools that will help you succeed in creating gourmet healthy food, the low-fat vegan way.

The Fat Factor

In This Chapter

- The 80 percent carbs, 10 percent fat, and 10 percent protein ideal
- Complex carbs—complete nutrition
- Low-fat eating for disease prevention
- Keeping your heart happy and healthy

When it comes to nutrition and the best diet, questions and answers, myths and misinformation, confusion and outrageous claims abound. So what's the answer? Is it different for everyone? Is there one miracle diet that supports perfect health for everyone?

A low-fat vegan diet sure is a great place to start. This way of eating can help you lose weight, lower your blood pressure and cholesterol, curb your cravings, balance your mood, and increase your energy. Eliminating animal products and excess fat from your diet reduces stress on your digestive system and significantly decreases your risk of numerous diseases. Eating a low-fat vegan diet supplies a vast range of nutrients essential for vibrant health and can help you transform a stagnant, fatigued body into a lean, fit one. It's no miracle, but a low-fat vegan lifestyle can effect some pretty miraculous changes in the way you look and feel!

The Ideal 80-10-10 Formula

The ideal balance of *macronutrients* follows a simple formula: 80-10-10. Don't worry, those aren't the measurements you'll end up with eating a low-fat vegan diet! Rather, it's the percentage of complex carbohydrates (80), protein (10), and fat (10) you need in your diet to obtain balance and well being. Therefore, 80 percent of your caloric intake will be from complex carbohydrates, those plant-based ingredients that are known to offer optimum health.

The 80-10-10 ratio closely mimics the diet of our nomadic ancestors, who—before the introduction of agriculture—survived by foraging for and eating mostly fruits, vegetables, nuts, and seeds. It was only after organized farming became widespread that humans began to rely on cereal grains as staple foods and to eat concentrated fats like oil and butter. Our modern eating habits have changed radically since then and, unfortunately, for the worse since the advent of industrialized food production.

Many health professionals still suggest you get up to 30 percent of your daily calories from fat and 30 percent from protein. That is a recipe for a health disaster, and when you consider the national epidemic of preventable diseases like diabetes and heart disease, you can see that we're suffering for it. The funny thing is, even the USDA says just 10 percent protein, and even less for fat, is adequate for most people during nearly any stage of life! So telling people they can eat up to 30 percent of their daily calories from fat alone lends justification to what's actually overindulgence.

A vegan diet that follows the 80-10-10 guidelines replaces artery-clogging animal fats and unnecessary protein with nutrient-packed whole foods that change your body from the inside out. Eating an 80-10-10 diet means you rely on vegetables and fruit for most of your complex carbs. You can eat a low-fat vegan diet using rice, bread, and potatoes as the mainstay of your meals, but doing so means missing out on the wonderful array of flavors, vitamins, minerals, enzymes, and other phytonutrients in fruits and vegetables. Bland, starchy foods also tempt you to use salt, sugar, or fat to enhance the flavor. For example, have you noticed how much tastier potatoes are when they're deep-fried and covered in salt? When you treat your potatoes like that, suddenly your vegan meal isn't very low-fat anymore! Getting the majority of your carbohydrates from fruits and vegetables instead opens the door to an endless variety of ingredients and makes every meal a feast.

The great thing about 80-10-10 is that you can pretty much eat whatever amount you like. Vegetables are nutrient-dense but are low in calories, so instead of restricting yourself to tiny portions, you can fill your plate. The more you eat, the more essential vitamins, minerals, and fiber you get!

You can end the cycle of overeating triggered by consuming nutrient-deficient processed foods. Giving your body the nutrients it needs squelches the cravings that result from nutritional imbalances. Not only can you eat low-fat vegan food in larger quantities than more calorie-dense foods, you also can eat *more* calories than someone who eats a high-fat diet, and still lose or maintain weight. Your body burns carbohydrates for fuel, so a regular supply of complex carbs stokes your metabolism and helps your body expend more calories.

By filling your body with nutrients and firing up your metabolism on the 80-10-10 low-fat vegan diet, you can prevent and combat a multitude of health problems. One of the main benefits to this diet is that you consume ample amounts of antioxidants that protect your body from *free radical* damage. Eating 80-10-10 keeps you lean, which protects against obesity-related illnesses like heart disease and diabetes.

> **DEFINITION**
>
> **Free radicals** are toxins that attack DNA, mitochondria, and other essential parts of your cells. Damage caused by free radicals—also called oxidative damage, or oxidation—is an underlying cause of illnesses such as cardiovascular disease, cancer, common colds, inflammatory diseases like arthritis and asthma, blindness, dementia, and Alzheimer's disease.

Another benefit you'll notice from your low-fat vegan diet is an improved balance in your mood and emotions. If you've ever hit the supermarket after a bad day and just *had* to buy a tub of ice cream or a big bag of nacho chips, you know food has a powerful effect on how you feel. Eating low-fat vegan food can banish cravings so you feel calm, balanced, and in control. Plus, cutting out all the trans-fats and chemical additives in snack foods helps your brain regain its own chemical balance.

Your body is a machine designed to run on complex carbohydrates. The ratio of nutrients offered in a vegan diet focused on maintaining the 80-10-10 guidelines provides optimum nutrition without the excess fat and protein that cause illness. It greatly improves your digestion, creates boundless energy, balances mood swings, and cuts cravings.

Transforming the way your body works from the inside makes changing your outer appearance a whole lot easier, too. All the water in those fruits and vegetables keeps you hydrated, which helps you lose weight and stay lean. The low-fat vegan diet not only gives you energy to burn, it also helps clear out chronic complaints—such as congestion, asthma, allergies, and irritable bowel syndrome—that slow you down and prevent you from feeling your best.

Craving Carbs?

If you turn to bread and pasta for comfort or think about eating a candy bar when struck with hunger pangs, it's because your body craves carbohydrates. You crave carbs because you need them for proper brain function and because your body utilizes simple sugars as an energy source. The high-carb foods you crave satisfy the body's call for carbohydrates, but there's a healthier and more efficient way to satisfy your body's needs than to gorge on low-nutrient bread and other "comfort foods." In fact, there's a drastic difference between the various types of carbohydrates and the way your body utilizes the energy they provide.

FRESH FACT

In the natural world, you actually obtain carbohydrates in proper ratios in regard to fats and proteins. Fruits, vegetables, and leafy greens all provide small amounts of both protein and fat in addition to carbs, and they do so in proportions that promote ideal health. On the other hand, food sources high in fat and protein are rare in nature and harder to access. Consider how many tiny sesame seeds you'd need to grow and harvest to make them a regular source of important nutrients. There's a good reason, aside from plant procreation, why nuts have such hard shells that are difficult to open: these concentrated foods are best when eaten in moderation.

You don't need to cut out carbs to cut out cravings; you just need to eat the right ones. Carbohydrates get a lot of bad press, but only some of them deserve it. The two major kinds of carbohydrates fall into the categories of either simple or complex. Simple carbohydrates include glucose and sucrose, which are found in sugar, alcohol, white rice, traditional pasta, and anything made with white flour such as bread, cakes, and cookies. Imagine your body is a furnace. Eating simple carbs is like throwing lighter fluid on a fire. Your energy flares as the sugar hits your bloodstream, but your body reacts by producing insulin to bring the "fire" under control. Insulin is like a bucket of cold water. Once it hits your bloodstream, your energy fizzles out and you crave more sugar.

By comparison, eating complex carbohydrates provided by a well-balanced, whole-food, low-fat vegan diet is like feeding a fire with good-quality firewood. The slow burn provides heat and energy over an extended period of time. Complex carbs are the long chains of simple sugars and various types of fiber found naturally in fruits, vegetables, legumes, and whole grains. Fiber, in particular, slows down the process of absorbing nutrients and prevents your body from panicking and throwing insulin into your bloodstream, which provides long-lasting energy and stops cravings cold. Slowed absorption ultimately protects you from developing diseases linked to insulin resistance caused by eating a diet high in simple carbohydrates.

How Much Fat Do You Really Need?

Should you eat up to one third of your daily calories from fat? The answer is a simple *no*. Your body only needs fat in very small quantities. Fat assists your body in the absorption of fat-soluble vitamins like A, D, K, and E, and helps produce hormones. Fats are very large molecules when compared to carbohydrates and proteins, and it takes up to 6 hours for your body to break them down! This makes fat a great source of long-lasting energy, but it also means that it should be eaten in moderation to save your body from the burden of digesting complex foods all day.

The most important fact about "healthy" fats is that they're still fats. Unsaturated fats, such as those found in olives, avocados, seeds, and nuts, are classified as healthy because they can help lower cholesterol when they replace animal-based saturated fats. But unsaturated fats don't have magical cholesterol-zapping properties; they simply don't have cholesterol, which occurs only in animal-based foods. You don't need to eat olive oil to reduce your risk of heart disease; you need to simply *stop* eating animal fats.

Eating excess amounts of fat is hard on your whole body. Fat slows digestion, makes the colon sluggish, and impairs proper liver function. It can also clog up the endocrine system and throw your hormones out of balance. Fat may be an important macronutrient, but it's incredibly important to eat the right amount of it.

Fat is also addictive—literally. When you eat fat, it releases endocannabinoids in your brain—these are the same class of chemicals triggered by smoking marijuana! Endocannabinoids boost your appetite and sense of taste, making you crave more fatty foods as well as salty and sweet foods. When you chow down on high-fat foods, the fat prompts cravings and encourages you to overeat.

Nuts, seeds, whole grains, legumes, and even fruits and vegetables contain fat, so you don't need to eat concentrated fats like oils to get the correct amount. Getting your fat from whole-food sources rather than oils boosts your diet's nutrient content. For example, nuts contain fat but they also provide protein, fiber, and a range of minerals. Studies show that 10 percent fat in your daily caloric intake is an ideal amount for preventing and reversing heart disease because that's the perfect amount to support essential metabolic functions without overwhelming your digestive system.

By itself, fat isn't bad. The fact is, you need some naturally occurring fat to maintain your body's functions and help deliver valuable nutrients.

The Protein Myths

The two things you absolutely need to know about protein are (1) your body doesn't require as much of it as you think it does and (2) there's no such thing as "quality" protein.

Consuming just 5 or 6 percent of your calories in the form of protein is enough to replace the amino acids lost by your body's daily functions, and 10 percent protein in your diet is perfect for health, fitness, and muscle growth. All plants contain some protein, and leafy greens, whole grains, nuts, seeds, and legumes are especially protein rich. Lentils have 18 grams of protein per 1 cup; black beans, 15; and peas, 9. Spinach has a whopping 12 grams of protein in a 100-gram serving! As long as you're eating a balanced, low-fat vegan diet, you'll get more than enough protein.

The myth of "quality" protein is the result of a meat-industry campaign to convince people eating meat is better than eating plants. This simply isn't so. All proteins are made up of different combinations of amino acids, of which 9 are essential amino acids. They're "essential" because your body doesn't manufacture them on its own, so you need to get them from your food.

Animal protein is called "quality" because it contains these 9 amino acids in a similar ratio to human tissue. But your body doesn't absorb protein from food; rather, it synthesizes it from amino acids. If you eat animal proteins, your body has to break them down to access the amino acids to build its own protein. The complex proteins in animal products make this process very time- and energy-consuming for your body and can use up the energy that protein is suppose to provide! On the other hand, plant sources of protein are very easily digested and are a far more efficient energy source.

A low-fat vegan diet provides all the amino acids you need, in an accessible form that doesn't burden your body, and allows you to get the most nutrition from the food you eat.

Discovering Your Lean, Mean Body

More than 65 percent of Americans are overweight or obese. The best way to avoid being part of that statistic is to eat a low-fat, high–complex carb vegan diet. But what about building muscle? Have you ever imagined that you can get the lean, mean body of your dreams from eating plants? A lot of diets are based on the premise that if you want to build muscle, you have to eat loads of protein. But the fact is, eating protein doesn't automatically make you lean and muscular; in fact, doing so can actually hinder your efforts.

Discovering your lean and mean body requires a proper diet and adequate exercise, and is influenced by factors such as sleep and stress. Vegan athletes prove you can build a world-class body without eating animal protein. What you do need is a nutrient-rich, energy-boosting diet to fuel your workouts. Excess fat and protein require your body to exert more effort toward digestion than carbohydrates and end up making you sluggish and bloated. However, the complex carbs in whole plant foods fuel you, providing the nutrients your body needs to support vigorous physical training, and they won't slow you down.

Following a low-fat vegan diet naturally boosts your energy and vitality, so you feel better and want to exercise more. The more you exercise, the leaner and more efficient your body becomes. This creates a virtuous circle in which eating right promotes exercise, which makes you fitter and happier, which encourages you to eat well. What could be simpler?

TASTY TIP

Cleaning up your diet can end the negative cycle of lethargy, inactivity, and depression caused by a diet rich in animal fats and proteins, heavily processed, refined foods, and inadequate nutrition. The low-fat vegan lifestyle can set you on a path for success if you stick with it and banish the negative, self-perpetuating cycle that keeps you from your ideal health. Just make this one change, and your mood, energy levels, and entire attitude about life will vastly improve!

How Fats Weigh on Digestion

You won't get very far trying to clean a greasy frying pan using plain water; you need detergent to break down the grease. Much of the fat you eat is similar to the fat in a frying pan; your body needs "detergent" to break it down. Bile is the substance in your body that acts like detergent, breaking down the fat you've eaten into microscopic droplets so your body can begin the process of digestion.

Bile is produced in your liver and stored in your gallbladder during fasting (such as when you're sleeping). After a meal, your body draws bile from your gallbladder to break down the fat you've just eaten. Your gallbladder stores a relatively small amount of bile, so when you eat a high-fat meal, your body can't break down all those fat molecules. Your body must then store some of the molecules as body fat, and the excess hangs around, clogging your digestive system and preventing it from dealing with the rest of the food it needs to process. This is why you feel sluggish and heavy after a high-fat meal; when your body has to break down all that fat, there's less energy for you!

The Effects of Excess Fat

Becoming overweight or obese are the most obvious effects of eating excessive amounts of unhealthy fat. Remember, we're designed to move and thrive on a lean diet of fruits, leafy greens, vegetables, nuts, and seeds. Our bodies are highly efficient at fat storage because our ancestors ate very little of it. The average American, however, eats more than 65 *pounds* of refined fats per year. No wonder the obesity rate is skyrocketing!

This is serious stuff. In the United States, 300,000 deaths are caused by obesity-related diseases every year. If you're overweight or obese, you dramatically increase your risk of heart disease, diabetes, reproductive problems, and cancer. Women who gain 20 pounds between adolescence and middle age have double the risk of postmenopausal breast cancer compared to women who maintain a healthy weight. Devastating chronic illnesses like multiple sclerosis, dementia, and Alzheimer's disease are linked to high-fat diets, as are asthma, arthritis, and depression.

The message is clear: eating a diet high in fat compromises your body, inside and out, and drastically affects your quality of life.

The Skinny on Healthy Fats

Fat is fat, right? Wrong! Among both saturated and unsaturated fats we find both healthy and unhealthy fats. Unsaturated fats are incredibly susceptible to rancidity, wherein the fat molecules oxidize, destroying the vitamin content. Rancid fats produce oxidized sterols, which are implicated in the onset of arteriosclerosis, they increase the incidence of heart disease, and are carcinogenic! You can detect rancid oils because they smell and taste "off" and they leave a sticky film on the outside of the container if allowed to sit for a few days.

Fatty foods like olives, flaxseeds, and hemp and chia seeds contain many healthy attributes. In particular, hemp, chia, and flaxseeds add very important *omega-3 fatty acids* to your diet. Keep them fresh by placing them in your freezer and grinding for smoothies or adding them to recipes as needed.

DEFINITION

Omega-3 fatty acids are one of the essential fatty acids the human body can't produce on its own and must be supplemented through diet. They're necessary for proper brain function and play an important role in heart health. Some important sources for this necessary nutrient are hemp seeds, chia seeds, flaxseeds, pumpkinseeds, AFA blue-green algae, chlorella, and spirulina.

These foods and others high in unsaturated fats are easily damaged by heat and are quick to go rancid, so they're incredibly sensitive to storage conditions and should never be used for cooking. In very small amounts, these oils—or better yet, the whole foods they come from—are a wonderful source of hormone-balancing fats. Just be sure to refrigerate your nuts, seeds, and oils.

All unsaturated fats become unstable and oxidize quickly when heated above about 120°F. Despite the negative propaganda surrounding saturated fats, they're a far more stable choice for long-term storage and high-heat cooking. The two best oils for cooking are coconut oil and "orangutan-safe" palm oil.

Saturated fats usually get the worst of the bad-fat rep, but in reality, some of them are the healthiest fats around. Palm oil is relatively benign, but coconut oil has amazing healing properties. Coconut oil is 66 percent medium-chain fatty acids, which don't need to be broken down by bile the way other fats do. They require almost no energy for absorption and support weight loss because they encourage the body to burn calories.

Used sparingly in your cooking, coconut oil does have immune-enhancing benefits. It's one of the only food sources containing lauric acid, aside from human breast milk, which suppresses viral replication and can inhibit the growth of bacteria and fungi in our bodies. Some research has revealed that coconut oil can be beneficial in treating HIV and cancer. Unrefined coconut oil in no way contributes to the diseases normally associated with saturated fats such as heart disease, high cholesterol, and diabetes and can even be used to reverse symptoms associated with these and other illnesses, according to Mary Enig, PhD, a biochemist and one of the world's leading authorities on fats and oils.

FRESH FACT

The main saturated fat in coconut oil is lauric acid, a medium-chain fatty acid (MCFA). Your body metabolizes each fatty acid differently depending on its size. MCFAs are absorbed directly into the bloodstream for use as opposed to long-chain fatty acids, which must first be broken down into MCFAs. MCFAs don't have a negative effect on cholesterol and have been known to actually protect against heart disease. Unlike other fats, your body converts the MCFAs in coconut oil into energy, rather than packing them on as body fat. Coconut oil provides energy, much like a carbohydrate, and does not contribute to body fat.

A Happy and Healthy Heart

The standard American diet will break your heart—literally. Heart disease is the biggest killer in the United States, outpacing even cancer as a cause of death. Contrary to what a lot of people believe, developing heart disease is not inevitable!

A low-fat vegan diet, in conjunction with other healthy habits, is key to a happy and healthy heart. Following a vegan diet that adheres to the 80-10-10 guidelines is an effective, inexpensive, and safe way to keep your heart healthy. It's never too late to change your heart's future. Like giving up smoking and other risk factors, eating a low-fat vegan diet prevents further damage to your cardiovascular system and actually reverses existing heart disease to help restore your heart health.

Just remember that your body has an innate ability to heal itself, and given the chance, it will do so effectively and efficiently. Removing from your diet the animal products, trans-fats, and denatured proteins that increase your risk for heart disease can help stop it in its tracks. Add to that a diet full of fresh fruits, vegetables, wholesome grains, leafy greens, and a small amount of healthy fats, and you have a recipe for a heart on its way to perfect health!

Understanding Heart Health

Heart disease kills about 40 percent of Americans—more than any other illness, including cancer. Many people assume heart problems are a normal part of aging, but that isn't true. If you follow a low-fat vegan diet and avoid other preventable risk factors, heart disease is a lifestyle illness.

Cholesterol, fat, salt, and sugar intake, combined with stress, are key factors in heart health. Dietary intake of fat and cholesterol sets the stage for heart problems. If you eat more fat than your body can metabolize, the excess is stored as body fat. Certain fats also accumulate in your arteries, where they combine with cholesterol and cause plaque to form. Eating a single high-fat meal of animal products causes your cholesterol levels to rise and prevents your blood vessels from dilating normally. Imagine the cumulative effects of eating a high-fat diet, day in and day out!

Cutting your fat intake to 10 percent or less of your total caloric intake lets your metabolism catch up so you burn excess fat. Losing body fat is the visible evidence of this process. Meanwhile, your body is cleaning those internal fat deposits from your arteries, sweeping away blockages, and reducing your risk of heart disease.

FRESH FACT

Stress is a major contributing factor of heart disease and many other maladies. Fortunately, a low-fat vegan diet promotes proper chemical balance in your brain and helps you cope with life's daily stressors. When your mind and body are functioning harmoniously, the things that normally stress you out begin to seem more manageable.

The kind of carbs you eat also plays a major role in heart health. Remember the link between sugar and insulin? Simple carbs cause blood sugar to flare up, and your body responds by raising its insulin production. One of the side effects of this insulin response is to increase the amount of fats (triglycerides) in your bloodstream, which raises your risk of heart disease and stroke. Eating complex carbohydrates, however, prevents this insulin response and helps keep your triglyceride levels low.

And believe it or not, heart health is inextricably linked to happiness. The clichéd highly stressed executive who keels over with a heart attack isn't pure fiction. When you're tense, anxious, or frightened, your body produces a stress hormone called cortisol, which increases heart attack risk by up to 5 times. Cortisol is also linked to shifts in blood sugar and causes you to store abdominal fat. So take a deep breath and relax!

A Heart Healthy Diet

A vegan diet tackles heart disease at every level. The first, vitally important thing is that it eliminates dietary cholesterol. Removing animal products allows you to cut your cholesterol consumption to absolute 0 because cholesterol occurs only with animal foods such as meat, milk, cheese, and eggs. Embracing plant-based eating may just be the best thing you can do for your heart!

You can also slash the amount of fat you consume and virtually erase the harmful kinds of saturated animal fats from your diet. As discussed, this gives your body a chance to scrub accumulated fat from your arteries and encourages you to burn incoming fat, rather than storing it. Eating a vegan diet high in complex carbohydrates also stops the dangerous sugar-insulin cycle that leads to unhealthy cravings and increases your risk of heart problems.

The beautiful thing about eating this way is that in addition to cutting out harmful substances, you gain even more health benefits from what you put in. A low-fat vegan diet with an abundance of fresh fruits and vegetables provides hundreds of substances, ranging from fiber to phenols, that protect your heart. We look at the benefits of a varied vegan diet in detail in the coming chapters. For now, just know that the array of nutrients you get from a plant-based diet is basically a cheap insurance plan for your long-term health.

The energy boost you get from a vegan diet encourages you to exercise, which is one of the single best ways to improve your heart health. Instead of leaving you heavy and groggy, your meals will fill you with vitality. The more you move, the better you'll feel and the more motivated you'll be to keep fit and healthy.

A vegan diet is also a great way to boost your mood. Complex carbs stabilize your blood sugar, getting you off the insulin-fuelled roller coaster of cravings and crashes that can cause extreme mood swings. Low-fat eating also protects you from the addictive effect of endocannabinoids, which trap you in a cycle of fat consumption. Curbing cravings is crucial to reducing emotional eating, which leaves you unhappy and out of control. Once you eliminate the chemical triggers (fat and sugar), you're back in charge and can enjoy food without guilt or stress.

Keep your heart and your whole body healthy by finding ways to reduce your stress while eating a low-fat vegan diet. You'll lengthen your life and make it a decidedly happier one!

The Least You Need to Know

- Excess fat is linked to a range of deadly diseases.
- A low-fat, complex carbohydrate diet is ideal.
- Ten percent protein is more than adequate for muscle-building.
- Not all fats are created equal, so focus on the best ones with omega-3.
- Small amounts of naturally occurring plant-based fat are a necessary component of a healthy diet.
- A low-fat vegan diet promotes heart health and overall wellness.

Successful Low-Fat Vegan Cooking

In This Chapter

- Boosting flavor without adding fat
- The truth about soy and some healthy alternatives
- Eating a varied diet
- Nutritious seeds and grains

Most people who are unfamiliar with a vegan diet think it's filled with nothing but salads. If you tell someone about your low-fat vegan diet, they may very well ask if you eat "rabbit food." And they may not believe you when you describe the complex and varied flavors of the incredible and healthy dishes you can create by using a plethora of aromatic herbs and spices.

In this chapter, I arm you with unrivaled secrets for creating the most delicious food you've ever tasted—low-fat or not. Soon, you'll be able to prove to friends and family that you eat a lot more than just lettuce. You may even make a few converts to the low-fat vegan lifestyle simply by preparing them some of the creative, world-fusion recipes in this book.

Without fail, you'll learn how to enhance the flavor of your dishes using a variety of spices, dried and fresh herbs, citrus, and salts. You'll also discover how to create the rich and creamy textures you love in your sauces, soups, and stews—without adding tons of extra fat.

Making Low-Fat Taste Delicious

You may have a hard time imagining that anything low in fat can be rich and decadent because these terms are usually applied to foods heavy in fat. But when you incorporate creamy textured foods—such as bananas, puréed beans, and cooked starchy vegetables like cauliflower—into your desserts, sauces, and soups, the resulting textures are just as smooth, silky, and memorable as a creamy hollandaise sauce or a rich, fluffy mousse.

> **TASTY TIP**
>
> Being able to create food that tastes amazing and satisfies your cravings can make or break a diet. We all want to be healthy, but we also want to eat foods we enjoy. The recipes in this book offer you the best of both worlds. You'll never again have to sacrifice your health just because you want to enjoy good food!

Herbs and Spice Make Everything Nice

Any dish that makes an imprint in your memory and leaves you dreaming of that next taste is certainly going to have an abundance of herbs, seasonings, and spices providing those signature flavors. Low-fat vegan dishes are no different. In fact, you'll rely heavily upon these indispensable components as you prepare the recipes in this book.

You should feel free to experiment with many different herbs while you're cooking. Dried herbs such as thyme, rosemary, tarragon, oregano, and dill are options, but also consider adding fresh herbs such as cilantro, parsley, and mint to your favorite vegan dishes, as they add complexity, aroma, and depth of flavor without adding fat. Herbs also add health benefits not found in other leafy greens and vegetables.

Spices like chili powder, cayenne, curry, sumac, turmeric, cumin, and coriander are must-haves for enhancing the earthiness and savor of simple dishes. Fresh spices like garlic, shallots, and ginger are another way to add pungent flavors and complexity to a meal. Just a small amount of these fresh spices goes a long way, so use them wisely!

Yet another way to boost flavor is to use specialty sea salts. Experiment with mineral-rich Himalayan pink, Hawaiian red, or Celtic grey salts, which boost the nutrient content of your meals and are better for your health than table salt because of their trace minerals.

The best way to use herbs and spices is to combine those that have complementary flavors. Try using traditional blends first. Italian seasoning, for example, may include oregano, rosemary, thyme, and garlic. You can make your own homemade curry powder by combining turmeric, cumin, coriander, garlic, ginger, and cayenne. After you get a feel for some of the more traditional combinations, you can play with new ones. Consider, for example, tossing a few fennel seeds and some fresh parsley into your marinara or combining caraway and dill with shallots and add to a veggie burger.

Using Nutritious Fats Sparingly

Low fat is best for your health, but low fat doesn't mean *no* fat. It's fine to use virgin coconut oil in small amounts to, for example, lightly coat vegetables to keep them from burning during sautéing or roasting. You should also feel free to blend a little nut butter or a few seeds into a creamy salad dressing for the nutrition they offer. But again, use these and all nuts sparingly.

Small amounts of foods that offer the body different fatty acids promote heart health and help preserve and improve the electrical conductivity in your brain. They help your joints stay lubricated and keep your skin looking young and supple. Conversely, using too much fat can have an almost completely opposite effect on your body because it clogs important pathways and overwhelms your body.

The Wonders of Plant-Based Proteins and Fats

As a vegan, you've probably been asked a hundred times, "Where do you get your protein?" This is a commonly asked question largely due to the misconception that plant proteins are incomplete compared to animal proteins. The funny thing is, nearly all plants can synthesize every one of the 20 amino acids that are standard in most living organisms, whereas animals need to get the 9 essential amino acids through their diet. So even if you eat an animal for its protein, that animal got its protein from plants. At some point, all 9 essential amino acids came from plants.

As you learned in Chapter 1, you can get adequate quantities of protein from a varied plant-based diet. You don't even need to consume every essential amino acid at the same time or every single day to supply your body with enough protein to function well. Plus, plants deliver their protein in a form that's easy for your body to break down and absorb without much digestive effort.

Your body thrives on a diet rich in essential nutrients. Both essential amino acids and essential fatty acids are best absorbed by the body from plants. In fact, if you really want to get a boost of high-quality protein, you should consume food sources of *globular proteins*. These proteins are the easiest to digest because they're closely related to enzymes and hemoglobin, which your body makes and breaks down easily for many essential functions.

> **DEFINITION**
>
> **Globular protein** is a water-soluble form of protein found in many plant foods. It's easily assimilated by your body because it requires very little digestion. Fibrous protein is found in animal products and requires much more energy to process. Globular proteins are what your body manufactures to produce hormones, insulin, and enzymes, and your body stores amino acids in the form of globular protein.

The best sources for both globular protein and essential fatty acids are hemp, chia, and flaxseeds, as well as algae. Common nutritious algae include spirulina, chlorella, and AFA blue-green algae. Each of these contains an impressive array of chlorophyll, vitamins, and minerals, as well as all 9 essential amino acids and omega fatty acids. Of the three commonly eaten algae, AFA blue-green algae supplies the body with EPA and DHA in addition to the more commonly found ALA.

Your body can convert ALA into EPA and DHA, but the conversion rate is inefficient, so getting them from your diet is important. Each of these fatty acids support proper neurological development in children and maintain long-term brain and circulatory health in adults. Many people try to acquire these omega-3 fatty acids through diet by taking fish oil supplements. Fortunately, you don't have to take fish oil to get these important oils—you just have to eat a bit of AFA blue-green algae from time to time and be sure you consume plenty of fresh fruits and vegetables!

The key is to enjoy a varied and well-balanced vegan diet full of fruits, vegetables, leafy greens, sea vegetables, beans, grains, and seeds. So many foods contain the best type of protein and essential fatty acids in the ideal amounts. So the next time you're asked where your protein comes from, you'll have a ready answer.

Beyond Soy

Soy is often used as a protein and dairy alternative, and many people believe it's healthy because it's a good source of protein. Soy also appears healthy because it's found throughout Asian cuisine, where the vegetable-rich fare is known for encouraging a long life span. I recommend using soy ingredients such as miso, tofu, tempeh, and tamari, all time tested for their health benefits.

These ingredients are fine in small amounts, but in reality, there are other sources of protein, such as rice or hemp protein powders, seeds, and nuts. It's also incredibly important to purchase organic soy products because more than 90 percent of conventionally grown soybeans are genetically modified beans.

The Truth About Phytoestrogens

You may have heard that soy can alleviate the symptoms of menopause or that it can have detrimental effects on male fertility. These myths have come about because soy contains phytoestrogens, which are plant versions of the human hormone estrogen. Rest assured, though, eating soy won't have the same effect as taking artificial hormones, despite anything you might have heard!

Phytoestrogens are very mild in comparison to synthetic hormones, but studies of their effects on humans have produced varying results. Some research suggests the estrogen-like soy isoflavones may offer women some protection against breast cancer; other very small studies seem to contradict this finding and show they can stimulate the growth of breast cancer cells grown in a laboratory. Studies on male reproduction show consuming large quantities of soy products may suppress testosterone levels.

Ultimately, as mentioned earlier, eating some soy is just fine, especially miso, tempeh, tofu, and tamari.

Superior Soy Alternatives

With the abundance of nondairy options available, there's no need for you to get stuck in a soy rut. One of the easiest ways to cut back on soy is to swap out soy milk for another type of nondairy milk. Almond, rice, and hemp milks are popular, and many brands of ready-to-drink coconut milks are available as well. If you're into doing it yourself, you'd be surprised at how easy it is to make your own low-fat nut and seed milks using raw almonds or hemp seeds (see Chapter 17 for a basic nut milk recipe). You can also make tasty vegan cheese from many different nuts or seeds; check out my recipe for Raw Cheesy Hemp Spread in Chapter 12 for some inspiration.

Years ago, the only options available for nondairy frozen desserts or for yogurt alternatives were made from soy products. Today, you can find a wonderful array of vegan ice creams made from coconut, hemp, and almond milk that come in nearly as many flavors as dairy versions. These alternatives contain higher-quality fat sources than soy or dairy, and some brands of almond milk ice cream contain about half the fat found in dairy ice cream and even most nondairy alternatives.

The same goes for traditional dairy yogurt. You can buy cultured coconut or almond yogurt instead of dairy or soy yogurt; both help support a healthy colon.

You Cannot Live on Pasta Alone

When you embark on a low-fat vegan diet, it may be tempting to rely on staples like pasta. After all, pasta is cheap, convenient, and fits the criteria (high-carb), yet there are a number of reasons to step away from the spaghetti packet.

Even if you're happy eating pasta every day, it isn't nutritious enough to be a dietary mainstay. When you eat pasta made from white flour, your body digests it rapidly, causing your blood sugar to spike. This triggers insulin production and starts a cycle of sugar cravings. This is bad news for your body because it can lead to insulin resistance, which causes heart attacks and diabetes. Whole-grain pasta offers more fiber and won't hit your blood sugar as hard. When made from rice, quinoa, or buckwheat, pasta can provide a great occasional addition to your diet.

Some grains are acid forming. Remember high school chemistry? Acidity is measured by pH. Neutral solutions, like water, have a pH of 7.0, meaning the solution is equally balanced between acids and bases. Your body prefers an alkaline environment, a pH between 7.2 and 7.8. What determines pH? Diet! The most acidifying foods are animal products such as eggs, milk, and cheese. Beans and grains are somewhat acidifying, too. Eating these foods regularly increases your risk of a range of diseases, including osteoporosis, high blood pressure, asthma, kidney problems, and age-related muscle wasting. For optimal health, eat alkaline foods at all meals.

Fruits Are Fabulous

The obvious healthy alternative to high-carb pastas and grains are high-carb fruits. It's certainly possible to get the daily calories you need from fruit. It may even be an ideal diet if you eat tons of leafy greens, a few nuts and seeds, and a few different types of algae for extra nutrition.

HEADS-UP

One pitfall to getting a large amount of your daily caloric value from fruits is that the fruit must be perfectly ripe for the sugars to develop in a way that meets your body's needs for carbohydrates. Unripe fruit doesn't offer the same nutritional or caloric value as their ripe counterparts. If you want to make fruits the mainstay of your diet, plan your meals well in advance and purchase fruit in bulk so you always have a good supply of ripe fruit on hand.

Of course, you'd spend much of your day eating fruit and salad if you chose this path, and you'd be missing out on the ample variety you can enjoy while eating a more complete vegan diet. Fruit is cleansing, nutritious, and a wonderful way to satisfy a craving for sweets. I suggest starting your day with a fresh fruit salad or smoothie.

Eat Your Veggies!

The great thing about a low-fat vegan diet is how simple it is to eat well. You can't go wrong eating an 80-10-10 diet packed with organic fruits and vegetables. Instead of thinking of food as the enemy, or worrying about harmful ingredients and chemicals, you can relax and enjoy eating. Every mouthful of a colorful salad or a delicious fruit smoothie offers vital nutrients. Low-fat plant-based vegan meals are a pleasure to eat because vegetables work in multiple ways to help you look and feel better, inside and out.

A low-fat vegan diet supplies your body with high-quality, fiber-rich, slow-burning fuel that dramatically reduces your risk of major illnesses. Eating an 80-10-10 diet can actually help reverse heart disease and diabetes, as I discussed in Chapter 1. Fiber is an integral part of this equation because it cleanses your body so it can function properly.

Fiber forms the structural support of the cell walls of plants and the names of different types of fiber, like pectin and cellulose, refer to the fiber in different parts of the cell. Insoluble fiber keeps your digestive system working properly, cleaning out toxins that cause bloating, gas, fatigue, headaches, body odor, and bad breath. It also protects against diseases like colon cancer, appendicitis, hemorrhoids, and deep vein thrombosis. Vegetables are a great source of insoluble fiber, especially green beans, celery, and peas, as are most fruits and leafy green vegetables. Soluble fiber is found in grapefruits, asparagus, brussels sprouts, sweet potatoes, carrots, beets, and broccoli, and regulates blood sugar levels, reduces cholesterol levels, and can decrease your risk of heart disease.

Sometimes what you don't eat is as important as what you do eat. By eating more veggies, you automatically eliminate a range of damaging substances. By avoiding meat, dairy, and eggs, you eliminate toxins and chemicals like antibiotics and growth hormones, which are routinely fed to farm animals. You also lower your risk of illnesses resulting from salmonella and E. coli, which occur in unsanitary agriculture conditions. Leaving fish and shellfish out of your diet reduces your exposure to heavy metals such as mercury and lead and chemicals like arsenic, polychlorinated biphenyls (PCBs), and benzene. Simply by switching to a vegan diet, you're reducing your risk of becoming ill from exposure to these toxins.

The Importance of Variety

There are hundreds, if not thousands, of fruits, vegetables, herbs, spices, nuts, and seeds to enjoy in your 80-10-10 diet, giving you the luxury of endless meal options. This makes eating a delicious and satisfying experience and includes a vast range of health-supporting substances in your diet.

In addition to familiar vitamins and minerals like vitamin C, iron, and calcium, plants are an exclusive source of healing compounds like phytochemicals and phenols. The greater the variety of fruits and vegetables you eat, the more you benefit from increased energy, enhanced well-being, and fewer illnesses.

Taking advantage of the huge variety of fresh produce, nuts, and seeds available can ensure you consume a perfect balance of these important *micronutrients*, which are essential to your health. Keeping a varied diet also helps you avoid getting too much of any one nutrient.

> **DEFINITION**
>
> **Micronutrients,** unlike macronutrients, don't offer much in the way of caloric value. Instead, these nutrients help maintain proper body functions. Vitamins, minerals, enzymes, and phytonutrients, also known as phytochemicals, are all part of the micronutrient group. They repair damaged tissues, create neurotransmitters in your brain, and provide antioxidant protection against free radicals and disease-causing substances, all while enhancing our immune system.

Protein

Eating a plant-based diet is the ideal way to support healthy protein synthesis. Remember, as I shared in Chapter 1, there's no such thing as "quality" protein. All amino acids are created equal, but they're combined into proteins in different ways and have different purposes. When you eat a wide range of plant foods, you easily get the protein you need without wasting the energy it takes to break down the complex protein combinations in animal products.

A few of the many excellent vegetable sources of protein include mung beans, quinoa, buckwheat, lentils, peas, broccoli, hemp seeds, and chia seeds. Spinach, kale, and other dark leafy greens are great, too. Even fruits like watermelon, pears, and oranges have protein value, so don't omit any of the many fruits and vegetables you eat while factoring your protein intake.

Vitamins

Thanks to modern science, we know we need vitamins. Unfortunately, the supplement industry has convinced a lot of people that they can make up for eating badly by popping pills. This just isn't true. In fact, supplements can be harmful to your health. Excessive doses of fat-soluble vitamins like A and E are toxic, and in some cases, supplements can accelerate certain illnesses.

The best health plan is to get your vitamins from whole foods. Brightly colored vegetables are full of antioxidants, which fight heart disease, cancer, obesity, and diabetes. Current research even suggests a low-fat vegan diet might help the symptoms and causes of macular degeneration, Alzheimer's disease, Parkinson's disease, and others.

You get an incredibly beneficial amount of vitamins from fruits and vegetables. For example, the vitamin C in kiwis, brussels sprouts, bell peppers, and parsnips boosts your body's immunity, helps your body heal wounds, and keeps your teeth strong. The B vitamins found in foods like lima beans, potatoes, peas, and okra support your nervous system and help fight stress. The vitamin A in butternut squash, pumpkin, carrots, and sweet potatoes supports healthy skin and eyes.

Minerals

Minerals provide the raw material you need to build and maintain strong bones and teeth, create blood and nerve cells, and regulate the transfer of nutrients in your body. Enjoying a wide variety of organic vegetables, especially green vegetables like brussels sprouts, artichoke, okra, kale, bok choy, and Swiss chard, ensures you get an abundant supply of minerals such as copper, zinc, phosphorus, and potassium.

What About Calcium?

The dairy industry wants you to believe you need to drink milk for healthy bones. Dairy is high in calcium, but it's also acidifying. When your body becomes acidic, it draws calcium from your bones to neutralize the pH in your bloodstream. Drinking milk can actually weaken your bones and make you more susceptible to osteoporosis.

On top of being packed with calcium and magnesium, which is necessary for proper calcium absorption, vegetables alkalize your body. So when you eat calcium-rich vegetables like broccoli, butternut squash, green beans, and kale, the calcium contributes directly to building strong bones and teeth. A more accurate slogan for calcium consumption is "Got greens?"

FRESH FACT

Strong evidence exists that our bodies can actually alter magnesium into calcium. We already know magnesium is necessary for calcium absorption, so it's not too far off to imagine that our bodies may, in fact, be manufacturing calcium from magnesium rather than absorbing it directly. This idea is further supported by the fact that certain microbes can turn manganese into iron.

Phytochemicals

The word *phytochemicals* literally means "plant chemicals" and describes a huge array of compounds plants produce for protection and propagation. Turns out that what's good for plants is good for people, too.

There are thousands of phytochemicals, and many examples show how important they are for good health. Many phytochemicals are antibacterial and antiviral, making them powerful infection fighters. Different colors indicate different phytochemicals, so eat a rainbow of vegetables to get the benefits all these plant foods have to offer.

Have you ever wondered why ginger and vanilla smell so incredible or why cayenne is so spicy? It's the *phenols*. Plants use these particular phytochemicals, also called phenolic acids, for growth, repair, and reproduction. These antioxidants fight cancer, heart disease, and strokes and protect against aging.

You may have heard about the antioxidant health benefits of chocolate, tea, coffee, and red wine. This is due to their phenolic acid content. But don't rush off to pour a glass of merlot and eat a chocolate bar just yet! Vegetables such as potatoes, lettuce, eggplant, bok choy, broccoli, artichokes, and carrots are all rich in phenols as well.

Carotenoids, flavonoids, and *sulphides* are also powerful antioxidants that protect your cells from free radical damage, reducing your risk of cancer, heart disease, and age-related illnesses. Carotenoids are found in orange and yellow vegetables, flavonoids are in beans and broccoli, and sulphides are in onions and leeks.

There are thousands of phytochemicals, and from a research perspective, we've learned what only approximately 10 percent of them do. Still, there's great evidence that these wonders of the plant kingdom give us lasting health and help reverse and prevent many known diseases. I wonder when science, nutrition, medicine, and the culinary world will come together to realize that when you eat a rainbow of colors from the plant kingdom, your body, and your palate, become healthy and vibrant all on their own.

FRESH FACT

Broccoli is inspiring researchers to devote millions of dollars to researching molecules that show evidence of slowing down tumor growth and cancers.

A low-fat vegan diet sets you up to live a healthy and happy life. Free from difficult-to-digest animal products, processed foods, and chemical additives, you'll find that optimal health is attainable and easy to maintain.

Is It a Seed or a Grain?

In some cases, it may be difficult to tell the difference between a seed and a grain. The simple explanation is that a seed is the embryo of a new plant, whereas a grain is more like a fruit and a seed fused together. The portion of the wheat grain we most often consume is the fruitlike part that makes flour, but the germ of the grain is actually the seed, and the two can be separated during processing.

In terms of nutrients, seeds are more nutritious than grains. They contain all the elements such as protein, fatty acids, and micronutrients a plant needs to successfully reproduce. One important distinction between seeds and grains is that many grains are acid-forming foods, while seeds, like vegetables, are alkalizing. You can use low-fat seeds to replace most or all of the grains in your diet.

Low-Fat Seeds

Low-fat seeds are the perfect ingredient to make a hearty meal that supplies necessary nutrients without burdening your body with allergenic proteins like the gluten found in wheat, oats, rye, and barley.

Quinoa is often mistaken for a grain, but it's actually a seed native to South America. Packed with protein, it supplies all the essential amino acids and is especially high in lysine, which supports tissue growth and repair. No wonder it was a favorite food of Incan warriors! Quinoa is also rich in minerals such as magnesium, iron, copper, and phosphorus. It's great in salads or as a substitute for rice or couscous, and is also available as flour. Please check out *The Complete Idiot's Guide Quinoa Cookbook* by Susan Irby for some great recipes using this amazing superfood.

Amaranth is another superseed from South America and was prized by the Aztecs. The amaranth seed is hugely popular in Mexico, where it's used to make crisp rice cereal–style treats. It can also be popped like popcorn, ground into flour, and cooked like oatmeal. You can eat amaranth greens as well. Like other seeds, amaranth is high in calcium, iron, phosphorus, and vitamins A, C, and E.

Don't let the name fool you; *buckwheat* has nothing to do with wheat. It's actually a seed from the rhubarb and sorrel family. As with rhubarb, the greens are mildly toxic, but the seed is a nutritional powerhouse. Buckwheat is packed with flavonoids that fight heart disease by lowering cholesterol, promoting circulation, preventing clotting of the arteries, and reducing blood pressure. You can add toasted buckwheat seeds to salads, or cook it as a hot cereal. Buckwheat flour makes great gluten-free pancakes and is used to make soba noodles.

These high-energy protein sources offer a wonderful amount of nutrition. Each of these seeds displays ratios of carbohydrates, fats, and proteins that are ideal for your dietary needs.

High-Fat Seeds

High-fat seeds are bursting with nutrients but also fat, which the seed stores to nourish the growth of new plants. Many of these seeds, like flax and hemp, are used to make oils, which are high in healthy unsaturated fat and omega-3 fatty acids. You're better off eating whole ground seeds, which provide fiber, protein, and nutrients in addition to healthy fats. As always, it's best to consume high-fat seeds in moderation so you can receive the most from their beneficial qualities.

TASTY TIP

Seeds are concentrated foods in general, and this is especially true for high-fat seeds. After all, entire plants arise from these tiny beads of super nutrition. When you eat a seed, you're eating a whole plant, in a way. That's how you should think about it when you reach for a second helping. A small amount is enough to give you the nutrition you need.

Pumpkinseeds are delicious, crunchy, and lower in fat than many other seeds. They're high in minerals such as manganese, magnesium, phosphorus, iron, copper, and zinc, which help maintain prostate health. They're also a good source of carotenoids. If the dark days of winter get you down, toasted pumpkinseeds might help! They're high in L-tryptophan, an essential amino acid that can ease depression.

Many people consider *hemp seeds* a nearly perfect food. The seeds are a "complete" protein because they contain all 9 essential amino acids. Because they come in the form of globular protein, they're also more easily absorbed than most other protein sources. They have a prefect ratio of omega-3 and -6 fatty acids, which protect your heart and brain health. Hemp seeds contain most minerals, ample fiber, and tons of phytonutrients, including chlorophyll.

You can grind hemp seeds and use them *au natural*, turn them into a seed butter, add them to your smoothies, and use them to make hemp milk, sour cream, ice cream, cheese, hemp tofu, and creamy sauces. You can sprinkle them on crudités or add them to veggie burgers and casseroles. They make a delicious, crunchy salad topping or a perfect snack all by themselves.

Our ancestors must have instinctively understood the benefits of *sesame seeds*, because people have been eating them since roughly 1500 B.C.E. A huge amount of nutrition is packed into tiny sesame seeds. Some of the main minerals include calcium, magnesium, iron, phosphorus, and zinc. Two unique compounds in sesame seeds, called *sesamin* and *sesamolin*, lower blood pressure and cholesterol and protect against liver damage.

Flaxseeds are another ancient favorite, and were cultivated as early as 3000 B.C.E. Flaxseeds contain soluble and insoluble fiber, which help prevent and treat digestive troubles like irritable bowel syndrome and regulate blood sugar. They're also loaded with antioxidants called lignans, which protect against a range of illnesses, and omega-3 fatty acids, which are good for your heart and help combat depression.

Flaxseeds are best absorbed when they're purchased whole and ground in a spice or flour grinder prior, or purchased ground for convenience. Sprinkle ground flaxseeds on your morning cereal, add to baked goods, and use as a binder for baked goods and sauces to power up your nutrition and give your food a thicker texture.

Chia: The Seed That Sustained Ancient Warriors

Chia seeds are small in size, but they're larger than life when it comes to nutrition. What makes chia seeds so special is their near-perfect combination of phytonutrients, fatty acids, and protein. They're a complete protein source, meaning they supply all the essential amino acids your body needs. They also have more of the omega-3 fatty acid ALA than any other food, and just 1 ounce of chia seeds provides 42 percent of your daily fiber!

The name *chia* comes from the Mayan language of Central America and means "strength," which is exactly what this powerhouse seed provides. Just 1 tablespoon of chia can keep you going for an entire day.

FRESH FACT

The Tarahumara Native Americans of Central America have been a subject of interest for many runners due to their ability to run hundreds of miles at a time. They eat a very simple diet, with corn and beans as major staples. They also eat chia seeds and attribute their extreme endurance to the energy provided by these tiny seeds.

As an added benefit, chia seeds are so full of antioxidants they stay fresh at room temperature for up to 2 years without going rancid. These potent antioxidants protect you from cancer, degenerative diseases, diabetes, and strokes. They're also an excellent food for athletes, especially those involved in endurance sports. Chia seeds are alkalizing, so their calcium contributes directly to strong bones. Iron supports the immune system and transports oxygen, while your body uses potassium to maintain electrolyte balance during exercise.

One unique thing about chia seeds is that they're water soluble. The Tarahumara use them to make chia iskiate, a lemonade-style drink composed of chia seeds, lemons or limes, water, and agave nectar. The chia seeds soften and take on a gel-like texture, and if you add enough chia to your lemonade, you'll end up with lemon jelly!

Not All Nuts Are Created Equal

Nuts are a delicious treat, but they have highly allergenic properties for some, which make them hard to digest and can cause adverse reactions. Also, keep nuts fresh by placing in a sealed glass jar or—for longer storage—in your refrigerator.

HEADS-UP

Cashews and pistachios are a part of the poison oak family and contain similar irritating oils throughout various parts of the trees that produce these nuts. As such, I haven't included these nuts in the recipes within this book.

Most nuts contain at least 50 percent fat, which makes them acid forming. You'll remember that acidity in your body is linked to a number of illnesses. Two exceptions to this 50 percent fat factor are almonds and Brazil nuts.

Almonds are a nearly perfect nut. They aren't acid forming, and they have the lowest amount of saturated fat of any nut. They're also a good source of calcium, zinc, iron, B vitamins, and vitamin E, which fights skin aging and protects heart and respiratory health. They're high in fiber and protein when compared to other nuts and are incredibly versatile when used as a nut milk or as a base for a low-fat soup or smoothie.

Eating one *Brazil nut* a day provides your recommended allowance of selenium and, like almonds, Brazil nuts are alkalizing. Selenium, found in Brazil nuts, is a cancer-fighting agent that protects against other degenerative conditions like heart disease, arthritis, neurological diseases, and infections. It also boosts the antioxidant power of vitamins C and E. Brazil nuts also are higher in protein and carbohydrates than many other nuts.

You may also use other nuts such as pine nuts and hazelnuts for their many health benefits. Still, 1 to 2 ounces of any nut is a good amount to eat in a day. Anything more goes beyond the suggested limits within the low-fat guidelines, so keep it light and healthy and you'll feel that way yourself!

The Least You Need to Know

- Fats are important, but use them sparingly to preserve and improve your health.
- A low-fat vegan diet gives you ample amounts of essential nutrients.
- Diets rich in fruits and vegetables provide healing phytochemicals.
- Grainlike seeds replace acid-forming high-gluten grains.
- Small amounts of nuts and seeds provide quality fats, important nutrients, and proteins.

The Valiant Vegan Kitchen

In This Chapter

- Filling your vegan pantry
- The best grains and legumes to keep handy
- Preparation and storage tips
- Handy and essential kitchen tools

In the previous two chapters, you became well versed in the health benefits of eating a low-fat vegan diet and learned tips and tricks for making every dish you create a memorable one. Now let's take a look at a few tried-and-true techniques to ensure creating delicious, nutritious low-fat vegan meals is as easy as walking into your kitchen and opening the pantry.

Stocking Your Pantry

To maximize your dining possibilities and inspire you in those moments when you lack a meal plan, it helps to keep a well-stocked pantry. Keep a healthy supply of staples like low-lectin grains and beans, fresh and dried fruits and vegetables, flours, sweeteners, and a variety of seasonings as well as a few specialty ingredients so you have free rein when you want to create the recipes in this book or go off on your own.

Fresh Fruits and Vegetables

Keep a nice variety of fruits and vegetables on hand. Stock often-used ingredients like lemons, apples, tomatoes, onions, and spinach. Of course, there are some veggies you probably don't eat every day, like eggplant and parsnips, and those will likely be spur-of-the-moment or planned purchases. Just be sure that whatever you keep in your pantry or refrigerator is always fresh and being used regularly. A good strategy is to have a nice supply of root vegetables like beets and daikon, as they tend to keep for long periods of time.

> **TASTY TIP**
>
> To complete your vegan pantry, dedicate some time to preparing a few bulk batches of the snacks from Chapter 12 and storing them in individual serving sizes in the pantry (or the refrigerator, if necessary). Then, when you feel like munching between meals, you'll always have a few healthy choices. You'll also be prepared for entertaining company and providing healthy food to hungry kids.

Spices and Herbs

Try to keep a staple of ingredients used for texture and flavor enhancement fully stocked. For example, keep a variety of dried and fresh spices like black pepper, ginger, and turmeric. Also stock up on various chile peppers, dried garlic, cinnamon, cloves, and different seeds like cumin, coriander, fennel, and fenugreek so you always have a variety to choose from and a good stock for making various curry and other spice combinations. Use or replace your spices regularly because they lose their flavor and potency over time.

Fresh herbs like cilantro, parsley, and dill are important staples in vegan cuisine, but because they're more perishable, you may want to buy these as needed or make bulk batches of certain herb-rich sauces to freeze for later use. If you have a batch of Argentinean Parsley Purée (recipe in Chapter 10) in your freezer, you can use it in place of fresh parsley in a recipe, creating a very convenient and tasty solution for your dish. Certain herbs do have a bit more staying power, though, so if you use things like lemongrass or lime leaves on a fairly regular basis, you can buy them up to a week in advance without having to worry about them spoiling before you get a chance to use them or freeze them for later use.

Flours and Sweeteners

Other must-haves include certain flours and sweeteners. Among the flours you'll find in this book are coconut, chickpea, brown or white rice, and occasionally amaranth or quinoa. Using your high-speed blender, you can make fresh flour from the whole grains and seeds in your pantry such as rice, quinoa, buckwheat, and flax. This keeps your ingredients fresh and makes your dishes even tastier. Experiment with using different flours as you become more comfortable with them. Keep them in your freezer for easy storage.

You can toss out your old white or brown sugar and replace them with *coconut sugar,* date sugar, and maple crystals, all of which can be used interchangeably in most of the recipes in this book. Also keep adequate amounts of maple and agave syrups on hand. You'll find yourself using these ingredients almost daily.

> **DEFINITION**
>
> **Coconut sugar,** similar to maple sugar, is made from the sap of the coconut palm, which is then dried into a powder. It has a malty flavor with a depth similar to brown sugar. It's less sweet than many other sugars and has a low-glycemic profile, making it ideal for anyone concerned about their blood sugar.

Low-Lectin Grains and Legumes

One very important aspect of a low-fat vegan diet is to keep your consumption of high-lectin grains and legumes to a minimum. Lectins are a group of proteins that bind to carbohydrates, make the blood clot, and have a high incidence of causing and complicating a variety of health problems. Anything from arthritis to diabetes and irritable bowel syndrome to autoimmune disorders are likely worsened by eating large amounts of high-lectin foods.

It's important to note that many foods have some lectin content and that this is completely safe and normal, but certain lectins cause more irritation than others and are concentrated in certain foods.

Cereal grains like wheat, rye, and barley are famous for their gluten content, which is another sticky, coarse protein that's difficult to digest and can cause health problems if you eat it in excess. Gluten, however, is not the only irritating factor in these and other grains. Most cereal grains have some lectin content and should be used in moderation. Some alternatives to cereal grains include quinoa, millet, buckwheat, and amaranth, all of which have much lower levels of lectins and are gluten free.

Legumes are a great source of fiber, carbohydrates, and of course, protein. Be very picky about the types of legumes you include in your diet, because certain beans also contain concentrated amounts of lectins. Among the more irritating legumes are lima beans, kidney beans, soy beans, and peanuts. Kidney beans in particular have such a high lectin content that eating them undercooked or improperly cooked can make you acutely ill. They're best avoided altogether, but if you do use them, soak, rinse, and cook them thoroughly to avoid toxicity.

The legumes that contain the least amount of lectins include lentils, mung beans, peas, and green beans, so stock up on those types.

When cooking with either low-lectin grains or legumes, it's best to soak and or sprout them before use. This minimizes the amount of lectins that make it into your food.

TASTY TIP

Soaking legumes, grains, nuts, and seeds prior to use leaches out tannins and lectins and deactivates enzyme inhibitors that might lead to indigestion and other problems. Soak these ingredients to derive the most nutrition from them and avoid toxins.

Another way to minimize lectin content is to consume cultured products like different types of tamari, miso, or tempeh.

Prepping and Storing Perishable Ingredients

You should always follow some specific guidelines when prepping and storing food. To ensure freshness and safety from bacterial pathogens, it's best to prepare your ingredients by cleaning, drying, and storing them in a cool place. You may clean with a bit of lemon or white vinegar in your water, or even one of the many available natural food cleaners.

You don't have to spend tons of time on food prep when you're cooking a recipe if you prep large batches to refrigerate or freeze ahead of time. It's always fun to think about what dishes you want to make for the next few days, and cleaning and prepping the available ingredients in advance will make your cooking even easier.

When it comes to storage, your pantry must be dark and cool. Store food in glass or neutral plastic containers. You can even vacuum-seal some items for long-term freshness.

Tools for the Vegan Kitchen

A lot of creativity takes place in the vegan kitchen. This means preparation can take a little time, especially when making specialty items like zucchini noodles and carrot ribbons for the first time. Numerous gadgets can make your life easier and cut your preparation time in half. Some of these items are eventual must-haves, but others are optional tools. As with anything new, the more you do it, the easier it becomes, and this is most true in the vegan kitchen. (In Appendix B, I share a list of resources where you can find many of these tools and gadgets.)

Gotta-Have Gizmos

Of all the gizmos out there—and there are a lot—some are essential for proper food prep.

First off, you'll need at least one high-quality, all-purpose *chef's knife*. Japanese foil knives are among some of the sharper knives out there and make cutting hard vegetables feel like you're slicing through soft butter. I prefer a ceramic knife, which is wonderful for daily use but must be handled with care to avoid breakage.

You should also invest in a *heavy cleaver* or *large serrated knife* for opening coconuts and cutting through hard squash.

Another very handy tool to have in the kitchen is a *mandoline*. A mandoline is a very sharp blade placed on a flat cutting surface. It usually comes with several attachments that allow you to vary slice thickness and may include a julienne blade and a fine shredding blade. Creating fun shapes with your ingredients is one of the best ways to make appealing dishes for even the most discerning palates.

HEADS-UP

The mandoline is an extremely sharp tool and should always be used with the accompanying finger guard or even kitchen gloves. You should also run your vegetables over the surface slowly to avoid slipping and accidentally cutting a finger.

Possibly the most basic and stone-age tool to have around is a *mortar and pestle*. It consists of a deep bowl and rounded pounder and is used for crushing herbs and spices into a meal or paste. It's fun and safe for kids to use, too!

A *zester* is a long, thin-handled grater that can be used to powder whole nutmeg and cinnamon sticks or to make fine peels of citrus rinds. A normal grater simply can't compare to the fine grate this tool offers.

What kitchen would be complete without a few *glass containers* for storing an extra batch of dressing or some yummy leftovers? Just be sure to vent the lid on anything hot, and don't store your dish until it has reached room temperature. Use glass containers for refrigeration and BPA-free plastic for freezing.

Fine-mesh colanders and *sieves* are great tools for rinsing and cleaning small ingredients like quinoa and amaranth. These also may be used for straining nut milks and teas. A *nut milk bag* or *cheesecloth* is the best choice for this purpose, though.

Nothing compares to a *spiral slicer* when it comes to making fresh noodles out of vegetables like zucchini or carrots. You can use a grater or mandoline for this purpose, but nothing equals a genuine spiral slicer for the perfect-size fresh vegetable pasta.

One of the most frequently used tools in my kitchen is the *food processor*. This tool is hard to do without. It can combine hard or soft ingredients into a fairly smooth batter, create the perfect salsa, and perfect a fabulous pâté. It has attachments for shredding, slicing, and julienning vegetables, which makes large batches easier to create.

Last but not least is the mighty *high-speed blender*. This high-powered appliance is powerful enough to blend even hard vegetables without added liquid and can completely purée anything. It can be used to make flour, confectioners' sugar, and grind spices as well as completely combine any ingredients you use it for. Its uses are virtually limitless.

FRESH FACT

One of the added bonuses of a high-speed blender is that it runs so fast, it can warm your food slightly. This is a nice way to warm a raw soup without actually heating it. This warming also makes it possible to blend solid coconut oil into a creamy liquid without having to melt it first.

Nice-to-Have Small Wares

Citrus presses are countertop equipment or handheld tools that help take some of the pressure off your fingers when you need to squeeze a large amount of juice. You can find a press for each different size of citrus or a universal one that will adequately press almost any size citrus fruit.

A *ricer* can help you make grain alternatives out of things like potatoes or squash. It looks similar to a large garlic press, and basically it pushes its contents through several small holes to create a rice texture.

If you're a fan of raw foods or preserving the seasonal bounty of your garden, you should absolutely invest in a *high-quality dehydrator* with a temperature control. With this appliance, you can preserve the enzymes of your kale chips and veggie crackers or make your own homemade sun-dried tomatoes. Look for a dehydrator that comes with multiple racks and Teflex sheets, which can be used for transforming moist ingredients, like fruit blends, into fruit leather.

A *juicer* is always nice to have on hand for those recipes that call for fresh juice. It's also very useful for making quick and easy fresh, healthy juice when you're craving a healthy liquid meal or snack.

The Least You Need to Know

- Having a well-stocked pantry helps keep you inspired when it comes to meal planning.
- Herbs, spices, seasonings, and other flavor enhancers can really make a difference in your low-fat vegan cooking.
- High-lectin beans and grains can be irritating and cause problems if consumed in large amounts, so stock up on and enjoy the low-lectin versions instead.
- Certain kitchen tools make prep work much easier, getting you out of the kitchen and to the dinner table faster.

Great Starts to Good Mornings

Because breakfast is the most-skipped meal of the day—but it's also the most important—in Part 2, I explain how sleep affects your digestion and how to best break your nightly fast without overloading your digestive system.

We then dive head first into delicious breakfast recipes, including a variety of quick-and-easy breakfast smoothies and light, fruit-based meals that help you start your day right.

Also included are hearty breakfast meals that bring new flavors to traditional favorites. These filling meals make being a low-fat vegan completely satisfying.

Morning Delights

In This Chapter

- Refreshing and revitalizing morning drinks
- Fruit and veggie blends
- Grab-and-go liquid breakfasts
- Light fruit salads

The first meal of the day breaks the nighttime fast, so *breakfast* literally means "break fast"! During the night, while your digestive system rests, your body utilizes this extra energy for cleansing and healing processes that maintain health and balance. So it's important to make a morning meal that's light and easy to digest.

The recipes in this chapter include simple and easily digestible smoothies and other delicious and light dishes that give you energy without burdening your digestive system first thing in the morning. Keeping your early morning meal light helps you absorb more of the nutrition these healthy recipes provide and allows your body to maximize its energy for the entire day.

Nighttime Digestive Duty

The typical human body requires a minimum of 4 hours to digest the average meal and 8 to 12 hours for a thorough intestinal cleansing. The most optimal time for this cleansing is the window between your last meal of the day and your breakfast the next morning, while you sleep.

After a night of thorough digestive cleaning, it's essential to replenish your body with clean and easily digestible food. Doing so jump-starts your metabolism and ensures you get the sustained energy you need for the day. Optimal replenishing breakfast options include freshly squeezed fruit and vegetable juices, fruit salads, or smoothies.

I'd also like to steer you away from energy drinks and caffeinated coffee as a means to start your day and encourage you to instead make a meal of a delicious and energy-giving smoothie for natural and sustained energy. Please check out my other book, *The Complete Idiot's Guide to Green Smoothies,* for some tasty and healthy options.

Blended Breakfasts

Breakfast in a cup is more nutritious for your body than you may think. Blended juices and smoothies are a cinch to make, and you can include pounds of fresh fruits and vegetables you may not otherwise get a chance to eat during your busy day. Using a blender to purée fruits, vegetables, seeds, and powdered superfoods such as spirulina and raw cacao gives you a bulk of fiber in a convenient format and allows the night's digestive work of sweeping the intestines to continue.

> **TASTY TIP**
>
> Smoothies and other liquid breakfasts are perfect when you're on the move. You can pour them into a travel-friendly mug, thermos, or cup and sip while on the go. If you can't drink them all at once, however, you can freeze them to enjoy later.

Blended drinks ease your waking body into action because they require less energy to digest. Nutrients enter the bloodstream faster, giving you energy quickly without the artificial jolt of stimulants like caffeine.

Try to consume liquids in the morning, including large amounts of fresh water, and increase the density of your food throughout the day. This approach reserves precious energy for accomplishing all the things you love to do. After all, the less energy you spend on digestion, the more energy you have for everything else.

Spirulina Splash Smoothie

Get a mega dose of nutrient-rich *spirulina* balanced by the juicy flavor of blueberries and pomegranate.

Yield:	Prep time:	Serving size:		
about 4 cups	5 minutes	2 cups		
Each serving has:				
303 calories	38 g carbohydrates	11 g fat	11 g fiber	17 g protein

1 cup fresh or frozen blueberries	1 TB. spirulina powder
1 cup pomegranate juice	2 TB. chia seeds
Water from 1 medium young coconut (1½ cups) or 1½ cups bottled coconut water	4 TB. vanilla hemp protein powder
	1 cup ice

1. In a high-speed blender, combine blueberries, pomegranate juice, coconut water, spirulina powder, chia seeds, and vanilla hemp protein powder. Blend on high until smooth.

2. Add ice, and blend until combined. Serve immediately.

Variation: Many super-greens powders contain spirulina, so if you don't have a bottle of spirulina, add 1 tablespoon of your favorite super-greens powder instead. Also, if you can't find pomegranate juice, use cranberry, blueberry, or black cherry juice as an alternative.

DEFINITION

Spirulina is a blue-green algae and a nutrient-rich food. It contains all essential amino acids and is 60 percent protein by weight! Spirulina is known to support the pH balance in the body, boost the immune system, and protect against cancer. You can find it in tablets, powders, and flakes. Just 1 teaspoon per day is sufficient to reap its magnificent health benefits.

Chocolate over Cherries Smoothie

Enjoy the decadent flavor of chocolate-covered cherries with the benefits of leafy greens, superfoods, and hydrating coconut water. The rich smoothness and sweet taste will make you forget how healthy this smoothie really is.

Yield:	Prep time:	Serving size:		
about 4 cups	5 minutes	2 cups		
Each serving has:				
355 calories	69 g carbohydrates	7 g fat	15 g fiber	14 g protein

3 cups fresh spinach

1 cup chopped kale leaves, stems removed

½ cup cucumber, chopped

1 medium Fuji apple, chopped (1 cup)

12 pitted fresh or frozen cherries

2 TB. chia seeds

2 tsp. spirulina or super-greens powder

2 tsp. maca powder

1 TB. raw cacao powder

Water from 1 large young coconut (2 cups) or 2 cups bottled coconut water

1. In a high-speed blender, combine spinach leaves, kale leaves, cucumber, Fuji apple, cherries, chia seeds, spirulina powder, maca powder, raw cacao powder, and coconut water.

2. Blend until thoroughly combined. Serve immediately.

Variation: This smoothie is just as delicious with fresh or frozen strawberries or raspberries or a combination of several red fruits. For added sweetness, include ½ large banana.

FRESH FACT

Cherries contain very high levels of disease-fighting antioxidants. They also contain 19 times the beta-carotene found in blueberries and strawberries, and vitamin C, potassium, magnesium, iron, fiber, and folate. Recent evidence links cherries to a reduction in arthritis and gout pain, and they reduce risk factors for heart disease, diabetes, and certain cancers.

Carrot Cake Smoothie

Indulge in this rich and creamy carrot smoothie, and enjoy the unique and delicate texture of extremely healthy flower pollen. This refresher is vibrant and filling and makes a great anytime-of-day drink.

Yield:	Prep time:	Serving size:		
about 4 cups	5 minutes	2 cups		
Each serving has:				
361 calories	47 g carbohydrates	18 g fat	11 g fiber	9 g protein

3 cups fresh carrot juice

1 cup vanilla almond milk

1 (1-in.) piece fresh peeled ginger

1 medium banana, peeled

3 TB. chia seeds

2 TB. almond butter

2 tsp. maca powder

¼ tsp. ground cinnamon

⅛ tsp. ground turmeric

⅛ tsp. ground nutmeg

1 cup ice

2 tsp. flower or pine pollen

1. In a high-speed blender, combine carrot juice, vanilla almond milk, ginger, banana, chia seeds, almond butter, maca powder, cinnamon, turmeric, nutmeg, and ice.

2. Blend until thoroughly combined.

3. Divide between 2 glasses and stir 1 teaspoon flower pollen into each glass. Serve immediately.

Variation: Use the same ingredients to make **Autumn Carrot Pudding.** Just increase the quantity of chia seeds to 6 tablespoons, reduce the almond milk to ½ cup, and reduce the carrot juice to 1½ cups. Blend on high until smooth, transfer to a jar or bowl with a tight-fitting lid, and refrigerate for 1 hour.

FRESH FACT

The cinnamon and flower pollen are hidden health gems in this smoothie. Cinnamon can lower LDL cholesterol, regulate blood sugar levels, inhibit the growth of yeast in the body, reduce arthritic pain, and boost cognitive function and memory. Flower pollen can help reduce the symptoms of allergies and asthma. You can find it at your health market; look for local pollen. If you have a severe allergy to pollen, seek guidance from your herbalist or naturopath prior to use.

Maui Morning Sunrise Smoothie

Imagine a cool island breeze and the flavor of the tropics. This smoothie has an abundance of pineapple and mango, and the texture is made silky by fresh banana and chia seeds.

Yield:	Prep time:	Serving size:		
about 4 cups	5 minutes	2 cups		
Each serving has:				
220 calories	45 g carbohydrates	5 g fat	10 g fiber	4 g protein

1 cup frozen pineapple bits
1 cup frozen mango cubes
½ small cucumber, peeled and chopped
1 medium banana, peeled

2 TB. chia seeds
Water from 1 small young coconut (1 cup) or 1 cup bottled coconut water
1 cup ice

1. In a high-speed blender, combine pineapple, mango, cucumber, banana, chia seeds, coconut water, and ice.

2. Blend until thoroughly combined. Serve immediately.

Variation: For a healthful and refreshing dessert, pour the blended contents into popsicle molds or ice-cube trays and freeze. To enliven sparkling water, drop in a couple of these flavored and nutritious ice cubes.

Ginger Jump-Start Smoothie

Sweet, creamy, and slightly spicy, this chilled smoothie will jump-start your energy for the day ahead.

Yield:	Prep time:	Serving size:		
about 4 cups	10 minutes	2 cups		
Each serving has:				
252 calories	65 g carbohydrates	1 g fat	7 g fiber	2 g protein

1 large banana, peeled

Water from 1 large young coconut (2 cups) or 2 cups bottled coconut water

1 (2-in.) piece fresh peeled ginger

2 small Fuji apples, cored and quartered

½ cup vanilla almond milk

4 large pitted medjool or deglet noor dates

1 cup ice

1. In a high-speed blender, combine banana, coconut water, ginger, Fuji apples, vanilla almond milk, medjool dates, and ice.

2. Blend on high until smooth and creamy. Serve immediately.

Variation: For **Ginger Jump-Start Frozen Custard,** spoon the ingredients into ice-cube trays or spread into freezer-safe bowls, and freeze.

Maca Madness Smoothie

If you love chocolate, this rich and velvety smoothie is sure to please. Raw cacao balances the earthiness of maca root in this sweet beverage you'll look forward to each morning.

Yield:	Prep time:	Serving size:		
about 4 cups	15 minutes	2 cups		
Each serving has:				
375 calories	75 g carbohydrates	8 g fat	14 g fiber	7 g protein

1 large banana, peeled

Water from 1 medium young coconut (1½ cups) or 1½ cups bottled coconut water

1 TB. raw cacao powder

2 TB. chia seeds

1 TB. maca powder

4 large pitted medjool or deglet noor dates

2 cups unsweetened vanilla almond milk

1. In a high-speed blender, combine banana, coconut water, raw cacao powder, chia seeds, maca powder, medjool dates, and vanilla almond milk.

2. Blend on high until smooth. Serve immediately.

FRESH FACT

Maca—touted as the "superfood of the Andes"—has been used in South America for centuries to strengthen the immune system, increase energy and endurance, and regulate the endocrine system. A member of the cruciferous family, maca is a radishlike tuberous root that's harvested and ground into a powder for easy consumption. Recent studies support the belief that consumption of maca is beneficial for regulating and supporting endocrine health. Benefits include metabolism regulation, hormonal support, increased energy levels, and a healthy libido.

Beet Blaster Smoothie

You can't go wrong with a hot pink beverage to get your morning going. This smoothie has a touch of tang from the lemon, sweetness from apples and young coconut water, and spice from a generous amount of fresh ginger.

Yield:	Prep time:	Serving size:		
about 4 cups	15 minutes	2 cups		
Each serving has:				
237 calories	29 g carbohydrates	8 g fat	10 g fiber	6 g protein

Juice of 1 medium beet (¼ cup)

Water from 1 medium young coconut (1½ cups) or 1½ cups bottled coconut water

1 large Fuji apple, chopped (1½ cups)

1 small red beet, peeled (½ cup)

1 TB. fresh lemon juice

1 (½-in.) piece fresh peeled ginger

2 TB. chia seeds

1 TB. Irish Moss Emulsifier (recipe in Chapter 10)

½ cup hemp milk

1. In a high-speed blender, combine beet juice, coconut water, Fuji apple, red beet, lemon juice, ginger, chia seeds, Irish Moss Emulsifier, and hemp milk.

2. Blend until thoroughly combined. Serve immediately.

Variation: You can also make this smoothie with golden or candy-striped beets. For a boost of nutrition, toss in a couple beet greens.

HEADS-UP

If you drink a lot of beet smoothies or other beet juices and elixirs, your urine or stool may take on a pink or reddish hue. This is harmless, but if you don't know this can happen, it can be alarming.

Green Tea-zer Smoothie

For those days when you need a little extra energy, whip up this vanilla-spiced, peachy green tea smoothie. There's no doubt this drink will get your body moving.

Yield:	Prep time:	Serving size:		
about 4 cups	15 minutes, plus 3 hours chill time	2 cups		

Each serving has:				
245 calories	61 g carbohydrates	2 g fat	6 g fiber	3 g protein

2 cups water

2 TB. loose green tea leaves or 4 green tea pouches

1 cup vanilla almond milk

1 large banana, peeled

½ cup frozen peaches

4 large pitted medjool or deglet noor dates

1 tsp. vanilla extract

2 tsp. maca powder

1. In a small saucepan over medium-high heat, bring water to a boil. Add green tea leaves, and remove the pan from heat. Cover, and allow tea to steep for about 5 minutes.

2. Pinch tea bags to release more of the tea extracts, and transfer to a glass jar. Chill for at least 3 hours.

3. In a high-speed blender, combine iced green tea, vanilla almond milk, banana, peaches, medjool dates, vanilla extract, and maca powder.

4. Blend until thoroughly combined. Serve immediately, or freeze to enjoy at a later time.

FRESH FACT

Green tea is loaded with antioxidants and contains less caffeine than black tea or coffee, which makes it the perfect option for your morning pick-me-up. You'll have sustained energy without jitters and reap the benefits of its nutritional profile.

Stone Fruit and Fig Salad

Welcome summer with this delightful breakfast fruit salad. Juicy nectarines, cherries, and plums pair perfectly with fresh figs and honey. Enjoy this salad on a typical morning, or increase the quantity to share it with a brunch crowd.

Yield:	Prep time:	Cook time:	Serving size:	
about 3 cups	10 minutes	5 minutes	1 cup	
Each serving has:				
421 calories	88 g carbohydrates	10 g fat	12 g fiber	5 g protein

1 medium nectarine, pitted and sliced (¾ cup)	8 medium fresh black mission figs, quartered
2 medium-small plums, pitted and sliced (1 cup)	2 TB. maple syrup
	2 TB. fresh orange juice
1 cup pitted fresh or frozen cherries, halved	½ tsp. vanilla extract
	2 TB. shredded unsweetened coconut

1. Place nectarine, plums, cherries, and black mission figs in a large bowl, and set aside.

2. In a small saucepan over low heat, combine maple syrup, orange juice, and vanilla extract. Cook for 5 minutes.

3. Pour maple-orange blend over fruit, and gently toss to coat.

4. Divide fruit salad among 3 bowls, sprinkle each with 2 teaspoons shredded coconut, and serve.

Variation: If stone fruits are difficult to find or out of season, try this salad with a mix of kiwi, persimmon, berries, or pear. You may also substitute coconut syrup for maple syrup.

HEADS-UP

Conventionally grown fruits and vegetables may be doused with up to 26 different pesticides on a single plant. The effects of pesticide exposure range from allergic reactions, to cancer, to reproductive problems. Babies and children are especially vulnerable to pesticides because their liver and immune system are less efficient at removing contaminants. Ideally, you should eat all organic or biologically grown produce. If organic options aren't available, check to see which produce items are on the Dirty Dozen list, which changes seasonally.

Skinny Scramble

Fragrant garlic and onion with leafy greens, mushrooms, and fresh herbs make this juicy tofu and veggie mélange a flavor-filled, savory start to the day.

Yield:	Prep time:	Cook time:	Serving size:	
about 3 cups	10 minutes	19 minutes	1 cup	
Each serving has:				
250 calories	9 g carbohydrates	18 g fat	3 g fiber	19 g protein

2 TB. virgin coconut oil

2 TB. sweet onion, minced

1 clove garlic, minced

1 (16-oz.) block extra-firm tofu, crumbled

½ cup mushrooms, sliced (your favorite)

8 cherry tomatoes, halved

⅔ cup fresh spinach

1 tsp. fresh basil leaves, minced

1 tsp. flat-leaf parsley, minced

1 tsp. fresh thyme, minced

1 tsp. nutritional yeast flakes

½ tsp. red chili flakes

1 TB. water

Pinch sea salt

Pinch ground black pepper

1. In a large sauté pan over medium heat, heat virgin coconut oil. Add sweet onion, and sauté for 5 minutes or until translucent.

2. Add garlic, and cook, stirring frequently, for 2 minutes or until fragrant.

3. Add tofu, and sauté for about 6 minutes or until golden brown.

4. Add mushrooms, cherry tomatoes, spinach, basil, parsley, thyme, nutritional yeast flakes, and red chili flakes, and stir to combine. Add water, and cook for 6 minutes or until spinach and herbs are softened.

5. Season with sea salt and black pepper, divide among 3 plates, and serve.

Variation: Customize your scramble with foods you have on hand. If you only have kale or collard greens, substitute them for spinach, or consider using sun-dried tomatoes instead of fresh cherry tomatoes.

Berries 'n' Whip

The creamy texture and slightly sweet flavor of this hemp seed whip will please any foodie's palate. When combined with succulent fresh berries, you'll wonder if you're eating breakfast or dessert.

Yield:	Prep time:	Serving size:		
about 2 cups	15 minutes	½ cup		
Each serving has:				
143 calories	16 g carbohydrates	8 g fat	4 g fiber	5 g protein

1 cup fresh blueberries	1 TB. pine nuts
½ cup fresh strawberries, sliced	1 TB. tahini
½ cup fresh raspberries	1 TB. maple syrup
½ cup fresh blackberries	¼ tsp. vanilla extract
2 TB. hemp seeds	2 TB. vanilla almond milk

1. In a large bowl, combine blueberries, strawberries, raspberries, and blackberries. Toss, and set aside.

2. In a high-speed blender, combine hemp seeds, pine nuts, tahini, maple syrup, and vanilla extract. Blend on high for 30 seconds or until smooth and creamy.

3. Continue to blend while slowly adding vanilla almond milk until desired consistency is achieved.

4. Divide berries among 4 bowls, top each with 2 tablespoons whip, and serve.

Variation: Serve this tasty whip with your favorite fruit. Pineapple, mango, pears, and peaches are especially good with it.

Apple Orchard Soup

This warm apple soup is scented with clove, cinnamon, and nutmeg. The sweet and creamy base creates a wonderful texture variation to soft chunks of fruit.

Yield:	Prep time:	Cook time:	Serving size:	
about 6 cups	15 minutes	40 minutes	1½ cups	
Each serving has:				
247 calories	61 g carbohydrates	1 g fat	5 g fiber	1 g protein

2 large Fuji apples, peeled, cored, and chopped (3 cups)

1 large green apple, cored and chopped (1½ cups)

1½ cups apple cider

1 cup almond milk

2 tsp. fresh lemon juice

4 TB. maple syrup

¼ tsp. ground cinnamon

½ tsp. vanilla extract

⅛ tsp. ground nutmeg

Pinch ground cloves

1. In a large saucepan over medium heat, combine 1½ cups Fuji apples, green apple, apple cider, almond milk, lemon juice, maple syrup, cinnamon, vanilla extract, and nutmeg. Cook for 20 minutes or until apples are tender.

2. Transfer contents to a high-speed blender, and blend on high until smooth.

3. Return soup to the saucepan, and set over low heat. Stir in remaining 1½ cups Fuji apples and cloves, and cook for 15 minutes.

4. Ladle soup into 4 soup bowls, and serve.

FRESH FACT

I know it's cliché to say "an apple a day keeps the doctor away," but a healthful reminder never hurts. Apples are one of the most convenient health foods and boast over 7,000 known varieties. Included in their list of health benefits is their possible ability to prevent cancer, lower cholesterol, prevent Alzheimer's, increase bone density, and manage weight loss—all while regulating blood sugar levels.

Wholesome and Hearty Breakfasts

In This Chapter

- Low-fat breakfasts with bold flavor
- Gluten-free breakfast creations
- Twists on traditional morning fare
- Brunch-friendly fare

If you've got a big day ahead of you, it might be a good idea to invest in a wholesome and hearty breakfast in lieu of something light like a smoothie. The recipes in this chapter have tons of nutrition and taste good, and they're filling enough to keep you satiated all morning.

Grab-and-Go Breakfast Bars

These oat and fruit bars are easy to prepare and perfect to take with you. They're baked with dried fruit, natural sugars, and a blend of healthy seeds, so you can count on a scrumptious and nutritious treat.

Yield:	Prep time:	Cook time:	Serving size:	
about 12 bars	15 minutes	about 1 hour	1 bar	
Each serving has:				
254 calories	32 g carbohydrates	12 g fat	5 g fiber	7 g protein

6 TB. water

2 TB. ground flaxseeds

½ cup hemp seeds, ground into butter

½ cup maple or coconut sugar

2 tsp. vanilla extract

¼ cup virgin coconut oil

½ tsp. ground cinnamon

½ tsp. sea salt

2½ cups rolled oats

1½ large bananas, peeled and mashed

¼ cup chia seeds

½ cup pitted medjool or deglet noor dates, chopped

½ cup dried cherries, chopped

½ medium apple, cored, and chopped (½ cup)

1. Preheat the oven to 350°F. Lightly grease a 9×11-inch baking dish with cooking spray.

2. In a small saucepan over low heat, heat water. Add flaxseeds, and stir for about 4 minutes or until a creamy consistency is achieved.

3. Add hemp seed butter, maple sugar, vanilla extract, virgin coconut oil, cinnamon, and sea salt. Stir to combine and cook for 3 minutes or until sugar is dissolved.

4. In a large bowl, combine rolled oats, bananas, chia seeds, dates, cherries, and apple.

5. Fold sugar and butter blend into oat mixture, and stir until combined. Press mixture into the prepared baking dish, and bake for 35 minutes or until top is golden.

6. Let cool completely, and cut into 12 equal-size bars.

Variation: If chia seeds are hard to come by, try a combination of other seeds like pumpkin or sunflower. These bars are also delicious with ½ cup unsweetened shredded coconut mixed in.

Pono Grind Granola

Granola doesn't need to be loaded with sugar and fat. This version is full of tropical flavor and satisfying crunch. Enjoy it by the handful, as a cereal with nut milk, or over ice cream for an elegant dessert.

Yield:	Prep time:	Cook time:	Serving size:	
about 4 cups	15 minutes	about 1 hour	½ cup	
Each serving has:				
377 calories	59 g carbohydrates	14 g fat	8 g fiber	8 g protein

4 cups rolled oats

1 medium Fuji apple, cored and diced (1 cup)

¼ cup hemp seeds

½ cup flaked unsweetened coconut

12 large pitted medjool or deglet noor dates, finely chopped

2 TB. pineapple juice

¼ cup maple syrup

2 TB. virgin coconut oil

1. Preheat the oven to 300°F.

2. In a large bowl, combine rolled oats, Fuji apple, hemp seeds, coconut, and medjool dates.

3. In a small saucepan over low heat, combine pineapple juice, maple syrup, and virgin coconut oil. Cook, stirring, for 2 minutes or until melted and combined.

4. Pour pineapple juice mixture into oat blend, and stir to coat evenly.

5. Divide granola between 2 large rimmed baking sheets, and spread into an even layer. Bake, shaking and tossing occasionally to ensure even cooking, for 50 to 60 minutes or until golden.

Variation: For a comforting breakfast cereal, add ½ cup nut milk to 1½ cups Pono Grind Granola, and warm in a small saucepan over medium-high heat for 1 minute or until warmed evenly. If you'd like, top it with a little extra sweetener such as maple syrup, some toasted seeds, or some warming spices like cinnamon and nutmeg.

Maple 'n' Oat Pancakes

Get ready to take a walk down memory lane as you enjoy what tastes like the steamy bowl of oatmeal your mom used to make. These dense, filling pancakes provide just a hint of sweetness and spice.

Yield:	Prep time:	Cook time:	Serving size:
about 8 pancakes	15 minutes	5 minutes per pancake	2 pancakes

Each serving has:				
417 calories	47 g carbohydrates	12 g fat	12 g fiber	7 g protein

1 cup rolled oats	1¼ cups unsweetened almond milk
¾ cup coconut flour	2 TB. virgin coconut oil, melted
¾ tsp. aluminum-free baking soda	¼ tsp. vanilla extract
1 TB. ground flaxseeds	½ tsp. ground cinnamon
3 TB. water	⅛ tsp. ground nutmeg
3 TB. plus ½ cup maple syrup	½ tsp. sea salt

1. In a medium bowl, combine rolled oats, coconut flour, and aluminum-free baking soda.

2. In a small saucepan over low heat, combine flaxseeds and water. Cook, stirring frequently, for about 4 minutes or until a creamy consistency is achieved.

3. Add 3 tablespoons maple syrup, almond milk, virgin coconut oil, vanilla extract, cinnamon, nutmeg, and sea salt, and cook for about 5 minutes or until honey is completely combined and blended thoroughly with other ingredients.

4. Fold honey mixture into oat and flour mixture, and stir until completely moistened. Batter should be thick yet pourable. If needed, add almond milk in 1 tablespoon increments until a smooth texture is achieved.

5. In a large cast-iron skillet over medium-high heat, heat 1 teaspoon virgin coconut oil, turning the skillet to coat. Pour batter in ⅓ cup servings onto a skillet and cook for about 3 minutes or until small bubbles form and remain hollow. Turn over pancake, and cook for 2 more minutes or until golden.

6. Serve pancakes warm topped with 2 tablespoons each maple syrup.

Variation: For added texture and a boost of flavor, add chopped dried cranberries, apples, raisins, or dates. You can also substitute hemp or rice milk for almond milk.

Ginger Pump-Cakes

You'll adore these ginger-spiced pumpkin pancakes. They're fluffy and rich with warming spices.

Yield:	Prep time:	Cook time:	Serving size:	
about 8 pancakes	10 minutes	20 minutes	2 pancakes	
Each serving has:				
305 calories	33 g carbohydrates	7 g fat	6 g fiber	3 g protein

½ cup brown rice flour	1 tsp. ground ginger
¼ cup coconut flour	½ tsp. sea salt
¼ cup tapioca flour	3 TB. hot water
2 tsp. aluminum-free baking powder	1 TB. ground flaxseeds
½ tsp. xanthan gum	½ cup pumpkin purée
½ tsp. ground cinnamon	2 TB. plus ½ cup maple syrup
¼ tsp. ground nutmeg	1 TB. virgin coconut oil, melted
⅛ tsp. ground cloves	1 cup almond or hemp milk

1. In a large bowl, combine brown rice flour, coconut flour, tapioca flour, aluminum-free baking powder, xanthan gum, cinnamon, nutmeg, cloves, ginger, and sea salt.

2. In a small bowl, combine hot water and flaxseeds until a creamy consistency is achieved.

3. In a medium bowl, combine flax mixture, pumpkin purée, 2 tablespoons maple syrup, virgin coconut oil, and almond milk.

4. Add wet ingredients to dry mixture, and stir until thoroughly combined. Batter should be pourable, so if needed, add more almond milk until batter pours nicely off a spoon.

5. In a large cast-iron skillet over medium-high heat, heat 1 teaspoon virgin coconut oil, turning the skillet to coat.

6. Pour batter in ⅓ cup servings onto the skillet. Cook for about 3 minutes or until small bubbles form. Turn over pancake, and cook for 2 more minutes or until golden.

7. Serve warm topped with 2 tablespoons each maple syrup.

Sweet and Spicy Corn Cakes

Bring a little southern love to your morning routine with these delightfully sweet and spicy corn cakes. They're so scrumptious, you may want to double the batch so you can go for a second serving.

Yield:	Prep time:	Cook time:	Serving size:	
about 10 cakes	10 minutes	25 minutes	2 cakes	
Each serving has:				
293 calories	37 g carbohydrates	3 g fat	4 g fiber	4 g protein

1 tsp. virgin coconut oil

Fresh sweet corn kernels cut from 1 large ear (1 cup)

1½ TB. ground flaxseeds

4 TB. warm water

2 TB. plus ⅔ cup maple syrup

1¼ cups vanilla almond milk

½ tsp. vanilla extract

3 TB. fresh orange juice

1 small jalapeño pepper, seeds removed, and minced

½ tsp. sea salt

¼ tsp. ground black pepper

¼ cup yellow cornmeal

¾ cup brown rice flour

1 tsp. aluminum-free baking powder

½ tsp. aluminum-free baking soda

1. In a large cast-iron skillet over medium-high heat, heat 1 teaspoon virgin coconut oil, turning the skillet to coat. Add corn kernels, and toast for 5 minutes or until slightly brown. Set aside.

2. In a small bowl, combine flaxseeds and warm water, and stir until mixture thickens.

3. In a large bowl, combine flax mixture, maple syrup, vanilla almond milk, toasted corn, vanilla extract, orange juice, jalapeño pepper, sea salt, and black pepper.

4. In another large bowl, combine yellow cornmeal, brown rice flour, aluminum-free baking powder, and aluminum-free baking soda.

5. Fold dry ingredients into wet ingredients, and stir until just combined. Do not overmix. Batter should be pourable yet slightly lumpy.

6. Heat a large, lightly greased griddle over medium heat. Pour in ⅓ cup batter at a time, leaving about 2 inches space in between cakes to allow for expansion. When small bubbles form on tops of cakes, flip cakes over, and cook for about 2 more minutes or until both sides are golden.

7. Serve 2 cakes each with 2 tablespoons warm maple syrup or orange preserves.

Variation: Just for fun, make these cakes with blue cornmeal. It doesn't alter the flavor much, but the cakes will be a rich purple-blue, and who can resist blue food? Altering the color may entice the kids to enjoy them, too.

HEADS-UP

Switching to aluminum-free baking soda and powder has been known to reduce your risk for Alzheimer's disease, attention deficit disorder, bone degeneration, Parkinson's disease, cancer, and kidney dysfunction. In addition, aluminum-free ingredients reduce the "tinny" flavor sometimes present in baked goods and other dishes that use baking sodas and powders containing aluminum.

Raw Sprouted Cacao Cakes

These cacao cakes are divinely decadent and full of fiber, protein, and antioxidants for a healthy dose of nutrition. Serve them with fresh fruit for breakfast or tea for dessert.

Yield:	Soak time:	Dehydrate time:	Serving size:	
about 12 cakes	12 hours	20 hours	1 cake	
Each serving has:				
272 calories	38 g carbohydrates	6 g fat	9 g fiber	6 g protein

½ cup ground flaxseeds	4 medium bananas, peeled and mashed
1½ cups water, slightly warm	½ cup chia seeds
2½ cups buckwheat sprouts	1 tsp. sea salt
½ cup raw cacao powder	2 tsp. vanilla extract
1¼ cup maple syrup	1½ cups unsweetened almond milk

1. In a medium bowl, combine flaxseeds and warm water, and stir until mixture thickens and a creamy texture is achieved. Set aside.

2. In a food processor fitted with an S blade, grind 2 cups buckwheat sprouts into a fine meal.

3. In a large bowl, combine ground buckwheat meal, flax mixture, remaining ½ cup buckwheat sprouts, raw cacao powder, ½ cup maple syrup, bananas, chia seeds, sea salt, vanilla extract, and almond milk.

4. Using your hands, scoop out ⅓ cup mixture at a time and roll into 12 balls. Transfer to dehydrator trays lined with Teflex sheets, and press balls into ½-inch-thick cakes. Place the trays in the dehydrator, and dehydrate at 115°F for 8 hours. Flip over cakes, and dehydrate another 12 hours.

5. Serve 1 cake each with 1 tablespoon warm maple syrup.

TASTY TIP

To sprout buckwheat, rinse groats thoroughly in cool water. Place in a large bowl, and cover with three times water. Cover with a towel and let sit at room temperature for 2 hours. Pour off water, rinse thoroughly, and place groats back in the bowl. Let sit at room temperature for 1 or 2 days or until green tails begin to form. Rinse with fresh water every 4 to 8 hours, and be sure to drain well. Your sprouted buckwheat is ready to use as soon as the tails appear.

Buckwheat Porridge

The nuttiness of roasted buckwheat groats complements the warm, earthy taste of vanilla and sweet maple in this comforting oatmeal alternative.

Yield:	Prep time:	Cook time:	Serving size:	
about 4 cups	5 minutes	10 minutes	1 cup	
Each serving has:				
449 calories	78 g carbohydrates	11 g fat	11 g fiber	11 g protein

4 cups water	¼ cup unsweetened shredded coconut
1 tsp. sea salt	2 tsp. vanilla extract
2 cups buckwheat *kasha,* rinsed	Pinch ground cinnamon
¼ cup maple syrup	1 cup hemp or almond milk

1. In a medium saucepan over high heat, bring water and sea salt to a boil. Add kasha, cover, reduce heat to low, and simmer for 10 minutes. Remove from heat, and fluff kasha with a fork.

2. Divide cooked kasha among 4 bowls, and top each with 1 tablespoon maple syrup, 1 tablespoon shredded coconut, ½ teaspoon vanilla extract, and pinch cinnamon. Stir to combine, and serve with ¼ cup hemp milk.

Variation: Personalize your porridge by adding dried fruit, crushed nuts, a sprinkle of raw cacao powder, or chia or hemp seeds.

DEFINITION

Kasha is another term for roasted buckwheat groats. Find this nutty-flavored grain in the bulk section of your health food market or with the packaged grains.

Powerhouse Potatoes

Boost your breakfast potatoes with added protein and fiber! Chia seeds and sweet potatoes make a sweet and savory combination that puts traditional skillet potatoes to rest and gives you an extra punch of power.

Yield:	Prep time:	Cook time:	Serving size:	
about 4 cups	10 minutes	30 minutes	1 cup	
Each serving has:				
231 calories	43 g carbohydrates	6 g fat	7 g fiber	4 g protein

1 TB. virgin coconut oil	2 TB. maple syrup
1 large sweet onion, thinly sliced	1 TB. chia seeds
3 large sweet potatoes, peeled and sliced into ¼-in. rounds	½ tsp. sea salt
	¼ tsp. ground white pepper
1 tsp. fresh thyme leaves, minced	

1. In a large cast-iron skillet over medium-high heat, heat virgin coconut oil, turning the skillet to coat. Add sweet onion, and cook for about 10 minutes or until caramelized. Remove onions from the skillet and set aside.

2. Add sweet potatoes to skillet in batches to maintain a single layer, and cook for about 6 minutes, turning to brown both sides. Repeat with remaining sweet potatoes. (About 20 minutes total.)

3. Return browned sweet potatoes to the skillet. Add caramelized onions, thyme, maple syrup, chia seeds, sea salt, and white pepper. Toss gently to coat, and serve immediately.

Variation: Experiment by adding different herbs such as rosemary or parsley, or use different seeds such as hemp or toasted pumpkinseeds to give this dish some extra dimension in flavor and texture.

FRESH FACT

Sweet potatoes are nutritionally superior to many other potatoes. These orange tubers are loaded with fiber, which keeps you full longer and helps regulate your digestive system. They also have a healthy dose of beta-carotene, vitamin C, and potassium. You can find sweet potatoes in a variety of colors, ranging from white to red and even purple. Purple sweet potatoes have the added nutritional benefit of purple anthocyanin, which has important antioxidant and anti-inflammatory properties.

Sunflower Buttered Toast

On mornings when you're feeling rushed, you can still eat a hearty breakfast. Gluten-free toast is a savory, nutritious breakfast when topped with fresh sunflower butter and hemp seeds.

Yield:	Prep time:	Serving size:		
about 4 slices	10 minutes	1 slice		
Each serving has:				
255 calories	22 g carbohydrates	16 g fat	3 g fiber	10 g protein

1 cup raw sunflower seeds	¾ tsp. sea salt
1 TB. virgin coconut oil, melted	4 slices gluten-free bread
2 TB. maple syrup	4 tsp. hemp seeds

1. In a small food processor fitted with an S blade, blend raw sunflower seeds, virgin coconut oil, maple syrup, and sea salt on high until thoroughly combined. Transfer to a jar with a tight-fitting lid. (Store leftover sunflower butter in the refrigerator for up to 2 weeks.)

2. Toast gluten-free bread to desired darkness. Spread 1 tablespoon fresh sunflower butter over each piece of toast, sprinkle each with 1 teaspoon hemp seeds, and serve.

Variation: You may substitute hemp or pumpkinseeds for sunflower seeds in this butter. You can also experiment with alternative oils such as hemp and flax.

Tempeh Scramble

This sizzling and spicy scramble is sure to please and will keep you satisfied for hours. Chipotle and cayenne give it a nice spicy kick, and earthy mushrooms are the perfect companion to the fresh flavors of cilantro and cumin.

Yield:	Prep time:	Cook time:	Serving size:	
about 4 cups	10 minutes	18 minutes	1 cup	
Each serving has:				
264 calories	14 g carbohydrates	13 g fat	3 g fiber	18 g protein

2 TB. coconut oil (optional)

½ medium red onion, thinly sliced

2 small cloves garlic, crushed

16 oz. tempeh, crumbled (2½ cups)

1 medium red bell pepper, ribs and seeds removed, and diced (1 cup)

½ cup portobello mushrooms, chopped fine

1 cup tomato, diced

2 cups fresh or frozen spinach, thawed, squeezed, and chopped

1 tsp. sea salt

1 TB. fresh lemon juice

1 tsp. chipotle powder

½ tsp. cayenne

1 tsp. ground cumin

½ tsp. ground coriander

½ tsp. ground black pepper

¼ cup vegetable stock

¼ cup fresh cilantro leaves, chopped

3 medium green onions, white and light green parts only, chopped

1. In a large skillet over medium heat, heat 1 tablespoon coconut oil (if using). Add red onion, and sauté for about 4 minutes or until softened.

2. Add garlic, and stir for about 1 minute or until fragrant. Transfer to a medium bowl, and set aside.

3. Add tempeh to the skillet, and cook for about 5 minutes or until lightly browned. Transfer to the bowl containing onions and garlic.

4. Add remaining 1 tablespoon coconut oil (if using) to the pan. Add red bell pepper, portobello mushrooms, tomato, spinach, and sea salt, and sauté for 6 minutes or until tender.

5. Stir in lemon juice, chipotle powder, cayenne, cumin, coriander, black pepper, and vegetable stock. Cook for 1 minute.

6. Pour tempeh and onion mixture into sauce, and stir to combine. Increase heat to medium-high, and add cilantro and green onions. Stir for 1 minute, and serve.

In the Lunchbox

Lunchtime is your midday chance to refuel for the rest of your workday. In Part 3, I share tons of tantalizing recipes worthy of packing in your lunchbox.

Discover the well-kept secrets of creating rich and velvety soups by learning techniques for creating creamy textures without added fat or dairy.

Or enjoy delicious salads, wilted and warm or cool and crisp, full of roasted veggies, light grains, seasonal fruits, or hearty beans. Drenching your healthy salads in tons of oil? Not anymore, now that you can rely on the robust flavors of low-fat vegan dressings in Chapter 8 to bring out the flavors of your gourmet salads.

Finally, you'll love noshing on the creative wraps and rolls that wrap up Part 3. With their distinctive flavors and convenient portability, these to-go lunches are a surefire way to keep you satisfied and nourished while you go about your day.

Silky Soups

In This Chapter

- Flavorful low-fat soups
- Filling, soul-warming soups
- Chilled, refreshing, and raw soups
- Soups that soothe

Soups are the perfect way to make an easy meal and add lots of veggies to your diet. In this chapter, along with more than a dozen delicious soup, stock, and curry recipes, I share some pointers on how to get the most flavor out of your vegetables so you can create amazingly rich soups.

I also provide important information about natural thickening agents, which help give low-fat vegan soups creamy textures that complement their rich flavors.

Low-Fat Roasting Tips

When roasting vegetables in the oven, you may use a rich vegetable stock, such as the Rich Herb Stock in this chapter, in place of oil. Toss 1 cup of vegetables in 2 tablespoons of stock, add seasoning to taste, cover with foil, and roast in the oven at a slightly lower temperature than what you might use for oil roasting, and cook slightly longer until the veggies appear roasted. Covering the vegetables and cooking longer prevents them from burning and provides the perfect flavor profile.

If you opt for roasting with oil, use only a very small amount of virgin coconut oil. One tablespoon of melted coconut oil should be sufficient to completely coat up to 4 cups of vegetables. Always toss the veggies with the oil in a bowl first to ensure even coating before placing the veggies in a roasting pan or on a baking sheet.

Thickening Soups

There's an incredible abundance of nutritious, starchy vegetables that are ideal for adding body to thick and creamy low-fat soups. Some used in the following recipes include cauliflower, butternut squash, purple sweet potatoes, parsnips, and sunchokes.

In most cases, cooking down these starchy delights enhances their sweetness and reduces their textural anomalies, giving rich, smooth consistency to the base of the soup.

Rich Herb Stock

This full-flavored vegetable stock makes a great base for creamy, broth-based, or puréed soups. A multitude of herbs and garlic, as well as some patience, are essential to the success of this satisfying stock.

Yield:	Prep time:	Cook time:	Serving size:	
about 8 cups	10 minutes	about 3 hours	1 cup	
Each serving has:				
49 calories	8 g carbohydrates	2 g fat	0 g fiber	1 g protein

2 medium scallions

4 sprigs thyme

1 sprig rosemary

2 sprigs tarragon

1 TB. virgin coconut oil

2 medium carrots, peeled and chopped (1 cup)

4 large celery stalks with leaves, roughly chopped (1½ cups)

1 medium yellow onion, roughly chopped (1 cup)

4 large cloves garlic, sliced

8 cups water

2 bay leaves

1 tsp. black peppercorns

2 medium leeks, cleaned and sliced (1 cup)

2 tsp. sea salt

1. Lay scallions horizontally on a flat surface. Place thyme, rosemary, and tarragon sprigs vertically in center hollow of scallions. Bring up scallion ends, and tie a knot to create an herb bouquet.

2. In a large cast-iron skillet over medium-high heat, heat virgin coconut oil, turning the skillet to coat. Add carrots and celery, and sauté for 5 minutes.

3. Add yellow onion, and sauté for 4 minutes.

4. Add garlic, and sauté for 1 minute.

5. In a large soup pot over medium heat, combine water, sautéed vegetables, herb bouquet, bay leaves, black peppercorns, leeks, and sea salt. Bring to a boil, reduce heat to low, cover, and simmer for about 3 hours or until stock has reduced by half.

6. Allow stock to cook, and pour through a strainer and into a glass container with a tight-fitting lid. Discard solids. Refrigerate stock for up to 10 days.

Variation: You can always add other vegetables you may have on hand to your broth, such as potato skins, or leeks, shallot, onion, and garlic skins.

TASTY TIP

One of the best benefits of making stock is being able to use up vegetable scraps from other dishes. When chopping vegetables and herbs, reserve any scraps in a zipper-lock plastic bag, and store them in the refrigerator or freezer. After a couple days of collecting, supplement your stash with the necessary ingredients, and you're ready to make your stock. Some scraps can add unpleasant flavors to stock, so avoid trimmings from broccoli, cauliflower, cabbage, asparagus, and other very strong-flavored vegetables.

Speedy Carrot and Ginger Soup

Bright orange carrots and spicy fresh ginger blend beautifully to create a rich soup you can enjoy as a savory starter or as an entire meal.

Yield:	Prep time:	Cook time:	Serving size:	
about 10 cups	5 minutes	about 15 minutes	2 cups	
Each serving has:				
169 calories	32 g carbohydrates	4 g fat	7 g fiber	4 g protein

9 medium carrots, peeled and chunked (6 cups)

2 TB. plus 4 cups Rich Herb Stock (recipe earlier in this chapter)

1 large sweet onion, chopped (1½ cups)

1 (2-in.) piece fresh peeled and grated ginger

2 medium cloves garlic, minced

2½ cups unsweetened almond milk

1 tsp. sea salt

¼ tsp. ground black pepper

2 TB. pumpkinseeds

1. In a vegetable steamer over high heat, heat 2 inches water. Add carrots, and steam for 5 minutes.

2. In a large soup pot over medium heat, heat 2 tablespoons Rich Herb Stock. Add sweet onion, and sauté for about 5 minutes or until translucent.

3. Add ginger and garlic, and stir for about 2 minutes or until fragrant. Add steamed carrots, and stir to coat.

4. Transfer vegetables to a high-speed blender, and add almond milk, remaining 4 cups vegetable stock, sea salt, and black pepper. Vent the lid slightly to prevent splatter, cover blender top with a kitchen towel, and blend on high for 1 minute.

5. In a small dry, cast-iron pan over high heat, toast pumpkinseeds for 1 or 2 minutes.

6. Divide soup among 5 bowls, sprinkle each with 2 teaspoons toasted pumpkin-seeds, and serve.

Variation: You may use ½ teaspoon ground ginger instead of the fresh ginger and coconut or hemp milk instead of the almond milk.

HEADS-UP

Always vent your blender's lid as you begin to blend anything hot. The air expansion caused by the steam literally can blow the lid off your blender if it's sealed too tightly. Even if your blender is equipped with vents, please take extra precaution by holding a kitchen towel over the lid and applying pressure to ensure your lid and soup don't go everywhere.

Sizzling Green Pea Soup

Jalapeño, lemon, and hints of mint and coriander bring bold flavors to this unusual soup and provide a uniquely spicy touch to the sweet taste of green peas.

Yield:	Prep time:	Cook time:	Serving size:	
about 8 cups	10 minutes	about 11 minutes	2 cups	
Each serving has:				
193 calories	31 g carbohydrates	6 g fat	9 g fiber	8 g protein

2 TB. fresh peeled and grated ginger	2 TB. fresh lemon juice
5 medium cloves garlic	1 TB. virgin coconut oil
¼ tsp. ground coriander	1 medium sweet onion, chopped (1 cup)
¼ tsp. dried mint	5 cups vegetable stock
1 medium green jalapeño pepper, chopped	3 cups frozen peas
1 tsp. sea salt	2 TB. fresh mint

1. Using a mortar and pestle, mash ginger, garlic, coriander, dried mint, jalapeño pepper, and sea salt into a paste. Add lemon juice, and stir to combine. Set aside.

2. In a large soup pot over medium heat, heat virgin coconut oil. Add sweet onion, and sauté for about 6 minutes or until just golden.

3. Add garlic-ginger paste, vegetable stock, and peas. Decrease heat to medium, and simmer for 5 minutes.

4. Transfer soup to a high-speed blender, and blend on high for 2 minutes or until puréed. Add fresh mint, and purée for 20 seconds. Season with additional sea salt, and thin soup, if needed, by adding a small amount of vegetable stock.

5. Divide soup among 4 bowls, and serve.

Variation: During the spring season, you can find fresh English shelling peas, which are incredibly sweet and rich in color and perfect for this soup. Remove 2½ pounds shelling peas from their pods, discard pods, and place peas in a bowl until you have about 3 cups. To prepare, bring 4 cups water to a boil in a medium saucepan with ¼ teaspoon sea salt over high heat. Add peas, and boil for 20 seconds. Using a strainer, drain peas immediately. The peas are now ready for use.

Roasted Tomato Fennel Purée

Enjoying a roasted vegetable purée is a perfect way to fill up on a light meal. The sweet plum tomatoes, anise-flavored fennel, and savory thyme in this creamy soup leave you feeling warm, cozy, and satisfied.

Yield:	Prep time:	Cook time:	Serving size:	
about 8 cups	10 minutes	1 hour	2 cups	
Each serving has:				
114 calories	24 g carbohydrates	1 g fat	5 g fiber	4 g protein

10 large roma tomatoes, quartered (6 cups)

1 large sweet onion, quartered (1½ cups)

1 medium fennel bulb, quartered (1 cup)

3 medium cloves garlic, unpeeled

2 TB. plus 1 cup Rich Herb Stock (recipe earlier in this chapter)

½ tsp. sea salt

1 cup water

1 tsp. crushed red pepper flakes

1 TB. maple syrup

1 tsp. fresh thyme, minced

¾ cup unsweetened almond milk

Pinch ground black pepper

2 TB. fresh flat-leaf parsley, chopped

1. Preheat the oven to 350°F.

2. In a large bowl, combine roma tomatoes, sweet onion, fennel, garlic, and 2 tablespoons Rich Herb Stock, and toss until vegetables are well coated. Sprinkle with sea salt, and turn out vegetables onto a large rimmed baking sheet.

3. Roast vegetables on the center rack for 50 minutes, turning every 10 minutes to ensure even cooking, or until tender and lightly browned. Remove garlic and onion after about 30 minutes to keep them from burning. Tomatoes and fennel will take about 45 minutes to complete roasting.

4. Remove the baking sheet from the oven, and pour water over tomatoes and fennel. Using a spatula, loosen any browned bits from the baking sheet.

5. Transfer vegetables and their liquid to a high-speed blender. Add onions, garlic, crushed red pepper flakes, maple syrup, remaining 1 cup vegetable stock, and thyme, and blend on high for 2 minutes or until smooth and creamy.

6. Place a large soup pot on the stove, and place a strainer over the top. Line the strainer with cheesecloth, and pour puréed soup through the strainer and into the soup pot.

7. Set heat to medium, pour in almond milk, and stir to combine. Heat for 15 minutes, stirring occasionally.

8. Season with more sea salt and black pepper. If needed, add a small amount of almond milk until desired texture is achieved.

9. Divide soup among 4 bowls, garnish each with 2 teaspoons chopped parsley, and serve.

Variation: To make a rich and creamy sauce, reduce the quantities of both the stock and milk by half and prepare remaining ingredients as suggested. Use this sauce atop quinoa noodles, cooked millet, polenta, or spaghetti squash.

Coconut Curry with Quinoa

The aroma of this exotic soup is intoxicating. Fragrant curry, hot chiles, and warming turmeric blend into creamy and sweet coconut milk, creating a soup bursting with complexity. Earthy quinoa, snow peas, and spinach enhance the soup's texture and nutrition.

Yield:	Prep time:	Cook time:	Serving size:	
about 12 cups	5 minutes	20 minutes	2 cups	
Each serving has:				
339 calories	32 g carbohydrates	21 g fat	6 g fiber	9 g protein

4 cups water

1 cup quinoa, rinsed well

1 cup fresh or frozen snow peas, halved

2 TB. virgin coconut oil

2 medium shallots, thinly sliced (¼ cup)

2 medium cloves garlic, minced

2 tsp. prepared red curry paste

1½ tsp. madras or Thai curry powder

½ tsp. ground turmeric

½ tsp. ground coriander

6 cups Rich Herb Stock (recipe earlier in this chapter)

1 (13.5-oz.) can lite coconut milk

2 TB. fresh lime juice

2 TB. maple syrup

1 TB. wheat-free tamari

4 cups fresh or frozen spinach, thawed, squeezed, and chopped

5 large scallions, thinly sliced (½ cup)

2 small red jalapeños or Thai bird chiles, minced

½ cup fresh cilantro, chopped

½ cup roasted peanuts, crushed

8 lime wedges

1. In a medium saucepan over high heat, bring 2 cups water to a boil. Add quinoa, and stir for 1 minute. Reduce heat to low, cover, and simmer for 15 minutes. Remove from heat, fluff with a fork, and divide among 6 soup bowls.

2. In a medium saucepan over high heat, bring remaining 2 cups water to a boil. Add snow peas, and cook for 30 seconds. Using a slotted spoon, remove snow peas from the saucepan and divide among soup bowls, on top of quinoa.

3. In a large soup pot over medium-high heat, heat 1 tablespoon virgin coconut oil. Add shallots, and sauté for about 5 minutes or until tender. Using a slotted spoon, remove shallots from the pot and add to snow peas and quinoa.

4. Add remaining 1 tablespoon coconut oil to the soup pot. Add garlic, and cook, stirring, for about 1 minute or until fragrant.

5. Add red curry paste, madras curry powder, turmeric, and coriander, and stir for 1 minute.

6. Pour in Rich Herb Stock and coconut milk, stir, and cook for about 5 minutes.

7. Add lime juice, maple syrup, and wheat-free tamari, and cook for 10 more minutes.

8. Divide spinach leaves among bowls, and ladle soup over top. Garnish each with 1 tablespoon scallions, 1 teaspoon red jalapeños, 1 tablespoon cilantro, 1 tablespoon crushed peanuts, and 1 lime wedge.

Variation: Turn this soup into a noodle soup by replacing the quinoa with cooked quinoa pasta or rice noodles. For added protein, try adding some sautéed cubed tofu or tempeh.

FRESH FACT

The active ingredient in turmeric is curcumin, which is known for its anti-inflammatory properties. Turmeric has been used for centuries as a natural antiseptic, as a preventative against cancers such as prostate and breast cancers and against Alzheimer's disease, as a liver detoxifier, and as an aid in fat metabolism.

Coconut-Lime Butternut Soup

With an abundance of squash available during the fall season, you'll have plenty of opportunities to make this creamy butternut squash soup. It has a bit of heat from the cayenne, tartness from the lime, and a touch of pepperiness from the ginger.

Yield:	Prep time:	Cook time:	Serving size:	
about 8 cups	10 minutes	16 minutes	2 cups	
Each serving has:				
299 calories	35 g carbohydrates	19 g fat	1 g fiber	4 g protein

1 TB. virgin coconut oil

¼ cup sweet onion, chopped

1 large clove garlic, smashed

1 medium butternut squash, peeled, seeded, and cut into chunks (4 cups)

Meat from 1 small young coconut (⅓ cup)

3 cups vegetable stock

2 TB. fresh lime juice

¼ tsp. cayenne

¾ tsp. ground ginger

1 tsp. curry powder

1 TB. maple syrup

1 tsp. sea salt

Pinch sea salt

Ground black pepper

¼ cup fresh cilantro leaves, coarsely chopped

1. In a large soup pot over medium heat, heat virgin coconut oil. Add sweet onion, and sauté for about 5 minutes or until translucent.

2. Add garlic, and stir for 30 seconds or until fragrant.

3. Add butternut squash and coconut meat, and stir until coated.

4. Add vegetable stock, lime juice, cayenne, ginger, curry powder, maple syrup, and sea salt, and cook over medium-high heat for 10 minutes or until squash is tender.

5. Transfer soup to a high-speed blender, and blend on high for 2 minutes or until smooth and creamy. Wipe reserved pot clean and return soup to the pot. Season with pinch sea salt and black pepper.

6. Divide soup among 4 bowls, sprinkle each with 1 tablespoon cilantro, and serve.

Variation: For a soup with even more sweetness and a bit more texture, use kabocha squash in place of butternut.

Smokin' Tortilla Soup

This creamy tortilla soup is thickened with puréed sweet corn. The sweetness of the corn is balanced with spicy jalapeños and serrano peppers, while a dollop of hemp sour cream adds a special cooling touch.

Yield:	Prep time:	Cook time:	Serving size:	
about 10 cups	5 minutes	15 minutes	2 cups	
Each serving has:				
193 calories	26 g carbohydrates	9 g fat	6 g fiber	7 g protein

4 (4-in.) corn tortillas, cut into ¼-in. strips

3 TB. plus 4 cups vegetable stock

1 medium yellow onion, diced (1 cup)

2 medium cloves garlic, minced

1 medium serrano pepper, ribs and seeds removed, and minced

1 medium green jalapeño pepper, seeds removed, and minced

1 (14-oz.) can diced tomatoes, with juice (1¾ cups)

1 cup whole kernel sweet corn, fresh or frozen

1 tsp. ground cumin

¾ tsp. ground chili powder

4 TB. fresh lime juice

½ tsp. sea salt

4 TB. Hemp Sour Cream (recipe in Chapter 10)

½ medium avocado, cubed (⅓ cup)

1. Preheat the oven to 400°F. Lightly coat a baking sheet with nonstick cooking spray.

2. Spread tortilla strips in a single layer on the prepared baking sheet, and bake for 10 minutes or until crispy. Remove and set aside.

3. In a large soup pot over medium heat, heat 3 tablespoons vegetable stock. Add yellow onion, and sauté for 3 minutes or until translucent.

4. Add garlic, serrano pepper, and jalapeño pepper, and heat for about 3 minutes.

5. Increase heat to high, and pour in remaining 4 cups vegetable stock, tomatoes with juice, and sweet corn. Add cumin, chili powder, and lime juice. Reduce heat to medium, and simmer for 10 minutes.

6. Remove soup from heat, and allow to cool slightly at room temperature. Pour ¾ of cooled soup into a high-speed blender. Vent the lid slightly to prevent splatter, and blend for about 2 minutes or until smooth.

7. Return blended soup to the pot, and season with sea salt.

8. Divide soup among 5 bowls, top each with 1 dollop Hemp Sour Cream, a few avocado cubes, and ⅕ of tortilla strips, and serve.

Variation: Another great way to prepare this recipe is with 1 cup hominy in place of the corn. The texture will be a bit creamier and the flavor a little sweeter. Adding some shredded romaine lettuce and freshly diced onions as a garnish adds a touch of fresh crispiness.

Purple Potato Soup

Get ready for a wildly bold soup! Purple sweet potatoes aren't grainy like some other varieties, so this puréed soup is incredibly smooth and creamy. Their deep purple flesh, when blended with almond milk, creates a soothing violet soup. Ginger, coriander, bay leaf, and white pepper complement the potatoes' sweetness beautifully.

Yield:	Prep time:	Cook time:	Serving size:	
about 10 cups	10 minutes	23 minutes	2 cups	
Each serving has:				
214 calories	46 g carbohydrates	2 g fat	7 g fiber	4 g protein

2 TB. plus 6 cups vegetable stock

1 small sweet onion, diced (½ cup)

2 medium cloves garlic, minced

2 medium-large purple sweet potatoes, peeled and chopped (3 cups)

¼ tsp. ground ginger

¼ tsp. ground coriander

1 bay leaf

¾ tsp. sea salt

½ tsp. ground white pepper

1 cup unsweetened almond milk

1. In a large soup pot over medium heat, heat 2 tablespoons vegetable stock. Add sweet onion, and cook for 7 minutes or until caramelized.

2. Add garlic, and cook for 1 minute.

3. Add purple sweet potatoes, ginger, coriander, bay leaf, remaining 6 cups vegetable stock, sea salt, and white pepper. Bring to a gentle boil, reduce heat to low, and simmer for 15 minutes or until potatoes are tender.

4. Add almond milk. Remove bay leaf, transfer soup to a high-speed blender, and purée for 2 minutes or until smooth. Wipe reserved pot clean, and return puréed soup to the pot. Season with additional sea salt and white pepper.

5. Divide soup among 5 bowls, and serve.

Variation: If you can't find purple sweet potatoes, use yams instead. The flavor will be similar, but the color will be orange instead of violet.

FRESH FACT

Purple sweet potatoes are indigenous to Peru and Okinawa, Japan. Their skin can range from pink to light and dark brown, and their flesh is a very deep purple. They're tremendously sweet and nutritious, containing a high amount of anthocyanin, the pigment that creates their vibrant purple color. These phytonutrients are also found in blueberries and purple cabbage and are known to reduce inflammation and decrease the risk of cancer.

Cream of Cauliflower Soup

Enjoy the decadence of this creamed soup, enhanced with a base of white beans. The flavor is rich with herbs and garlic and will warm you from your head to your toes.

Yield:	Prep time:	Cook time:	Serving size:
about 10 cups	10 minutes	about 50 minutes	2 cups

Each serving has:				
147 calories	27 g carbohydrates	3 g fat	8 g fiber	8 g protein

2 TB. plus 6 cups Rich Herb Stock (recipe earlier in this chapter)

1 medium sweet onion, chopped (1 cup)

4 medium cloves garlic, smashed

1 large cauliflower head, chopped (5 cups)

1 tsp. fresh thyme, minced

1 tsp. fresh parsley, minced

½ tsp. fresh tarragon, minced

1 tsp. sea salt

½ tsp. ground black pepper

2 tsp. ground paprika

1 bay leaf

1 (13-oz.) can cannellini or northern beans, drained and rinsed

1. In a large soup pot over medium heat, heat 2 tablespoons Rich Herb Stock. Add sweet onion, and sauté for 5 minutes or until translucent.

2. Add garlic, and stir for about 2 minutes or until fragrant.

3. Reduce heat to medium, and add cauliflower, remaining 6 cups Rich Herb Stock, thyme, parsley, tarragon, sea salt, black pepper, paprika, and bay leaf. Bring to a boil. Reduce heat to low, and simmer for 15 minutes or until cauliflower is tender.

4. Add cannellini beans, and simmer for 10 more minutes.

5. Remove bay leaf, and transfer soup, in batches, to a high-speed blender and blend on high for 2 minutes, or until puréed. Return puréed soup to the soup pot, reduce heat to low, and simmer for 20 more minutes.

6. Season with additional sea salt and black pepper, divide soup among 5 bowls, and serve.

Variation: For **Cream of Broccoli Soup,** use broccoli in place of the cauliflower. Add 2 tablespoons lemon juice and ¼ teaspoon red chili flakes prior to blending.

FRESH FACT

For years, cauliflower has received less praise than its other cruciferous vegetable relatives, such as broccoli and brussels sprouts. But dozens of studies link diets rich in cauliflower to cancer prevention. Cauliflower is an excellent source of vitamin C, manganese, and vitamin K as well as omega-3 fatty acids. It's also high in fiber.

Aromatic Lemongrass Soup

This traditional Thai soup is incredibly aromatic. A blend of kaffir lime leaf, fresh lemongrass, chiles, and ginger provide a perfect cocktail of spice, pepper, and tang. This soup is intended to be very spicy. Add single chiles, one at a time, until you achieve the desired spice level.

Yield:	Prep time:	Cook time:	Serving size:	
about 10 cups	5 minutes	15 minutes	1¼ cups	
Each serving has:				
130 calories	17 g carbohydrates	7 g fat	4 g fiber	4 g protein

2 large cloves garlic	2 TB. virgin coconut oil
1 (2-in.) piece fresh peeled ginger, thinly sliced	1 medium white onion, thinly sliced (1 cup)
3 medium stalks lemongrass, tough skins removed, and inner soft flesh, smashed and chopped	8 cups vegetable stock
	3 TB. wheat-free tamari
	¼ cup fresh lime juice
8 kaffir lime leaves, cut into thin strips	1 cup brown or white mushrooms, quartered
10 to 15 dried chiles de arbol or other small dried red chiles	2½ cups plum tomatoes, chopped
	½ cup fresh cilantro, roughly chopped

1. Using a mortar and pestle, mash garlic, ginger, lemongrass, kaffir lime leaves, and chiles de arbol into a paste.

2. In a large soup pot over medium-high heat, heat virgin coconut oil. Add white onion, and sauté for about 5 minutes or until softened.

3. Add chili paste, vegetable stock, wheat-free tamari, lime juice, brown mushrooms, and plum tomatoes. Decrease heat to medium, and simmer for about 10 minutes or until tomatoes are tender but not mushy.

4. Divide among 8 bowls, top with 1 tablespoon cilantro, and serve.

Middle Eastern Quinoa Noodle Soup

Seasoned with aromatic Middle Eastern spices and full of herbs, greens, beans, and quinoa noodles, this soup can easily be a complete meal. Hemp Sour Cream and fresh lemon juice add a bit of tang, while turmeric, mint, coriander, and fresh ginger provide flavor.

Yield:	Prep time:	Cook time:	Serving size:
about 12 cups	10 minutes, plus overnight soak time	40 minutes	2 cups

Each serving has:				
474 calories	51 g carbohydrates	23 g fat	13 g fiber	22 g protein

3 TB. virgin coconut oil	8 cups Rich Herb Stock (recipe earlier in this chapter)
3 medium yellow onions, thinly sliced (3 cups)	10 oz. dried quinoa linguini
1 (1-in.) piece fresh peeled ginger, chopped	1½ cups cooked chickpeas
5 medium cloves garlic, minced	1 cup Hemp Sour Cream (recipe in Chapter 10)
1½ tsp. sea salt	½ cup fresh dill, chopped
1 tsp. ground turmeric	½ cup fresh cilantro, chopped, plus extra for garnish
2 tsp. dried mint	1 cup fresh parsley, chopped
¾ tsp. ground coriander	4 cups fresh spinach
1 tsp. ground black pepper	3 medium lemons, halved
¾ cup dried green or brown lentils	

1. In a soup pot over medium heat, heat virgin coconut oil. Add yellow onions and ginger, and sauté for about 7 minutes, stirring occasionally, or until onions are slightly caramelized.

2. Add garlic, sea salt, turmeric, mint, coriander, black pepper, green lentils, and Rich Herb Stock. Bring to a boil, reduce heat to low, cover, and simmer for about 20 minutes or until lentils are tender.

3. Increase heat to high, add quinoa linguini and chickpeas, and boil for 5 minutes.

4. Reduce heat to low, and stir in Hemp Sour Cream, dill, cilantro, parsley, and spinach for about 10 minutes or until herbs and spinach wilt.

5. Season with additional sea salt and black pepper. Divide soup among 6 bowls, sprinkle with chopped cilantro leaves and a generous squeeze of fresh lemon juice, and serve.

Variation: Improvise with ingredients you have available. If your pantry is stocked with quinoa and white beans, they will be excellent substitutes for the chickpeas, lentils, and quinoa noodles.

HEADS-UP

The gas often caused by beans can be greatly reduced and even avoided by soaking, draining, and rinsing the beans and slowly bringing them to a boil. Otherwise, you might experience unpleasant side effects such as gas and bloating.

Raw Beautifying Beet Soup

It might be the vibrant pink color that will have you adoring this soup, or it could be the unique combination of sweet carrots, apples, red beets, and spicy ginger. This soup is completely raw and is served chilled.

Yield:	Prep time:	Chill time:	Serving size:	
about 5 cups	20 minutes	1 hour	1 cup	
Each serving has:				
169 calories	15 g carbohydrates	10 g fat	3 g fiber	6 g protein

1 large red beet, peeled and chopped (1½ cups)

2 large beets, skin on, and juiced (1½ cups)

8 large carrots, skin on, and juiced (2 cups)

2 medium carrots, peeled and chopped (1½ cups)

2 medium Fuji apples, cored and sliced (2 cups)

1 (2-in.) piece fresh peeled ginger, chopped

¼ cup hemp seeds

1 TB. chia seeds

¼ cup almond butter

2 TB. fresh lemon juice

½ tsp. sea salt

2 cups water

1. In a high-speed blender, purée red beet, beet juice, carrot juice, carrots, Fuji apples, ginger, hemp seeds, chia seeds, almond butter, lemon juice, sea salt, and water on high for 2 minutes or until smooth.

2. Transfer to a container with a lid, and refrigerate for about 1 hour or until chilled.

3. Divide soup among 5 bowls, sprinkle with hemp seeds, and serve.

Variation: Many of the ingredients are already juiced, so for a **Cleansing Beet Smoothie,** put the remaining whole carrots, apples, beet, 1-inch piece of ginger, and ½ lemon with peel removed through a juicer. Mix with carrot and beet juices, and enjoy this smoothie first thing in the morning to encourage cleansing and kick-start your digestive activity.

FRESH FACT

Beets are hard to beat when it comes to detoxification. They contain phytonutrients called betalains that have been shown to provide antioxidant, anti-inflammatory, and deep detoxification support of the blood. They're also known to lower blood pressure, reduce cancer risk, and bring a glow to the skin.

Raw Watermelon Gazpacho

Succulent, sweet watermelon combined with fresh mint and a bit of spice is a perfect savory summer treat.

Yield:	Prep time:	Chill time:	Serving size:
about 2 cups	15 minutes	1 hour	1 cup

Each serving has:				
70 calories	17 g carbohydrates	0 g fat	2 g fiber	2 g protein

1 small seedless watermelon, chopped (2 cups)	2 medium jalapeño peppers, cored and minced
3 TB. aged balsamic vinegar	1 tsp. sea salt
¼ cup fresh lime juice	2 TB. green onions, white and light green parts only
1 TB. fresh mint, finely chopped	¼ cup fresh cilantro, finely chopped

1. In a large bowl, combine watermelon, aged balsamic vinegar, lime juice, mint, jalapeño peppers, and sea salt, and toss to combine.

2. Using a large spoon, mash watermelon until all large pieces are broken down. You will want to maintain some texture in soup. Refrigerate for 1 hour.

3. Divide soup among 2 bowls, stir in green onions and cilantro, and serve.

Variation: For **Raw Watermelon Salsa,** rather than mashing the watermelon, transfer it to a strainer set over a bowl. Let watermelon rest for 30 minutes or until most of the juice has been released. (Reserve juice for a refreshing beverage or freeze it into a few popsicles.) Mix cubed watermelon with remaining ingredients, and refrigerate for 1 hour. Serve with plantain or blue corn chips.

Sensational Salads

In This Chapter

- Hearty grain and bean salads
- Grilled, dried, and fresh fruit salads
- Light and refreshing slaws
- Robust entrée-worthy greens

Step aside, iceberg lettuce. There's no room for bland, watery, white lettuce in this chapter! Instead, prepare your palate for myriad bold flavors and varied textures of the sensational salads that follow.

Warmed or fresh, accompanied by grains, beans, or fruits, I share an herbal array of glorious, healthy leafy green dishes here that will reform your every notion of the traditional salad.

From Light and Refreshing to Complete Meals

One thing I love about salads is their versatility. Play around with inventing a complete meal on a single plate. Experiment with creations such as sautéed greens with herbs, spices, and hearty mushrooms or tofu, or toss a fruit salad with warm grains. If you have the time, roast root vegetables and combine them with hearty greens, such as rapini or kale, and a serving of cooked and seasoned beans.

For a lighter meal or a side salad, have fun with delicate yet robust flavored greens like watercress, arugula, endive, and frisée. Make slaws using shredded cabbage and sprouts, or introduce more distinctly flavored veggies such as sunchokes, kohlrabi, and fennel into your repertoire. Herbs such as cilantro, mint, basil, and parsley and sea vegetables like arame and wakame also are excellent for livening up salads.

Beet Tartar Salad

Sweet and robust steamed beets are enhanced with a creamy and unique dressing of nutty tahini, silky white beans, and fresh dill.

Yield:	Prep time:	Cook time:	Serving size:	
about 4 cups	10 minutes	15 minutes	1 cup	
Each serving has:				
130 calories	13 g carbohydrates	7 g fat	4 g fiber	6 g protein

4 medium red beets, skin on, scrubbed, ends trimmed, and quartered

1 small clove garlic, peeled

½ tsp. fine sea salt

2 TB. tahini

¼ cup cooked white beans

1 TB. fresh dill, minced

1 TB. fresh lemon juice

2 TB. water

1 TB. nutritional yeast flakes

1 tsp. balsamic vinegar

1 TB. extra-virgin olive oil

1 TB. fresh basil leaves, minced

Pinch cracked black pepper

1. Fill a vegetable steamer with 2 inches water, and bring to a boil over high heat. Add red beets, and cook for 15 minutes or until just tender. Check for doneness at 12 minutes by inserting a fork in center of beet. If the fork inserts with ease, beets are ready. Remove beets, and set aside to cool completely.

2. When beets are cooled, and wearing rubber gloves, peel beets and chop into small-dice cubes. Place in a medium bowl, and set aside.

3. Using a mortar and pestle, mash garlic and fine sea salt into a paste.

4. In a small bowl, combine garlic paste, tahini, white beans, dill, lemon juice, water, and nutritional yeast flakes. Mash together until thoroughly combined and creamy.

5. In the medium bowl, add balsamic vinegar and extra-virgin olive oil to beets, and stir to coat evenly.

6. Divide beets among serving plates, top with 1 or 2 tablespoons tahini blend, sprinkle with basil, and season with black pepper.

Variation: For a warm, fall salad, instead of steaming the beets, roast them in a 350°F oven for 35 minutes or until tender. While still warm, peel beets, and toss with tahini blend. Turn out onto plates, and sprinkle with basil and black pepper.

Roasted Corn and Quinoa Salad

This robust salad combines fluffy quinoa, roasted sweet corn, and a dressing of succulent orange juice, honey, hot cayenne, and fragrant cumin. Its light flavor and rich texture will leave you feeling sufficiently full.

Yield:	Prep time:	Cook time:	Serving size:	
about 3½ cups	10 minutes	23 minutes	¾ cup	
Each serving has:				
280 calories	58 g carbohydrates	3 g fat	6 g fiber	9 g protein

Kernels from 2 large ears of sweet corn (2 cups)

2 cups water

1 cup quinoa, rinsed

¼ cup fresh orange juice

3 TB. maple syrup

1 tsp. chili powder

½ tsp. cayenne

1 tsp. ground cumin

1 tsp. dried Mexican oregano

½ tsp. sea salt

3 medium green onions, whites and light green parts only, chopped

1 TB. chopped fresh cilantro leaves

2 TB. pine nuts (optional)

1. In a small cast-iron skillet over high heat, dry-toast corn kernels for about 8 minutes or until soft and slightly browned. Set aside.

2. In a medium saucepan over high heat, bring water to a boil. Add quinoa, cover, reduce heat to low, and simmer for 15 minutes. Fluff with a fork, and transfer to a large bowl.

3. In a small bowl, combine orange juice, maple syrup, chili powder, cayenne, cumin, Mexican oregano, and sea salt.

4. Pour dressing into quinoa, add green onions and cilantro, and stir to combine. Serve topped with pine nuts (if using).

Variation: Make a healthy and complete meal in a bowl using this salad as the base. Top with steamed or roasted vegetables, or sautéed greens and cooked white beans. Finish with your favorite dressing, such as Jalapeño Cilantro Lime Dressing (recipe in Chapter 8).

FRESH FACT

Technically a seed, quinoa is suitable for gluten-free diets or for those who have wheat and grain sensitivities. This superseed is full of amino acids and is a superior source of protein, weighing in at between 8 and 22 percent protein depending on the variety. Simple to cook and highly versatile, quinoa is perfect for salads, as a side dish, in morning porridge, or baked into sweets and snacks.

Southwestern Quinoa and Black Bean Salad

Nutty quinoa and black beans make this cool and hearty salad a perfect entrée. Flavorful lime, serrano, and cumin bring a spicy flair and the addition of Hemp Sour Cream and salsa make this a worthy dish for a fiesta.

Yield:	Prep time:	Cook time:	Serving size:	
about 6 cups	10 minutes	15 minutes	1½ cups	
Each serving has:				
355 calories	49 g carbohydrates	12 g fat	10 g fiber	14 g protein

1½ cups water

½ cup red or black quinoa, rinsed

½ cup white quinoa, rinsed

2 small cloves garlic

1 tsp. sea salt

4 TB. fresh lime juice

½ tsp. ground cumin

⅛ cup extra-virgin olive oil

1 small red bell pepper, ribs and seeds removed, and diced small (½ cup)

¼ medium red onion, minced (¼ cup)

1 medium serrano pepper, seeded and minced

½ cup fresh cherry tomatoes, quartered

1½ cups cooked black beans

3 TB. fresh cilantro leaves, minced

⅓ cup Hemp Sour Cream (recipe in Chapter 10)

¼ cup salsa (your favorite)

1 medium avocado, peeled and cubed (optional)

1. In a medium saucepan over high heat, bring water to a boil. Add red quinoa and white quinoa, reduce heat to low, cover, and cook for 15 minutes. Remove from heat, fluff with a fork, and set aside to cool completely.

2. Meanwhile, using a mortar and pestle, mash garlic and sea salt into a paste. Transfer to a medium bowl, add lime juice and cumin, and stir to combine. Slowly whisk in extra-virgin olive oil until thoroughly combined. Set aside.

3. In a large mixing bowl, combine cooled quinoa, red bell pepper, red onion, serrano, cherry tomatoes, black beans, cilantro, and dressing.

4. Transfer to serving bowls, and top each with 1 tablespoon Hemp Sour Cream and salsa to your liking. Finish with cubed avocado (if using).

Variation: This salad is easy to customize with ingredients you have on hand. Use millet or brown rice instead of quinoa and white beans instead of black. Vary the level of heat by using less or more serrano, or bring on a smoky heat by using 1 or 2 chopped chipotle peppers.

Fennel, Orange, and Black Olive Salad

The light and refreshing blend of juicy oranges, crunchy fennel, and buttery black olives makes this a perfect summertime salad. It's drizzled with a mouthwatering sweet orange dressing that's a definite palate pleaser.

Yield:	Prep time:	Serving size:		
about 4 cups	10 minutes	1 cup		
Each serving has:				
111 calories	22 g carbohydrates	3 g fat	6 g fiber	2 g protein

2 medium fennel bulbs

1 cup fresh arugula leaves

2 medium naval oranges, peeled and segmented

1 (3.8-oz.) can sliced black olives, drained

½ cup Cider Orange Dressing (recipe in Chapter 8)

Pinch ground black pepper

1. Remove and discard greens from fennel bulbs, scrub bulbs, and cut into long and thin strips (1½ cups total). Add to a large bowl.

2. Add arugula, naval oranges, and black olives to fennel, and toss well.

3. Divide salad among serving plates, drizzle each with 2 tablespoons Cider Orange Dressing, and season with black pepper.

Variation: Enjoy this salad with blistered white beans for a complete meal. In a large skillet over medium-high heat, heat 1 tablespoon coconut oil. Add fennel, and cook for 8 minutes or until soft and slightly caramelized. Add 1 cup cooked white beans, and sauté for about 6 minutes or until beans begin to blister. Stir in dressing, oranges, and olives, and heat for 2 minutes. Omit arugula in this variation.

FRESH FACT

Fennel has a celery-like texture and is slightly sweet with a notable licorice flavor. It's refreshing and versatile and can be enjoyed raw or cooked to caramelized perfection. Fennel is a member of the *Umbellifereae* family, which also includes parsley, dill, and coriander. It's a good source of fiber, vitamin C, folate, potassium, and the phytonutrient anethole, which is helpful in reducing inflammation and has been shown to prevent cancer. Shop for fennel during fall and through the early months of spring, when it's most abundant.

Warm Garlic Greens Salad

Hearty greens sweeten and relax pungent garlic a bit while citrus jazzes up this succulent salad accented by hot chili flakes and aromatic thyme.

Yield:	Prep time:	Cook time:	Serving size:	
about 2 cups	10 minutes	about 10 minutes	½ cup	
Each serving has:				
88 calories	9 g carbohydrates	5 g fat	2 g fiber	4 g protein

1 TB. virgin coconut oil

2 medium shallots, sliced (¼ cup)

3 medium cloves garlic, thinly sliced

3 medium rainbow chard leaves, roughly chopped (2 cups)

4 medium lacinato kale leaves, stems removed and roughly chopped (2 cups)

3 medium collard greens, stems removed and roughly chopped (2 cups)

1 tsp. red chili flakes

½ tsp. dried thyme

¼ cup vegetable stock

2 TB. fresh lemon juice

½ tsp. sea salt

¼ tsp. ground black pepper

1 TB. hemp seeds

1. In a large cast-iron skillet over medium-high heat, heat virgin coconut oil, turning the skillet to coat. Add shallots, and sauté for 2 minutes.

2. Add garlic, and sauté for 1 minute.

3. Add rainbow chard, kale, collard greens, red chili flakes, thyme, and vegetable stock. Cook for about 7 minutes or until greens wilt.

4. Remove from heat, stir in lemon juice, and add sea salt and black pepper.

5. Sprinkle with hemp seeds, and serve.

Variation: You could make a similar dish with different textures using broccolini or rapini instead of, or in addition to, the greens. Follow the directions as outlined, but when cooking the broccolini or rapini, cook for 3 or 4 more minutes or until tender.

Beet, Hemp Patty, and Arugula Salad

The combination of sweet steamed beets, warm hemp patties, peppery arugula, and crispy frisée is highlighted by a rich balsamic vinaigrette that adds a touch of tang.

Yield:	Prep time:	Cook time:	Chill time:	Serving size:
about 5 cups	10 minutes	about 20 minutes	25 minutes	1½ cups

Each serving has:				
187 calories	9 g carbohydrates	15 g fat	2 g fiber	8 g protein

¼ cup hemp seeds	¼ cup ground almonds or almond flour
⅛ cup water	1 TB. virgin coconut oil
1 TB. nutritional yeast flakes	3 cups baby arugula
1 tsp. fresh lemon juice	1 cup fresh frisée
½ tsp. sea salt	½ cup Balsamic Vinaigrette (variation in Chapter 8)
2 medium red or golden beets, scrubbed and ends trimmed	Pinch ground black pepper

1. In a food processor fitted with an S blade, blend hemp seeds, water, nutritional yeast flakes, lemon juice, and sea salt until smooth and creamy. Transfer to a small bowl, and refrigerate for at least 25 minutes.

2. Meanwhile, fill a vegetable steamer with 2 inches water, and bring to a boil. Add red beets, and steam for 15 minutes or until tender. Remove beets, and set aside to cool slightly.

3. When beets are cooled enough to handle, and wearing rubber apply gloves, peel beets and cut into ½-inch cubes. Set aside.

4. Sprinkle ground almonds onto a plate.

5. Roll chilled hemp batter into (1-inch) balls and press into ½-inch-thick patties. Coat hemp patties in ground almonds on all sides.

6. In a medium skillet over high heat, heat virgin coconut oil. Add hemp patties, and cook for about 2 minutes per side or until golden brown. Remove hemp patties from the skillet, and set aside on a paper towel.

7. Divide arugula and frisée among plates, divide beets among greens, drizzle with Balsamic Vinaigrette, and top with hemp fritters. Season with black pepper.

Variation: Turn this salad into a savory appetizer by topping gluten-free crackers with a small dollop of warmed hemp batter, several arugula leaves, a few chopped beets, and a drizzle of dressing.

FRESH FACT

Arugula, also known as "rocket" for its peppery flavor, is a member of the *Brassicaceae* family. Relatives of arugula include kale, mustard greens, and cauliflower. Arugula is full of phytochemicals that have been known to suppress the growth of cancer cells. It's also a supreme source of vitamins A, C, K, and several B vitamins, which are essential for healthy metabolic functions. In addition, it has notable quantities of minerals such as copper and iron.

Strawberry Pine Nut Salad

You might be surprised at how well sweet strawberries pair with peppery arugula and cheesy nutritional yeast flakes. The garlicky balsamic dressing is mellowed slightly with maple syrup.

Yield: about 3 cups	Prep time: 15 minutes	Serving size: 1 cup		
Each serving has:				
363 calories	12 g carbohydrates	35 g fat	4 g fiber	8 g protein

3 cups arugula

6 large fresh strawberries, greens removed, and sliced (1 cup)

½ small red onion, thinly sliced (¼ cup)

½ cup Balsamic Vinaigrette (variation in Chapter 8)

2 TB. pine nuts

1 TB. nutritional yeast flakes

Pinch ground black pepper

1. In a large bowl, toss arugula, strawberries, and red onion with Balsamic Vinaigrette.

2. Divide salad among plates, and sprinkle each with 2 teaspoons pine nuts, 1 teaspoon nutritional yeast flakes, and pinch black pepper.

Variation: Make a unique snack or appetizer by rolling chopped strawberries, a couple red onion slices, a few arugula leaves, nutritional yeast flakes, and pine nuts inside a few radicchio leaves. Serve with a side of dressing.

Fig, Avocado, and Fennel Salad

The distinct licorice flavor of fresh fennel harmoniously blends with the natural sugars of fresh figs and buttery avocado, while a light sweet citrus dressing completes this dish.

Yield:	Prep time:	Serving size:		
about 4 cups	15 minutes	1 cup		
Each serving has:				
292 calories	39 g carbohydrates	17 g fat	6 g fiber	2 g protein

½ medium fennel bulb

3 TB. fresh lemon juice

2 TB. agave nectar

½ tsp. sea salt

¼ tsp. ground black pepper

¼ cup extra-virgin olive oil

3 cups fresh arugula

8 large fresh figs, stems removed, and quartered (3 cups)

½ medium avocado, cubed

1. Remove and discard greens from fennel bulb, scrub bulb, and thinly slice. Add to a large bowl.

2. In a small bowl, combine lemon juice, agave nectar, sea salt, and black pepper. Slowly whisk in extra-virgin olive oil until thoroughly combined and emulsified.

3. Add arugula to fennel, and toss with dressing.

4. Divide salad among 4 plates, and top each with ¼ of figs and ¼ of avocado. Season with more black pepper.

Variation: Alter the flavor of this recipe significantly by cooking the figs and fennel. In a large skillet over medium heat, heat 1 teaspoon coconut oil. Add fennel and caramelize. Remove fennel from the skillet, and repeat with the figs until warm. Return fennel to the skillet, add arugula and dressing, and heat for 1 minute, stirring to coat evenly with dressing. Omit the avocado when serving this variation.

FRESH FACT

Figs reign supreme on the health charts and are an incredibly delicate and intoxicating fruit. Fresh figs are abundantly sweet with a leathery skin and tiny crunchy seeds. They can be devoured raw, grilled, roasted, or dried. They contain significant levels of dietary fiber and are rich in minerals calcium and potassium. They've been shown to increase cardiovascular health, protect against cancer, regulate insulin levels, and promote healthy weight management.

Lemony Lentil Salad

This Mediterranean-flavored dish is lemony, earthy, and laced with salt and savor. Lentils are cooked *al dente* to provide a firm heartiness, and fresh herbs, sweet cherry tomatoes, and olives provide balance and layered texture.

Yield:	Prep time:	Cook time:	Serving size:	
about 3 cups	10 minutes	25 minutes	¾ cup	
Each serving has:				
322 calories	37 g carbohydrates	13 g fat	15 g fiber	15 g protein

1¾ cups vegetable stock	1 tsp. Dijon mustard
1 cup dried brown lentils, rinsed	1 small clove garlic, peeled and minced
1 TB. fresh thyme, minced	½ tsp. sea salt
½ tsp. lemon zest	¼ tsp. ground black pepper
2 TB. fresh lemon juice	3 TB. extra-virgin olive oil
1 tsp. apple cider vinegar	¼ cup fresh parsley, minced
1 TB. shallots, minced	½ cup cherry tomatoes, halved
2 tsp. maple syrup	¼ cup pitted kalamata olives, chopped

1. In a medium saucepan over medium-high heat, bring vegetable stock to a boil. Add brown lentils and thyme, and return to a boil. Reduce heat to low, cover, and simmer for 20 to 25 minutes or until just tender.

2. Meanwhile, in a small bowl, combine lemon zest, lemon juice, apple cider vinegar, shallots, maple syrup, Dijon mustard, garlic, sea salt, and black pepper. Slowly whisk in extra-virgin olive oil until thoroughly combined. Set aside.

3. In a large bowl, toss lentils, parsley, and dressing. Stir in cherry tomatoes and kalamata olives.

Variation: The ingredients of this salad also make a delicious soup. Increase the vegetable stock to 3½ cups and use carrots and celery instead of tomatoes and olives. Combine all ingredients in a medium saucepan, add 1 bay leaf, and simmer for 40 to 50 minutes. Remove bay leaf, stir in 3 cups chopped kale or spinach, and heat until warm and relaxed.

TASTY TIP
Lentils are a superior vegan protein source, with around 30 percent of their calories being protein. They're high in dietary fiber, which is also around 30 percent of calories. They also contain iron, folate, phosphorus, and zinc. Lentils come in at least a dozen varieties, ranging in size and colors of orange, red, pink, brown, yellow, green, and black.

Heirloom Tomato and Torn Basil Salad

Simple, fresh, and especially enjoyable when heirlooms are abundant, this version of a traditional Italian salad is savory and sweet and makes a delightful start to any meal.

Yield:	Prep time:	Serving size:		
about 3½ cups	15 minutes	¾ cup		
Each serving has:				
112 calories	10 g carbohydrates	7 g fat	3 g fiber	3 g protein

1 small clove garlic

½ tsp. sea salt

1 TB. red wine vinegar

½ tsp. Dijon mustard

½ tsp. maple syrup

¼ tsp. ground black pepper

⅛ cup extra-virgin olive oil

4 medium heirloom tomatoes, quartered (3 cups)

½ cup heirloom cherry tomatoes, halved

1 TB. nutritional yeast flakes

½ cup fresh basil leaves, torn

1. Using a mortar and pestle, mash garlic and sea salt into a paste. Transfer to a small bowl.

2. Add red wine vinegar, Dijon mustard, maple syrup, and black pepper to garlic paste, and stir to combine. Slowly whisk in extra-virgin olive oil until thoroughly emulsified. Set aside.

3. In a large bowl, toss heirloom tomatoes and cherry tomatoes with dressing, sprinkle in nutritional yeast flakes and basil, and stir to combine. Let salad rest for 15 minutes before serving.

Variation: For a scrumptious bruschetta topper, finely chop tomatoes and basil and toss with dressing and nutritional yeast flakes until thoroughly combined. Spread on gluten-free toast points.

Warm Kale and White Bean Salad

Warm kale is combined with browned and blistered white beans, garlic, onions, and lemon juice for a creamy, rich, and savory salad that you can enjoy as a side dish or main meal.

Yield:	Prep time:	Cook time:	Serving size:	
about 3½ cups	10 minutes	about 10 minutes	¾ cup	
Each serving has:				
270 calories	38 g carbohydrates	8 g fat	10 g fiber	16 g protein

2 TB. virgin coconut oil

1 small sweet onion, thinly sliced (½ cup)

4 small cloves garlic, minced

2 cups cooked Great Northern or cannellini beans

3 medium lacinato kale leaves, stems removed and chopped (2½ cups)

¼ cup vegetable stock

1 TB. fresh lemon juice

½ tsp. sea salt

2 TB. nutritional yeast flakes

Pinch cracked black pepper

1. In a large skillet over medium-high heat, heat virgin coconut oil. Add sweet onion and garlic, and stir for 1 minute.

2. Add Great Northern beans, and cook for 8 minutes or until browned and blistered.

3. Add kale, vegetable stock, lemon juice, sea salt, and nutritional yeast flakes, and stir for 2 minutes or until kale is warmed and wilted.

4. Divide among 4 plates, and finish each with pinch black pepper.

Variation: To create **Homemade Veggie Patties,** follow instructions for this recipe but instead of dividing among plates, transfer warmed beans and kale to a large bowl, add another 3 tablespoons vegetable stock and 1 tablespoon flax meal, and form mixture into 10 (2-inch) patties. Brown patties in a large skillet over medium heat with a bit of virgin coconut oil for 2 minutes per side.

Raw Sea Vegetable Salad

Crunchy, colorful, and filled with a mix of sweet, peppery, and succulent veggies, this sea vegetable salad is fresh, light, and full of important micronutrients.

Yield:	Prep time:	Soak time:	Serving size:	
about 4 cups	10 minutes	20 minutes	1 cup	
Each serving has:				
67 calories	14 g carbohydrates	2 g fat	9 g fiber	2 g protein

½ cup dried kombu

½ cup dried arame

½ cup dried wakame seaweed

½ small head purple cabbage, shredded (¾ cup)

½ small head green cabbage, shredded (¾ cup)

1 medium carrot, julienned (½ cup)

1 medium celery stalk, julienned (½ cup)

½ cup fresh mung bean sprouts

¼ small daikon radish, julienned (¼ cup)

½ cup Toasted Sesame and Soy Dressing (recipe in Chapter 8)

¼ cup fresh cilantro leaves, chopped

1. In a medium bowl, soak kombu, arame, and wakame seaweed for 20 minutes. Drain, press out excess water, chop, and set aside.

2. In a large bowl, toss purple cabbage, green cabbage, carrots, celery, kombu, arame, wakame seaweed, bean sprouts, and daikon radish.

3. Pour in Toasted Sesame and Soy Dressing, and toss to coat.

4. Divide among plates, and top each with 1 tablespoon cilantro.

Variation: For a delicious grab-and-go snack or lunch, wrap some of the cabbage, carrots, celery, sea vegetables, bean sprouts, radish, and cilantro in collard leaves, nori, or rice paper. Serve with a side of dressing for dipping.

FRESH FACT

We should all be eating more sea vegetables! Kelp, nori, Irish moss, arame, wakame, hijiki, and dulse contain alginic acid, a polysaccharide known to cleanse the body of heavy metals, free radicals, and environmental toxins. They protect the body against radiation, stabilize blood sugar levels, and support healthy endocrine function and thyroid health. Iodine content is generally high, and this incredible mineral is being considered as prevention for attention-deficit hyperactivity disorder (ADHD), obesity, and fibromyalgia.

Raw Relaxed Kale and Carrot Salad

If you've ever questioned the tastiness of kale, this salad will convert you into a kale lover. The citrus and salt wilts the raw kale, making it very tender, while fresh carrots and seeds add crunch and boost the flavor of this nutrient-rich salad.

Yield:	Prep time:	Serving size:		
about 4 cups	15 minutes	1 cup		
Each serving has:				
257 calories	18 g carbohydrates	19 g fat	4 g fiber	8 g protein

4 curly kale leaves, stems removed and chopped into bite-size pieces (4 cups)

3 medium carrots, peeled and grated (1¼ cup)

1 cup fresh sunflower or broccoli sprouts

⅓ cup fresh lemon juice

¼ cup wheat-free tamari

¼ cup extra-virgin olive oil

2 TB. hemp seeds

2 TB. sesame seeds

1 cup pearl tomatoes, halved

Pinch cracked black pepper

1. In a large bowl, combine kale, carrots, and sunflower sprouts.

2. In a small bowl, combine lemon juice and wheat-free tamari. Whisk in extra-virgin olive oil until thoroughly combined.

3. Pour dressing over salad, and using your hands, massage kale and dressing together until kale begins to soften.

4. Divide among plates, sprinkle each with ½ tablespoon hemp seeds and ½ tablespoon sesame seeds, top with ¼ cup pearl tomatoes, and finish with black pepper.

Variation: Roll salad in large romaine or collard leaves for a savory and convenient wrap.

Raw Thai Green Papaya Salad

True to traditional Thai flavors, this salad is balanced with citrus, salt, spices, and natural sweetness. Green papaya is crunchy and mild, unlike its ripe orange counterpart, making it the perfect base for this light lunch salad.

Yield:	Prep time:	Serving size:		
about 5 cups	20 minutes	1 cup		
Each serving has:				
181 calories	43 g carbohydrates	1 g fat	9 g fiber	6 g protein

1 large green papaya	¼ cup maple syrup
3 small cloves garlic	2 medium carrots, julienned (1 cup)
½ tsp. sea salt	8 cherry tomatoes, halved
4 small Thai red chiles	1 small head green cabbage, cut into 4 even wedges
8 fresh green beans, each cut on the bias into 3 pieces	½ cup fresh cilantro sprigs
¼ cup wheat-free tamari	½ cup peanuts (optional)
¼ cup fresh lime juice	

1. Peel papaya, cut in half lengthwise, and scoop out and discard seeds. Using a mandoline fixed with a julienne blade, run papaya through the blade to achieve 4 cups fresh julienne strips. Place in a large bowl, and set aside.

2. Using a mortar and pestle, mash garlic and sea salt together to form a paste. Add Thai red chiles and green beans, and mash to bruise and flatten.

3. Transfer paste to a small bowl, and mix with wheat-free tamari, lime juice, and maple syrup.

4. Add carrots, cherry tomatoes, and dressing to papaya, and toss to coat evenly.

5. Place 1 wedge green cabbage on each serving plate, and divide papaya salad among plates. Top with a few sprigs cilantro and peanuts (if using).

Variation: If unripened green papaya is hard to come by, you may enjoy a similarly refreshing salad by using 4 cups shredded green cabbage or even shredded kohlrabi.

HEADS-UP

Look for papaya that has completely green skin because when this superfruit ripens, its color changes from green to yellow or orange. A mature papaya won't work for this salad.

Raw Shaved Brussels Sprouts and Sunchoke Slaw

Enjoy brussels sprouts raw in this delicious slaw. Shredding brussels sprouts allows them to easily absorb a refreshing dressing of citrus, olive juice, olive oil, and sea salt. Nutty sunchokes and crunchy fennel add texture to this unique slaw.

Yield:	Prep time:	Serving size:		
about 3 cups	15 minutes	¾ cup		
Each serving has:				
85 calories	10 g carbohydrates	5 g fat	3 g fiber	2 g protein

½ cup Lemon Garlic Dressing (recipe in Chapter 8)

⅛ cup olive juice from jar of olives

10 brussels sprouts, washed and stems and bruised leaves removed

1 small fennel bulb, greens discarded, and bulb scrubbed

6 medium fresh sunchokes, peeled

Pinch sea salt

Pinch cracked black pepper

10 pitted Castellano olives, halved

1. In a small bowl, blend Lemon Garlic Dressing and olive juice. Set aside.

2. Remove a few leaves from brussels sprouts, and add leaves to a medium bowl. Using a mandoline, shave sprouts into the same bowl. Break apart larger brussels sprouts shavings so you have a nice slaw.

3. Cut fennel in ½, and shave both halves into the bowl. Break apart larger fennel shavings.

4. Shave sunchokes into the bowl, breaking apart larger shavings.

5. Pour in dressing, and toss to coat. Season with sea salt and black pepper.

6. Divide among plates, and top each with 4 to 6 Castellano olive halves.

Variation: If organic brussels sprouts are out of season, substitute 1½ cups shredded cabbage or julienned broccoli stalks.

Divine Dressings

In This Chapter

- Rich and flavorful low-fat dressings
- Creamy and smooth bean and seed-based dressings
- Simple and versatile dressings for a variety of dishes
- Citrus and fruit dressings

Dressings are a great condiment for jazzing up salads or sprinkling over some roasted veggies, but the commercial varieties are usually dripping with oil and have a very high fat content. Rather than relying on heavy oils to give these dressings their exciting flavors and creamy texture, the delicious dressing recipes in this chapter are packed full of mineral-dense vegetables, creamy beans, zesty lemon, pungent garlic, and savory and sweet herbs and spices.

There's surely a dressing for everyone in this chapter, and you'll find a perfect dressing for fruit salad as well as one for a bowl of quinoa and braised kale. You'll love the nutrition and powerful flavors they add to your favorite foods.

Garlic Tahini Dressing

Salt and garlic blend with nutty sesame in this versatile and addictive dressing. Drizzle it on bowls of grains and beans, spread it on veggie burgers, and use it to dress leafy greens salads. This dressing is also delicious served atop collards, kale, or rainbow chard.

Yield:	Prep time:	Serving size:		
about ½ cup	5 minutes	2 tablespoons		
Each serving has:				
94 calories	12 g carbohydrates	4 g fat	3 g fiber	5 g protein

2 TB. tahini	1 TB. nutritional yeast flakes
2 large cloves garlic, chopped	¼ cup water
2 TB. lemon juice	3 TB. cooked white beans
1 tsp. sea salt	

1. In a high-speed blender, combine tahini, garlic, lemon juice, sea salt, nutritional yeast flakes, water, and white beans.

2. Blend until smooth and silky. Transfer to an airtight glass container, and refrigerate for up to 4 days.

Variation: Turn this into **Lemony White Bean Hummus** by increasing the quantity of tahini to ¼ cup, the white beans to 2 cups, and reducing the quantity of water to 2 tablespoons. Season with sea salt, lemon, and nutritional yeast flakes, and serve with freshly cut carrots, celery, cucumbers, and blanched asparagus for a quick and refreshing low-fat snack.

TASTY TIP

I like to use white beans, chickpeas, and black beans as bases for sauces and dressings. They add creamy texture—without fat—and a good dose of fiber. You can use either home-cooked or canned beans to achieve the same creamy consistency. Buying organic beans is quite inexpensive, so learn how to cook and store them to save time and money.

Carrot Ginger Dressing

This bright orange dressing is perfect for serving over butter and romaine leaf salads. It's also delicious as a dip for crispy Asian vegetables wrapped in sheets of nori seaweed.

Yield:	Prep time:	Serving size:		
about ¾ cup	5 minutes	2 tablespoons		
Each serving has:				
19 calories	3 g carbohydrates	1 g fat	1 g fiber	1 g protein

2 medium carrots, peeled and chopped

1 (1-in.) piece fresh peeled ginger

2 tsp. chili garlic sauce

2 TB. wheat-free tamari

¼ cup rice vinegar

1 TB. rice wine

3 TB. water

2 tsp. raw sesame seeds

½ tsp. ground black pepper

⅛ tsp. sea salt

1. In a high-speed blender, combine carrots, ginger, chili garlic sauce, wheat-free tamari, rice vinegar, rice wine, water, raw sesame seeds, black pepper, and sea salt.

2. Blend until completely smooth. Transfer to an airtight glass container, and refrigerate for up to 5 days.

Variation: Omit the rice vinegar for a sweet, salty, and spicy dip. Enjoy with fresh spring rolls or mushroom lettuce wraps.

FRESH FACT

Tamari is a fermented soy sauce that's slightly sweeter and less pungent than its close relative. Most all soy sauces contain wheat, but there are wheat-free varieties. Look for wheat-free tamari in the Asian foods section of almost any health food store.

Maple Lime Dressing

Pucker up with this tart, sweet, and nutty dressing. It's perfect for Asian cabbage slaw or for tossing with a light salad of watercress, sprouts, daikon radish, cucumbers, and slivered almonds.

Yield:	Prep time:	Serving size:		
about ½ cup	5 minutes	2 tablespoons		
Each serving has:				
94 calories	10 g carbohydrates	7 g fat	0 g fiber	0 g protein

3 TB. fresh lime juice	½ tsp. sea salt
1 TB. water	1 TB. rice vinegar
2 TB. maple syrup	2 TB. sesame oil

1. In a small bowl, combine lime juice, water, maple syrup, sea salt, and rice vinegar.

2. Slowly whisk in sesame oil until thoroughly combined. Transfer to an airtight glass container, and refrigerate for up to 4 days.

Variation: Make a creamy version of this dressing to use as a delectable dip or spread by blending in 3 tablespoons almond butter.

Low-Fat Creamy Caesar Dressing

Enjoy the true taste of Caesar salad without the raw eggs and anchovies in this dressing thickened with Irish moss paste and *dulse* flakes to achieve a hint of the salty sea.

Yield:	Prep time:	Serving size:		
about 1 cup	5 minutes	2 tablespoons		
Each serving has:				
26 calories	4 g carbohydrates	1 g fat	1 g fiber	2 g protein

¾ cup water

3 TB. Irish Moss Emulsifier (recipe in Chapter 10)

4 TB. hemp seeds

1 TB. apple cider vinegar

2 tsp. maple syrup

2 TB. nutritional yeast flakes

½ tsp. sea salt

1 large clove garlic

¼ tsp. ground black pepper

1 tsp. dulse flakes

2 TB. fresh lemon juice

1. In a high-speed blender, combine water, Irish Moss Emulsifier, hemp seeds, apple cider vinegar, maple syrup, nutritional yeast flakes, sea salt, garlic, black pepper, dulse flakes, and lemon juice.

2. Blend until completely smooth. Transfer to an airtight glass container, and refrigerate for up to 5 days.

Variation: This creamy dressing is also yummy made with dillweed. Omit the dulse flakes and nutritional yeast and stir in 1 tablespoon freshly minced dill. Serve with beet salads or freshly sliced cucumbers, add to potato salad, or spread on grilled quinoa cakes.

DEFINITION

Dulse is red algae harvested along the northern coasts of the Pacific and Atlantic oceans that contains high quantities of fiber, protein, B vitamins, and iron. It's used in vegan dishes as a flavor enhancer and source of key nutrients. Find dried dulse leaves or flakes at your local health food market, online, or from specialty grocers.

Cider Vinaigrette

This tangy and simple dressing enhances mixed greens and fall fruit salads. Pair it with pomegranate seeds, pears, and apples, or drizzle on top of a salad of roasted parsnips, carrots, turnips, and brussels sprouts.

Yield:	Prep time:	Serving size:		
about ¾ cup	5 minutes	2 tablespoons		
Each serving has:				
101 calories	5 g carbohydrates	9 g fat	0 g fiber	0 g protein

¼ cup apple cider vinegar	1 TB. maple syrup
¼ cup apple juice	½ tsp. sea salt
1½ TB. shallots, minced	¼ cup extra-virgin olive oil
1 TB. Dijon mustard	

1. In a small bowl, combine apple cider vinegar, apple juice, shallots, Dijon mustard, maple syrup, and sea salt.

2. Slowly whisk in extra-virgin olive oil until thoroughly combined. Transfer to an airtight glass container, and refrigerate for up to 5 days.

Variation: For a simple **Balsamic Vinaigrette,** omit the Dijon mustard and apple juice, substitute aged balsamic for the apple cider vinegar, and add 1 clove garlic, crushed. Season with sea salt and ground black pepper.

Jalapeño Cilantro Lime Dressing

This vinaigrette is light, refreshing, and delicious served over romaine and butter leaf salads or grilled asparagus and can be used as a dressing for mushroom tacos and Mexican casseroles. Or drizzle it on corn before grilling.

Yield:	Prep time:	Serving size:		
about ⅔ cup	5 minutes	2 tablespoons		
Each serving has:				
55 calories	3 g carbohydrates	4 g fat	0 g fiber	0 g protein

1 TB. sunflower oil

1 TB. extra-virgin olive oil

2 TB. water

1 small jalapeño, seeds removed, and chopped

¼ cup packed fresh cilantro leaves

3 TB. fresh lime juice

2 small cloves garlic

1 TB. maple syrup

2 TB. white wine vinegar

½ tsp. sea salt

1. In a high-speed blender, combine sunflower oil, extra-virgin olive oil, water, jalapeño, cilantro, lime juice, garlic, maple syrup, white wine vinegar, and sea salt.

2. Blend until completely smooth. Transfer to an airtight glass container, and refrigerate for up to 5 days.

Variation: For a delicious **Jalapeño Cilantro Lime Dip,** blend in 1 cup white or black beans and omit the oil for a completely fat-free chip dip. Refrigerate in an airtight glass container for up to 4 days.

Creamy Ginger Miso Dressing

This vegan and gluten-free version of the traditional Japanese dressing is delicious drizzled on spinach salads and braised bok choy. It's the perfect dressing for an Asian slaw.

Yield:	Prep time:	Serving size:		
about 1 cup	5 minutes	2 tablespoons		
Each serving has:				
44 calories	4 g carbohydrates	3 g fat	1 g fiber	1 g protein

1 (1-in.) piece fresh peeled ginger	½ cup water
1 TB. chia or hemp seeds	1 TB. sesame oil
1 small clove garlic	1 tsp. wheat-free tamari
¼ cup yellow miso	1 TB. rice vinegar
1 TB. maple syrup	2 tsp. red jalapeño, with seeds

1. In a high-speed blender, combine ginger, chia seeds, garlic, yellow miso, maple syrup, water, sesame oil, wheat-free tamari, rice vinegar, and red jalapeño.

2. Blend until completely smooth. Transfer to an airtight glass container, and refrigerate for up to 5 days.

Variation: Balance the sweetness and heat to your liking by adding more maple syrup or red jalapeño. To make a fat-free version, substitute 1 tablespoon Irish Moss Emulsifier (recipe in Chapter 10) for the chia or hemp seeds and omit the sesame oil.

Toasted Sesame and Soy Dressing

The perfect dressing for serving over edamame and tofu salads, the nuttiness of toasted sesame and the saltiness of tamari dress up simple ingredients. Drizzle over cooked Japanese pumpkin, eggplant, asparagus, and zucchini just before grilling to add savor.

Yield:	Prep time:	Serving size:		
about ⅔ cup	5 minutes	2 tablespoons		
Each serving has:				
57 calories	2 g carbohydrates	4 g fat	0 g fiber	1 g protein

2 TB. wheat-free tamari

¼ cup rice vinegar

1 TB. tahini

2 tsp. maple syrup

1 TB. toasted sesame oil

1. In a small bowl, combine wheat-free tamari, rice vinegar, tahini, and maple syrup.

2. Slowly whisk in toasted sesame oil until thoroughly combined. Transfer to an airtight glass container, and refrigerate for up to 5 days.

Variation: For a fat-free dressing, substitute 2 tablespoons cooked white beans for the tahini and omit the sesame oil. Then add a few drops of liquid smoke, and blend in a food processor to achieve a smooth texture. Liquid smoke enhances the taste, creating a delicious dressing that can dress up salads and vegetables.

Lemon Garlic Dressing

You can't go wrong with lemon and garlic for topping salads of leafy greens, braised greens, blanched green beans, lentils, or roasted root vegetables. This dressing is simple to make, and a little goes a long way.

Yield:	Prep time:	Serving size:		
about ½ cup	5 minutes	2 tablespoons		
Each serving has:				
125 calories	2 g carbohydrates	14 g fat	0 g fiber	0 g protein

2 small cloves garlic

½ tsp. sea salt

3 TB. fresh lemon juice

¼ tsp. ground black pepper

¼ cup extra-virgin olive oil

1. Using a mortar and pestle, mash together garlic and sea salt until a paste forms. Transfer paste to a small bowl.

2. Add lemon juice and black pepper, and stir to combine.

3. Slowly whisk in extra-virgin olive oil until thoroughly combined. Transfer to an airtight glass container, and refrigerate for up to 3 days.

Variation: For a creamy **Lemon Garlic Mayo,** add 2 tablespoons Irish Moss Emulsifier (recipe in Chapter 10). Spread on bean and grain patties, or dress up wraps and potato salads with this creamy mayo alternative. Refrigerate in an airtight glass container for up to 3 days.

Zippy Dijon Dressing

You're sure to use this simple yet bold Dijon vinaigrette often. It's low in fat and packs a flavorful punch. Enjoy it atop field greens, brussels sprouts, endive, radicchio, arugula, spinach, green beans, asparagus, zucchini noodles, or grains.

Yield:	Prep time:		Serving size:		
about ½ cup	5 minutes		2 tablespoons		
Each serving has:					
27 calories	2 g carbohydrates	2 g fat	0 g fiber		0 g protein

1 medium clove garlic	1½ tsp. Dijon mustard
½ tsp. sea salt	¼ tsp. ground white pepper
2 TB. champagne vinegar	2 TB. water
2 TB. fresh lemon juice	2 tsp. extra-virgin olive oil

1. Using a mortar and pestle, mash together garlic and sea salt until a paste forms. Transfer paste to a small bowl.

2. Add champagne vinegar, lemon juice, Dijon mustard, white pepper, and water, and mix well.

3. Slowly whisk in extra-virgin olive oil until thoroughly combined. Transfer to an airtight glass container, and refrigerate for up to 4 days.

Variation: For a low-fat and decadent **Zippy Dijon Spread,** blend ingredients with 1 cup cooked chickpeas. Enjoy spread on lentil burgers or atop grilled portobello mushrooms. Refrigerate in an airtight glass container for up to 4 days.

FRESH FACT

A mortar and pestle is essential for grinding spices, nuts, and seeds, and for making homemade pastes such as garlic and curry pastes. You can find them anywhere that sells small housewares. They come in a variety of finishes such as wood, granite, volcanic stone, marble, brass, and porcelain.

Cider Orange Dressing

Bursting with citrus, vinegar, and spices, this dressing pairs magnificently with mixed greens, radicchio, frisée, watercress, sprouts, figs, cranberries, oranges, grapefruit, beets, and candied nuts. It's also delicious drizzled over vegetable pâtés.

Yield:	Prep time:	Serving size:		
about ½ cup	5 minutes	2 tablespoons		
Each serving has:				
102 calories	10 g carbohydrates	7 g fat	0 g fiber	0 g protein

¼ cup apple cider vinegar

¼ cup fresh orange juice

½ tsp. orange zest

¼ tsp. sea salt

⅛ tsp. ground cloves

2 TB. maple syrup

2 TB. sunflower oil

1. In a small bowl, combine apple cider vinegar, orange juice, orange zest, sea salt, cloves, and maple syrup.

2. Slowly whisk in sunflower oil until thoroughly combined. Transfer to an airtight glass container, and refrigerate for up to 3 days.

Variation: Dressings made with fruit juices are light and refreshing, perfect for summer salads. Omit the cloves, substitute olive oil for the sunflower oil, and blend in 2 tablespoons fresh raspberries with the other ingredients for a unique spin on a traditional raspberry vinaigrette. Refrigerate in an airtight container for up to 3 days.

TASTY TIP

I've used sunflower oil for this dressing because it's very mild and doesn't compete with the sweet flavor of fresh orange the way olive oil might. Opt for cold-pressed, unrefined, organic sunflower oil. This sunflower seed oil is extracted at a low temperature, and is made in small batches. It doesn't contain hydrogenated fats, saturated fats, or trans-fatty acids.

Miso Vin Dressing

This dressing with a subtle vinegar finish pairs nicely with a salad of fresh zucchini noodle salads, shredded purple cabbage, bean sprouts, shredded carrots, and freshly chopped cilantro. Top it off with toasted sesame or hemp seeds.

Yield:	Prep time:	Serving size:		
about ⅔ cup	5 minutes	2 tablespoons		
Each serving has:				
83 calories	3 g carbohydrates	7 g fat	0 g fiber	1 g protein

½ tsp. ground dry mustard	2 TB. rice vinegar
2 TB. red or yellow *miso* paste	2 tsp. maple syrup
2 tsp. fresh peeled ginger, minced	1 tsp. sesame oil
1 TB. fresh lime juice	2 TB. sunflower oil
2 TB. water	

1. In a small bowl, combine dry mustard, red miso paste, and ginger. Add lime juice, water, rice vinegar, and maple syrup, and stir until combined.

2. Slowly whisk in sesame oil and sunflower oil until thoroughly combined. Transfer to an airtight glass container, and refrigerate for up to 3 days.

Variation: If miso isn't available, you can substitute 2 teaspoons wheat-free tamari instead. You'll still achieve the salty flavor this dressing is known for.

DEFINITION

Miso is a traditional Japanese seasoning made by fermenting rice, barley, soybeans, or chickpeas with salt and kojikin (a fungus). It's a thick yellow, brown, or red paste, and the darker the color, the more full-bodied the flavor will be. To maintain freshness, refrigerate miso in an airtight glass container for up to 3 months.

Wraps and Rolls

In This Chapter

- Quick-and-easy wraps
- Simple and elegant rolls
- Veggie-packed on-the-go lunches
- Fiesta-worthy tamales, enchiladas, and tacos

Wraps and rolls make great convenience foods. You can prepare them in advance and pack them for lunch, or you can take the filling and wraps separately to keep your wrapper fresh. They're a great party food if you cut them into slices, with the added benefit of a beautiful presentation when served with your favorite garnish and low-fat vegan dip.

Whatever your reason for choosing a healthy, low-fat wrap, you'll find great taste and extreme versatility among these recipes.

Creative Wraps and Rolls

There's no limit to what you can wrap! Some of my favorite wrappers include large collard leaves, fresh cabbage leaves, large romaine leaves, rice paper, and sheets of nori seaweed. You can stuff a filling of cooked or raw veggies, marinated mushrooms, spreads, pâtés, sprouts, and grains in any of these wrappers for a convenient and healthy meal that adds something special to your daily fare.

Or make a variety of homemade raw wrappers out of dehydrated layers of thinly sliced cucumber or zucchini. You even can make raw ice-cream cones out of blended flax wrappers that you shape into a cone when they're dry but still pliable. You can also find specialty wrappers made from things like coconut meat and ground flax (see Appendix B).

Experiment with warm and cold ingredients. Use a cool lettuce leaf to hold sautéed mushrooms, for example, or warm a collard leaf to blanket a blend of cooked grains and beans.

Make a batch of Sweet Pea Hummus Dip (recipe in Chapter 12), Zucchini Spread (recipe in Chapter 12), or Arugula and Pumpkinseed Pesto (recipe in Chapter 10) to keep on hand to spread in your wraps. And always have dips and dressings like Tamarind Dip (recipe in Chapter 12), Garlic Tahini Dressing (recipe in Chapter 8), or Creamy Ginger Miso Dressing (recipe in Chapter 8) close by to enhance your wraps and rolls.

Grab-and-Go Meals

I love to make a variety of wraps ahead of time to take with me when I'm on the go. Sometimes I make a batch of five or six wraps and store them in airtight containers so I can quickly and easily have a meal when I need to run out on short notice or friends drop by unexpectedly. If you know you're going to be out for a while, you can bring along a cup of soup to make a satisfying, filling, and convenient meal.

TASTY TIP

Many of the wraps in this chapter are perfect for air travel dining. Just be sure you package your accompanying dips in containers smaller than 3 ounces, and store them separately in a zipper-lock plastic bag to prevent an unnecessary encounter with airline security.

Smoked Pepper Tempeh Wraps

Smoky chipotle peppers combine with cumin, garlic, maple syrup, liquid smoke, and the nutty flavor of tempeh. Sweet, succulent pineapple and a tangy dressing with a touch of spice finishes these scrumptious wraps.

Yield:	Prep time:	Marinate time:	Serving size:	
4 wraps	10 minutes	1 hour	1 wrap	
Each serving has:				
325 calories	30 g carbohydrates	15 g fat	3 g fiber	22 g protein

2 canned chipotle peppers in adobo sauce, seeds removed and chopped

1 small clove garlic, peeled

¼ tsp. ground cumin

1 TB. adobo sauce from chipotle pepper can

2 TB. apple cider vinegar

3 TB. maple syrup

1 TB. liquid smoke

½ tsp. sea salt

½ tsp. ground black pepper

½ tsp. ancho chili powder

16 oz. tempeh, sliced into 2-in. strips

4 large collard leaves

¼ medium pineapple, cut into bite-size bits (½ cup)

¼ medium head green cabbage, shredded (1 cup)

¼ cup Jalapeño Cilantro Lime Dressing (recipe in Chapter 8)

2 TB. fresh cilantro leaves, chopped

1. In a blender, combine chipotle peppers, garlic, cumin, adobo sauce, apple cider vinegar, maple syrup, liquid smoke, sea salt, black pepper, and ancho chili powder.

2. Add tempeh, and stir to combine. Let tempeh marinate in the refrigerator for 1 hour.

3. Place collard leaves on a flat surface. Top each with ¼ of marinated tempeh, ⅛ cup pineapple, ½ cup green cabbage, 1 tablespoon Jalapeño Cilantro Lime Dressing, and 1½ teaspoons cilantro. Roll tightly, cut in ½, and serve with additional dressing for dipping if desired.

Variation: This dish may be made using 2 cups chopped tofu or portobello mushrooms instead of tempeh. Let marinate at least 2 hours in the refrigerator when using this variation to allow the flavor of the sauce to absorb and distribute thoroughly.

Southwestern Mushroom Collard Wraps

Hearty mushrooms are the perfect filler for peppery collard leaves. When simmered with onions and tamari, they soak up the exotic flavor and blend harmoniously with creamy and spicy black bean spread, bell peppers, romaine, and sweet tomatoes.

Yield:	Prep time:	Cook time:	Serving size:
4 wraps	15 minutes	about 15 minutes	1 wrap

Each serving has:				
250 calories	29 g carbohydrates	13 g fat	10 g fiber	10 g protein

1 TB. virgin coconut oil

1 small red onion, thinly sliced (½ cup)

2 cups mixed oyster, chanterelle, or porcini mushrooms

1 TB. wheat-free tamari

½ cup vegetable stock

1 cup cooked black beans

1 small serrano pepper, stem and seeds removed, and minced

1 small clove garlic, minced

1 TB. maple syrup

2 TB. tahini

2 TB. fresh lime juice

¼ cup water

½ tsp. chili powder

¼ tsp. cayenne

¼ tsp. ground cumin

½ tsp. sea salt

¼ tsp. cracked black pepper

4 large collard leaves

½ large red bell pepper, diced (½ cup)

¼ cup halved cherry tomatoes

1 large romaine leaf, shredded (½ cup)

1 medium-small avocado, peeled, pitted, and cubed (½ cup)

¼ cup Hemp Sour Cream (recipe in Chapter 10)

Dash hot sauce

1. In a large skillet over medium heat, heat virgin coconut oil. Add red onion, and sauté for 5 minutes or until translucent.

2. Add mixed mushrooms, wheat-free tamari, and vegetable stock. Reduce heat to low, and simmer for 8 minutes.

3. Meanwhile, in a high-speed blender, purée black beans, serrano pepper, garlic, maple syrup, tahini, lime juice, water, chili powder, cayenne, cumin, sea salt, and black pepper until smooth and creamy. Set aside.

4. Place collard leaves on a flat surface. Spread each with ¼ of black bean mixture. Top with ⅛ cup bell pepper, 1 tablespoon cherry tomatoes, ⅛ cup romaine, and ⅛ cup avocado. Roll tightly, cut in ½, and serve with 1 tablespoon Hemp Sour Cream and hot sauce to taste.

Variation: For a **Delicious Morning Hash,** sauté the oil, onions, mushrooms, wheat-free tamari, chili powder, cayenne, cumin, salt, pepper, serrano, garlic, maple syrup, lime juice, and water. Add 1 cup crumbled extra-firm tofu and sauté for 8 minutes. Stir in bell pepper, tomatoes, and avocado, and serve with gluten-free toast.

Five-Spice Eggplant Wraps

Sweet, sour, tart, salt, and spice give roasted eggplant a perfect balance of aroma, savor, and texture in this simple wrap. Add silky thin rice noodles, crunchy bean sprouts, and cooling herbs for a tasty low-fat Asian dish.

Yield:	Prep time:	Cook time:	Serving size:	
8 wraps	5 minutes	30 minutes	2 wraps	
Each serving has:				
157 calories	28 g carbohydrates	5 g fat	4 g fiber	3 g protein

3 small Japanese eggplant, cut into (2-in.) strips (3 cups)

1 TB. Chinese five-spice powder

2 TB. vegetable stock

2 TB. rice wine

2 TB. fresh peeled and minced ginger

1 TB. fresh lime juice

1 tsp. toasted sesame oil

1 TB. virgin coconut oil

4 cups water

2 oz. thin rice noodles

8 large fresh romaine leaves

1 cup fresh bean sprouts

¼ cup green onions, white and light green parts only, finely chopped

2 TB. fresh Thai basil, minced

1. Preheat the oven to 375°F.

2. In a large bowl, toss Japanese eggplant with Chinese five-spice powder, vegetable stock, rice wine, ginger, lime juice, toasted sesame oil, and virgin coconut oil. Turn out mixture onto a baking sheet, and roast for 15 to 20 minutes, or until tender.

3. Meanwhile, in a large saucepan over high heat, bring water to a boil. Add thin rice noodles, turn off heat, cover, and let rest for 15 minutes. Drain, chop into bite-size strands, and set aside.

4. Place romaine leaves on a flat surface. Top each with ⅛ cup cooked rice noodles, ⅓ cup roasted eggplant, ⅛ cup bean sprouts, 1½ teaspoons green onions, and 1 tablespoon Thai basil. Roll tightly, cut in ½, and serve.

Variation: Create a warming and hearty bowl by topping a generous serving of thin rice noodles, cooked brown rice, cooked and chopped sweet potatoes, or cooked quinoa with roasted eggplant, bean sprouts, green onions, and basil. Drizzle with an extra serving of the eggplant marinade before serving.

FRESH FACT

Chinese five-spice powder is a blend of spices used predominately in Asian cuisine. The most common spices include cloves, cinnamon, star anise, fennel, and Sichuan peppers. All these spices have internal warming properties, making them ideal for flavoring hearty vegetable, rice, and potato dishes.

Raw Pesto Collard Wraps

These rich, creamy, and crunchy wraps with layers of chewy sun-dried tomatoes, crunchy cabbage, crisp beets and carrots, and hearty spinach leaves may likely become your go-to favorite when you're in need of a travel-friendly treat.

Yield:	Prep time:	Serving size:		
about 4 wraps	15 minutes	1 wrap		
Each serving has:				
146 calories	14 g carbohydrates	9 g fat	5 g fiber	6 g protein

4 large collard leaves

½ cup Arugula and Pumpkinseed Pesto (recipe in Chapter 10)

½ cup Zucchini Spread (recipe in Chapter 12)

1 cup fresh spinach leaves

¼ cup sun-dried tomatoes, rehydrated and chopped

¼ small head purple cabbage, shredded (½ cup)

1 small raw beet, peeled and julienned (½ cup)

2 medium carrots, peeled and julienned (1 cup)

1. Place collard leaves on a flat surface. Spread one side of each with 2 tablespoons Arugula and Pumpkinseed Pesto. Spread 2 tablespoons Zucchini Spread on the other side.

2. Top one side with ¼ cup spinach leaves, 1 tablespoon sun-dried tomatoes, ⅛ cup purple cabbage, ⅛ cup beets, and ¼ of carrots. Roll tightly, cut in ½, and serve.

Variation: Experiment with different wrappers such as rice paper, romaine leaves, or cabbage leaves. Try customizing your wrap with different vegetable fillings like sunflower sprouts, bean sprouts, or radishes, or proteins such as beans and grains. Add extra crunch with hemp seeds or crushed Brazil nuts.

Thai Salad Rolls

These fresh salad rolls are perfect as a snack or appetizer. Crisp carrots, bell peppers, cucumbers, and bean sprouts are wrapped snugly in red cabbage leaves. A tart and mildly sweet Tamarind Dip enhances each bite.

Yield:	Prep time:	Cook time:	Serving size:	
12 rolls	15 minutes	15 minutes	3 rolls	
Each serving has:				
177 calories	36 g carbohydrates	3 g fat	5 g fiber	4 g protein

6 cups water

3 oz. thin rice noodles

12 red cabbage leaves

2 medium carrots, peeled and julienned (1 cup)

½ cup bean sprouts

1 small cucumber, peeled and sliced into thin rounds (½ cup)

½ medium red bell pepper, ribs and seeds removed, and julienned (½ cup)

¼ cup fresh cilantro leaves, chopped

⅛ cup fresh mint leaves, chopped

⅛ cup Brazil nuts, chopped

½ cup Tamarind Dip (recipe in Chapter 11)

1. In a large pot over high heat, bring water to a boil. Add thin rice noodles, turn off heat, cover, and let sit for 15 minutes. Drain, rinse with cold water, and set aside.

2. Place red cabbage leaves on a flat surface. Top each with $\frac{1}{12}$ of rice noodles, $\frac{1}{12}$ of carrots, $\frac{1}{12}$ of bean sprouts, $\frac{1}{12}$ of cucumber, $\frac{1}{12}$ of red bell pepper, $\frac{1}{12}$ of cilantro, $\frac{1}{12}$ of mint, and $\frac{1}{12}$ of Brazil nuts. Roll tightly, cut in $\frac{1}{2}$, and serve each with 2 teaspoons Tamarind Dip.

Variation: For a more traditional Thai salad roll, use rice papers instead of cabbage leaves and serve with a peanut sauce instead of Tamarind Dip.

Yam Rice and Nori Rolls

Enjoy the sweetness of yams mixed with the South Pacific flavors of red jalapeño, miso, ginger, and refreshing cilantro. These rolls are satisfying and convenient for when you're on the go.

Yield:	Prep time:	Cook time:	Serving size:	
8 rolls	15 minutes	20 minutes	2 rolls	
Each serving has:				
310 calories	52 g carbohydrates	9 g fat	7 g fiber	7 g protein

4 cups water

¾ tsp. sea salt

2 medium yams, peeled, and cut into 1½-in. cubes

1 small red jalapeño, seeds removed, and minced

1 TB. maple syrup

2 tsp. virgin coconut oil, melted

8 nori sheets

2 TB. fresh cilantro leaves, chopped

½ medium English cucumber, peeled and cut into thin (2-in.) long strips

1 medium beet, peeled and cut into thin matchsticks (⅔ cup)

¼ small head purple cabbage, shredded (½ cup)

3 TB. hemp seeds

½ cup Creamy Ginger Miso Dressing (recipe in Chapter 8)

1. In a medium saucepot over medium-high heat, bring water, sea salt, and yams to a boil. Reduce heat to low, and simmer for 7 minutes. Drain yams, transfer to a bowl, and set aside to cool completely.

2. Push cooled yams through a *ricer*, or pulse briefly in a food processor fitted with an S blade until a ricelike texture is achieved. Transfer to a medium bowl.

3. Add red jalapeño, maple syrup, and virgin coconut oil to yams, and stir gently to combine. Set aside.

4. Place nori sheets on a flat surface. Spread ¼ cup yam rice over the bottom half of each nori sheet, top with 1 teaspoon cilantro, 2 or 3 English cucumber strips, 4 beet matchsticks, ⅛ cup purple cabbage, and 1 teaspoon hemp seeds.

5. Roll tightly, starting with the bottom edge (the edge covered with vegetables). Seal by dipping your finger in water and running it along the top of nori sheet. Cut in ½, and serve 2 halves with 1 tablespoon Creamy Ginger Miso Dressing.

Variation: The best part of making wraps with nori is the nearly endless combinations of flavors and textures you can play with. If you prefer, use cooked brown rice, quinoa, or even a creamy hummus as your base. Top with cut tropical fruits like pineapple and mango or a variety of slivered veggies like carrots, radishes, or sundried tomatoes.

DEFINITION

A **ricer** is a convenient utensil used to take large pieces of soft foods such as cooked potatoes, cauliflower, or carrots and break them down into smaller bits. It has a larger chamber and a plunger that's connected to a large handle. To use, add cooked foods to the chamber and press down on the food using the plunger. This forces the food through the small holes in the bottom, resulting in what looks like grains of rice.

Asian Tofu Lettuce Cups

The extra-firm tofu in these lettuce wraps soaks up the succulent Asian flavors of garlic, ginger, chiles, sesame, and tamari. Crisp water chestnuts, carrots, and ground rice add a bit of crunch.

Yield:	Prep time:	Cook time:	Serving size:
8 lettuce cups	10 minutes	about 20 minutes	2 lettuce cups

Each serving has:				
325 calories	38 g carbohydrates	15 g fat	4 g fiber	15 g protein

16 oz. extra-firm tofu

4 TB. uncooked white rice

3 TB. minced garlic

1 TB. fresh peeled and minced ginger

3 TB. maple syrup

3 TB. wheat-free tamari

1 tsp. toasted sesame oil

1½ TB. chile-garlic sauce

3 TB. water

3 TB. rice wine

2 TB. virgin coconut oil

8 large romaine leaves

2 medium carrots, peeled and grated (1 cup)

1 (8-oz.) can water chestnuts, drained and diced

1 TB. fresh mint leaves, chopped

2 TB. fresh cilantro leaves, chopped

3 medium green onions, whites and light green parts only, minced

1. Rinse tofu and drain to release excess water. Dice into small cubes, and set aside.

2. In a large, dry cast-iron skillet over medium heat, toast white rice for 2 minutes or until brown but not black. Transfer to a spice grinder, mortar and pestle, or food processor fitted with an S blade, and grind into flour. Set aside.

3. In a small bowl, combine garlic, ginger, maple syrup, wheat-free tamari, toasted sesame oil, chile-garlic sauce, water, and rice wine. Set aside.

4. In the same skillet over medium heat, heat virgin coconut oil. Add tofu, and cook, stirring often, for 5 to 7 minutes or until lightly browned. Pour in sauce, reduce heat to low, and simmer for 10 minutes.

5. Place romaine leaves on a flat surface. Divide ¼ cup tofu mixture among leaves, and top each with ⅛ cup carrots, 1 teaspoon water chestnuts, 1 teaspoon mint leaves, 2 teaspoons cilantro, and 2 teaspoons green onions. Finish with 1½ tablespoons ground rice flour, roll tightly, cut in ½, and serve.

Variation: For a soy-free recipe, use 2 cups hearty mushrooms such as crimini or portobello in place of the tofu, and substitute coconut aminos for the tamari.

Roasted Vegetable Tamales

These roasted vegetable tamales are low in fat and high in authentic Mexican flavor. Sweet butternut squash, earthy portobellos, and zucchini pair with hot peppers, smoky paprika, and Mexican spices and herbs, all wrapped in sweet corn masa dough.

Yield:	Prep time:	Cook time:	Serving size:
12 tamales	25 minutes	about 30 minutes	2 tamales

Each serving has:				
254 calories	44 g carbohydrates	9 g fat	5 g fiber	6 g protein

4 cups water

1¾ tsp. sea salt

2 tsp. plus 2 TB. virgin coconut oil

2 cups *masa harina*

1 small butternut squash, peeled and chopped into ½-in. pieces (2 cups)

2 medium portobello mushrooms, diced (1 cup)

2 large fresh green poblano chiles, stem and seeds removed, and diced

2 small zucchini, peeled and diced (1 cup)

1 TB. chili powder

2 tsp. granulated garlic

2 tsp. ground cumin

¼ tsp. ground black pepper

1 tsp. ground smoked paprika

1 tsp. dried Mexican oregano

1½ medium serrano chile, stem and seeds removed, and minced

4 medium cloves garlic, minced

1 medium sweet onion, minced (1 cup)

½ cup vegetable stock

¼ cup fresh cilantro leaves, minced

12 dry corn husks, soaked in hot water for 10 to 15 minutes

1. Preheat the oven to 375°F.

2. In a large saucepan over high heat, bring water, 1 teaspoon sea salt, and 2 teaspoons virgin coconut oil to a boil. Turn off heat, and gradually stir in masa harina until a thick dough is reached. Set aside to cool to room temperature.

3. Roll masa dough into 12 (2-inch) balls, and set aside.

4. In a large bowl, combine butternut squash, portobello mushrooms, poblanos, and zucchini. Add remaining 2 tablespoons virgin coconut oil, chili powder, granulated garlic, cumin, black pepper, remaining ¾ teaspoon sea salt, smoked paprika, and Mexican oregano. Stir to coat vegetables evenly.

5. Turn out vegetables to a baking sheet, and spread into a single layer. Roast for 15 minutes or until butternut squash is tender.

6. Transfer roasted vegetables to a large skillet over medium heat. Add serrano chile, garlic, sweet onion, and vegetable stock, and sauté for about 5 minutes or until liquid is absorbed and onions are tender.

7. Stir in cilantro, and set aside.

8. Place corn husks on a flat surface. Place 1 masa dough ball in center of each husk. Dip your fingers in water, and spread masa into a ¼-inch layer down length of husk, leaving 1 inch at each end free. Spoon ¼ cup roasted vegetable mixture on top of masa dough, turn in ends of husks, and wrap into tight tamales.

9. In a large pot with a steamer insert over high heat, heat 2 inches of water. Add tamales, 2 at a time, to the steamer, and steam for 2 minutes. Repeat with remaining tamales, and serve.

Variation: Make a tamale pie by pressing dough into a 9-inch pie dish and filling with roasted vegetables. Top vegetables with small spoonfuls of masa dough. Cover and bake in a 375°F oven for 20 minutes. Uncover and bake for 10 more minutes to brown the top.

DEFINITION

Masa harina is a Mexican flour made from lime-treated corn and is used for making tamales, tortillas, corn cakes, and other traditional Mexican dishes. You can find masa harina at your local store in the baking supplies isle, next to the other flours.

Mushroom and Bean Enchiladas

Get ready for a unique twist on traditional enchiladas. These hearty delights are abundant in citrus and tangy tomatillos, which boost the flavor of buttery white beans and earthy mushrooms.

Yield:	Prep time:	Cook time:	Serving size:	
10 enchiladas	20 minutes	25 minutes	2 enchiladas	
Each serving has:				
663 calories	87 g carbohydrates	26 g fat	19 g fiber	21 g protein

1 TB. virgin coconut oil	2 medium Swiss chard leaves, chopped (2 cups)
1 medium sweet onion, diced (1 cup)	1 TB. fresh lemon juice
½ tsp. red chili flakes	10 (8-in.) gluten-free tortillas, warmed
2 medium portobello mushrooms, diced (1 cup)	4 cups Tangy Green Chile Sauce (recipe in Chapter 10)
1 cup crimini mushrooms, diced	1 cup grated vegan jack cheese
1 TB. wheat-free tamari	
2 cups cooked white beans	

1. Preheat the oven to 400°F.

2. In a large skillet over medium heat, heat virgin coconut oil. Add sweet onion, and sauté for about 5 minutes or until tender.

3. Add red chili flakes, portobello mushrooms, crimini mushrooms, and wheat-free tamari, and cook for about 8 minutes or until mushrooms are tender.

4. Stir in white beans, Swiss chard, and lemon juice, and cook for 1 more minute. Set aside.

5. To assemble enchiladas, place gluten-free tortillas on a flat surface. Distribute mushroom and bean mixture evenly among tortillas, top each with 2 tablespoons Tangy Green Chile Sauce, tightly roll, and place in a 9×11-inch ovenproof casserole dish. Cover enchiladas with remaining sauce, and sprinkle vegan jack cheese over the top. Bake for 15 minutes or until cheese melts.

Variation: For an extra-hearty wrap, replace the white beans with 2 cups cubed tempeh and 1 cup fresh cut corn, and cover with 4 cups Chia Mole (recipe in Chapter 10) instead of the Tangy Green Chile Sauce.

Spinach and Parsnip Enchiladas

These creamy, gooey enchiladas are as close to dessert as an entrée can get. Sweet roasted parsnips and decadently creamy spinach are an unparalleled combination with rich and smoky Chia Mole.

Yield:	Prep time:	Cook time:	Serving size:
10 enchiladas	15 minutes	45 minutes	2 enchiladas

Each serving has:				
768 calories	92 g carbohydrates	37 g fat	21 g fiber	27 g protein

1 cup cooked white beans	3 medium-large parsnips, peeled and chopped to ½-in. cubes (2 cups)
½ cup unsweetened almond milk	2 TB. virgin coconut oil, melted
½ cup Hemp Sour Cream (recipe in Chapter 10)	1 (10-oz.) pkg. frozen chopped spinach, thawed and drained (about 2 cups)
½ tsp. sea salt	10 (8-in.) gluten-free tortillas, warmed
4 TB. nutritional yeast flakes	1½ cups Chia Mole (recipe in Chapter 10)
½ cup vegetable stock	1 cup shredded vegan jack cheese

1. Preheat the oven to 375°F.

2. In a high-speed blender, blend white beans, almond milk, Hemp Sour Cream, sea salt, nutritional yeast flakes, and vegetable stock until smooth and creamy. Set aside.

3. In a medium bowl, toss parsnips with melted virgin coconut oil. Turn out parsnips onto a baking sheet, and roast, stirring occasionally, for 25 minutes or until tender. Remove and transfer to a large bowl.

4. Add white bean mixture and spinach to parsnips, and stir to combine.

5. Place gluten-free tortillas on a flat surface. Evenly divide spinach and parsnip mix among tortillas, tightly roll, and place in a 9×11-inch ovenproof casserole dish. Top enchiladas with Chia Mole and vegan jack cheese, and bake for 20 minutes or until cheese melts.

Variation: Make a delicious casserole by replacing the tortillas with 3 cups cooked quinoa. Fill the bottom of a 9×11-inch casserole dish with quinoa, and top with parsnip and spinach blend. Pour Chia Mole over the top, sprinkle with vegan jack cheese, and bake as directed.

Tangy Squash Tacos

Pickled red onions top sweet kabocha squash and rich tomato sauce in these vibrantly colored and uniquely flavored tacos.

Yield:	Prep time:	Chill time:	Cook time:	Serving size:
8 tacos	15 minutes	2 hours	40 minutes	2 tacos
Each serving has:				
321 calories	56 g carbohydrates	10 g fat	7 g fiber	10 g protein

2 small jalapeños

¾ cup water

1 small red onion, thinly sliced (⅓ cup)

1 small clove garlic, thinly sliced

¼ medium red beet, peeled and diced (⅓ cup)

¼ tsp. whole cumin seeds

1 TB. maple syrup

¼ cup apple cider vinegar

½ tsp. plus ¾ tsp. sea salt

½ medium kabocha squash, peeled and cut into ½-in. cubes (3⅓ cups)

2 TB. plus 1 tsp. virgin coconut oil

1 small clove garlic, minced

1 tsp. ground cumin

1 tsp. ground coriander

1½ tsp. chili powder

⅔ (15-oz.) can fire-roasted tomatoes, drained (1¼ cups)

2 TB. fresh lemon juice

¼ tsp. granulated garlic

2 TB. nutritional yeast flakes

1 tsp. balsamic vinegar

¼ tsp. ground black pepper

8 (4-in.) corn tortillas, warmed

8 lime wedges

¼ cup fresh cilantro leaves, chopped

1. Preheat the oven to 400°F.

2. Fire-roast jalapeños by holding stems tightly and rotating them over a flame for about 2 minutes. Or dry-roast them in a cast-iron skillet over medium-high heat for 6 to 8 minutes, turning often to roast evenly. When skin is evenly blackened, transfer jalapeños to a paper bag or set out on a cutting board to cool. When cool enough to handle, remove skin from the jalapeños, and chop.

3. In a small saucepan over high heat, combine water and red onion. Bring to a boil, remove from heat, and let sit for 5 minutes. Drain, transfer onions to a small bowl, and set aside.

4. In the saucepan, combine sliced garlic, red beet, cumin seeds, maple syrup, apple cider vinegar, and ½ teaspoon sea salt. Bring to a boil, reduce heat to low, add red onions, and simmer for 15 minutes. Transfer to a glass jar with a tight-fitting lid, and refrigerate for 2 hours or until cool.

5. In a large bowl, combine kabocha squash, 2 tablespoons virgin coconut oil, minced garlic, cumin, coriander, chili powder, and remaining ¾ teaspoon sea salt. Toss to coat, and turn out onto a baking sheet. Roast for 20 minutes, tossing occasionally to coat evenly.

6. Peel jalapeños, remove seeds, and mince.

7. In a small skillet over medium-high heat, heat remaining 1 teaspoon virgin coconut oil. Add minced jalapeños, fire-roasted tomatoes, lemon juice, granulated garlic, nutritional yeast flakes, balsamic vinegar, and black pepper. Reduce heat to medium-low, and simmer for 10 minutes or until sauce is reduced by ⅓.

8. Place corn tortillas on a flat surface. Divide squash among tortillas, top with tomato sauce and pickled red onions, and serve with lime wedges and cilantro.

Variation: You can make a delicious raw taco salad by grating raw squash, omitting the roasting directions, and tossing with minced garlic, cumin, coriander, chili powder, and sea salt. Lay some romaine leaves on a plate, top with squash mixture, add a layer of tomato blend, and top with pickled red onions and cilantro. Add a drizzle of Hemp Sour Cream (recipe in Chapter 10) for extra decadence.

FRESH FACT

I use kabocha squash, also known as Japanese pumpkin, as much as possible when it's in season. Kabochas look like smashed round balls, and their skin ranges in color from light to dark green. Sometimes you'll find them with a single dark yellow or orange spot if the squash ripened on the ground. The flesh of kabocha is bright orange, incredibly sweet, dry, and flaky.

Sauces, Spreads, Snacks, and More

A sauce a day keeps boredom at bay! Sauces and marinades really are the cornerstone of any amazing dish. They hold the key to the flavor combinations that make food interesting and memorable. Every great chef has a signature sauce!

In Part 4, I offer dozens of delicious sauces and marvelous marinades. Armed with these flavor enhancers, you'll soon have the tools you need to make any ordinary dish taste completely gourmet!

Also in this part, I share a healthy dose of basic and exotic spreads and dips, along with healthy snacks that are sure to become staples in your child's lunch bag, at social gatherings, and everywhere snacks are called for!

Saucy Secrets

In This Chapter

- The fundamentals of flavorful sauces
- Trade secrets of low-fat sauces
- Rich and flavorful gravies
- Sweet syrup recipes

Sauces add distinct character to regional cuisines from around the world. The mention of a béchamel calls to mind France. For a Bolognese, you may think of Italy. A cool and creamy tzatziki is reminiscent of Greece. Sauces have become culinary cornerstones because they're as important as the dishes they dress. And in many cases, they make a dish what it is! This is especially true when creating low-fat vegan dishes, as you'll see by the recipes in this chapter.

What Makes a Memorable Sauce?

"What's in this sauce?" is a question vegans often ask to ensure the sauce is safe. It's not always easy to veganize a sauce because of the simple mechanics of sauces. There are three basic components to sauce structure: liquids, thickening and binding agents, and seasonings.

Liquids give the sauce volume and body. Water, stock, oil, citrus juice, wine, liquor, vegetable and fruit juices, or vinegar all qualify here.

Traditionally, thickening and binding agents include roux, egg yolk, or cornstarch. In the vegan world, we use thickeners and binders such as *agar agar*; Irish moss, beans, squash, nuts, flax, chia, and other seeds.

> **DEFINITION**
>
> **Agar agar** is a plant-based gelatin produced from red marine algae. You can find it at health food markets in flake and powder forms. Use it in your vegan cooking to thicken sauces, puddings, and custards. Simply mix agar agar with liquid in a small saucepan and bring to a boil. Reduce heat and simmer until the mixture thickens slightly. Transfer to a glass jar and refrigerate until it's cool and sets into a gel.

When it comes to seasonings, this is where you get to customize your sauces using seasonings like fresh or dried chilies, fresh or dried herbs, exotic spices, extracts, or tinctures.

It doesn't take a culinary genius to create memorable sauces, but it does take some creativity and trial and error. Of course, you can avoid much of the learning curve by creating sauces from a world of flavors in the following recipes.

The Secret to Creamy, Low-Fat Sauces

You might ask yourself how you can possibly create a creamy sauce without the fat. You might even doubt it's possible.

Rich, low-fat sauces can be easily achieved by using ingredients that become smooth and silky when puréed and blended with liquid. Take beans, for example. When puréed with a little liquid, chickpeas, white, black, cannellini, and Great Northern beans create a smooth and creamy sauce without any added fat. You can then enhance the sauce with seasonings, thin or thicken the sauce with liquid, and bind it with a natural ingredient such as Irish moss or agar agar.

Similarly, you can cook and purée starchy vegetables like cauliflower, potatoes, parsnips, or sunchokes to get a creamy sauce base.

White and brown rice flour also work brilliantly when heated and mixed with broth or water. Be patient with this method; add only small amounts of flour and liquid at a time until desired texture and density is achieved.

For body and silkiness, and to keep the sauce from separating, you may want to use a binder such as Irish moss, flax meal, or chia seeds. These natural binders greatly enhance the texture and density of creamy foods without adding loads of calories and fat. You can find Irish moss, flax meal, chia seeds, and other texture enhancers at your local health food store.

Carrageenan and Irish Moss

Carrageenan, also known as Irish moss or *Chondrus crispus,* is a food that comes from red seaweed. For decades, carrageenan has been used as a thickener and emulsifier in ice cream, yogurt, and other processed foods. It's also found in many fine cosmetics because of its purity and unique qualities.

It's important to understand the difference between pure carrageenan, or Irish moss, and processed carrageenan known as degraded carrageenan, which is the type most commonly found in packaged foods. The pure carrageenan used in the following recipes is 100 percent natural. It's also very nutritious, with its iodine, phosphorus, zinc, calcium, magnesium, potassium, and B vitamins. It contains polysaccharides, which are long-chain sugars that help release nutrients from food into the body over a slower period of time, reducing unhealthy spikes in blood sugar.

One of the best ways to use Irish moss is to create a paste using the powder—I give you an easy Irish Moss Emulsifier recipe later in this chapter. Add it to puddings, baked goods, frozen desserts, sauces, dips, nut and seed milks, and spreads for a creamy, rich texture.

Chia Seeds

Chia seeds are rich in fiber, protein, and omega-3 fatty acids. In fact, chia has even more omega-3 than flax and does not need to be ground in order for the nutrients to be digestible. In addition to 5 grams fiber and 3 grams protein per tablespoon, these superseeds contain calcium, phosphorus, magnesium, copper, niacin, zinc, manganese, and iron.

Even more amazing is that chia seeds can expand up to nine times their size when combined with a liquid. This blend makes a perfect gel when combined with water, nut milk, or juice, as you'll see with my Chia Seed Gel recipe later in this chapter. You can use this gel to thicken smoothies, dressings, sauces, puddings, desserts, and ice cream. And because the seeds expand so much, the caloric intake and fat content of each serving is greatly reduced.

TASTY TIP

Knowing which sauce to use with what is sometimes a stumper. To steer you in the right direction, I've paired many of the sauces in this chapter with other recipes throughout the book. Use this as a guide for learning which sauces complement particular ingredients. I also encourage you to experiment with using sauces to enhance single-dimensional dishes such as steamed vegetables or bean and grain bowls. With the right sauce, a bowl of quinoa and steamed kale, for example, can become a culinary masterpiece.

Irish Moss Emulsifier

Irish moss paste is a versatile thickening and binding agent used to stabilize and add body to seed cheeses, nondairy ice cream, nut and seed milk, sauces, dressings, and other creamy delights.

Yield:	Prep time:	Soak time:	Serving size:	
about 1½ cups	10 minutes	24 hours	2 tablespoons	
Each serving has:				
3 calories	1 g carbohydrates	11 mg fat	0 g fiber	0 g protein

1 cup raw Irish moss
6 cups water

1. Rinse raw Irish moss under cold water until all debris and particles have been removed.

2. In a large bowl, combine Irish moss and 4 cups water, and let soak for 24 hours.

3. Pour off soaking water, and rinse thoroughly.

4. In a high-speed blender, combine Irish moss with remaining 2 cups water and process on high until a well-combined paste is achieved. Run a small dab of paste through your fingers to ensure the texture is smooth. If paste is at all bumpy or grainy, continue blending.

5. Transfer to an airtight glass container, and refrigerate for up to 10 days.

Chia Seed Gel

Chia seed gel is used to enhance the texture and thickness of smoothies, drinks, sauces, ice cream, puddings, and other desserts.

Yield:	Prep time:	Chill time:	Serving size:	
about 2 cups	5 minutes	1 hour	2 tablespoons	
Each serving has:				
23 calories	2 g carbohydrates	1.5 g fat	2 g fiber	0.7 g protein

⅓ cup raw chia seeds

2 cups water

1. In a high-speed blender, process raw chia seeds and water until well combined.

2. Transfer to a glass jar with a tight-fitting lid, and allow to set for at least 1 hour before use.

3. Refrigerate in airtight glass container for up to 2 weeks.

Hemp Sour Cream

Just like traditional sour cream, this hemp version is dense, smooth, and a bit tart. It can be used in aromatic soups, atop bean dishes, and as an accompaniment for Mexican or southwestern fare.

Yield:	Prep time:	Serving size:		
about 1 cup	5 minutes	⅛ cup		
Each serving has:				
125 calories	2 g carbohydrates	10 g fat	1 g fiber	8 g protein

2 TB. water	2 TB. apple cider vinegar
¾ cup hemp seeds	¼ small red onion, minced (2 TB.)
2 TB. fresh lemon juice	½ tsp. sea salt

1. In a high-speed blender, combine water, hemp seeds, lemon juice, apple cider vinegar, red onion, and sea salt.

2. Blend until smooth and creamy.

3. Transfer to an airtight glass container, and refrigerate for up to 5 days.

Variation: Enhance your sour cream with additions such as jalapeño-lime, chipotle, red chili, and lemon-garlic and then spread the cream on sandwiches or crackers.

Argentinian Parsley Purée

This sauce gets its savor from an abundance of fresh parsley and has a little bite thanks to crushed red pepper flakes. It pairs beautifully with grilled vegetables such as artichokes and eggplant, and adds an earthy zest to grains and beans.

Yield:	Prep time:	Serving size:		
about 1 cup	5 minutes	⅛ cup		
Each serving has:				
39 calories	3 g carbohydrates	3 g fat	1 g fiber	1 g protein

1 cup packed fresh flat-leaf parsley	½ tsp. sea salt
¼ cup packed fresh cilantro leaves	¼ tsp. ground black pepper
⅛ cup fresh lemon juice	1 tsp. dried oregano
3 medium cloves garlic	2 TB. extra-virgin olive oil
½ tsp. crushed red pepper flakes	2 TB. red wine vinegar
½ tsp. ground cumin	2 TB. water

1. In a food processor fitted with an S blade, pulse flat-leaf parsley, cilantro, lemon juice, garlic, crushed red pepper flakes, cumin, sea salt, black pepper, oregano, extra-virgin olive oil, red wine vinegar, and water.

2. Pulse until well combined.

3. Transfer to an airtight glass container, and refrigerate for up to 2 days.

Variation: Blending the ingredients with Great Northern or cannellini beans and vegetable stock makes for a creamy and savory soup.

FRESH FACT

This purée, also called chimichurri, is a rich sauce full of parsley or cilantro and a staple in Argentinian cuisine.

Arugula and Pumpkinseed Pesto Sauce

The spicy bite of arugula leaves adds zip to this versatile pesto. Pumpkinseeds boost the nutritional content and provide creaminess while nutritional yeast flakes add the flavor of cheese without the fat.

Yield:	Prep time:	Serving size:		
about 1¼ cups	5 minutes	⅛ cup		
Each serving has:				
65 calories	2 g carbohydrates	6 g fat	1 g fiber	3 g protein

2 cups packed arugula leaves	1 tsp. sea salt
2 TB. fresh flat-leaf parsley, chopped	2 TB. extra-virgin olive oil
3 small cloves garlic	2 TB. water
2 TB. fresh lemon juice	1 tsp. apple cider vinegar
2 TB. nutritional yeast flakes	¼ cup raw pumpkinseeds

1. In a food processor fitted with an S blade, combine arugula leaves, flat-leaf parsley, garlic, lemon juice, nutritional yeast flakes, and sea salt.

2. Pulse until blended yet still coarse.

3. Add extra-virgin olive oil, water, apple cider vinegar, and raw pumpkinseeds, and purée until smooth.

4. Transfer to an airtight glass container, and refrigerate for up to 5 days.

Variation: Change up this simple pesto with the nuts and seeds you have on hand. Try a batch made with pistachios, walnuts, or pine nuts, and substitute basil for arugula for a more traditional recipe.

FRESH FACT

Pumpkinseeds, also known as pepitas, are the green edible kernels of the pumpkin that have been removed from the white husk. These small seeds are packed full of fiber, B vitamins, magnesium, manganese, potassium, vitamin E, amino acids, and zinc. In addition to adding texture and creaminess to sauces, you can grind them and sprinkle them over salads, drinks, porridge, and grain dishes.

Thai Curry Simmer Sauce

Aromatic lemongrass is soothing to the soul while the chiles build inner heat, making this sauce a perfect accompaniment to a fall dish of grains, roasted pumpkin, and steamed vegetables, or a bowl full of rice noodles, bean sprouts, herbs, and Asian greens.

Yield:	Prep time:	Cook time:	Serving size:	
about 2 cups	20 minutes	10 minutes	½ cup	
Each serving has:				
88 calories	9 g carbohydrates	5 g fat	1 g fiber	2 g protein

2 medium stalks lemongrass, outer layers removed and soft inside chopped (3 TB.)

5 medium cloves garlic

2 fresh jalapeños or Thai green chiles, stems removed, and minced

1 (1-in.) piece fresh peeled and sliced ginger

¼ tsp. sea salt

1 cup fresh cilantro

½ cup fresh Thai or regular basil

½ tsp. ground coriander

¼ tsp. ground cumin

1 TB. wheat-free tamari

1 TB. maple syrup

1 cup unsweetened almond milk

1 cup lite coconut milk

1. Using a mortar and pestle, crush together lemongrass, garlic, jalapeños, ginger, and sea salt.

2. Transfer to a food processor fitted with an S blade. Add cilantro, Thai basil, coriander, cumin, wheat-free tamari, maple syrup, and almond milk, and purée until smooth.

3. Transfer mixture to a medium saucepan over low heat. Add coconut milk, and simmer for 10 minutes. Cool slightly for 5 minutes at room temperature.

4. Transfer to an airtight glass container, and refrigerate for up to 4 days.

Variation: Enjoy this sauce as a delicious soup by adding more coconut milk and some vegetable stock and then pouring the hot liquid over a bowl of cooked buckwheat soba noodles and mushrooms.

TASTY TIP

Instead of purchasing lite coconut milk, divide a regular can of coconut milk and dilute each half with equal parts of water. This allows you to achieve 2 cans' worth of lite coconut milk from 1 can of regular. Freeze the unused portion for future use.

Kansas City Barbecue Sauce

Barbecue sauces don't have to be fattening and full of refined sugars to be delicious. This tangy sauce is fat free and layered with flavor. Use it to coat and grill tofu, tempeh, or hearty mushrooms such as king oyster or portobello.

Yield:	Prep time:	Serving size:		
about 1½ cups	5 minutes	¼ cup		
Each serving has:				
57 calories	14 g carbohydrates	0 g fat	0 g fiber	0 g protein

½ cup organic ketchup	½ tsp. celery salt
½ cup water	½ tsp. ground allspice
⅛ cup apple cider vinegar	¼ tsp. cayenne
3 TB. maple syrup	1 tsp. garlic powder
1½ tsp. ground black pepper	

1. In a high-speed blender, combine ketchup, water, apple cider vinegar, maple syrup, black pepper, celery salt, allspice, cayenne, and garlic powder.

2. Blend on high until completely smooth.

3. Transfer to an airtight glass container, and refrigerate for up to 2 weeks.

Variation: Bake a batch of fresh-cut french fries and use this BBQ sauce as your dipping sauce.

Pad Thai Sauce

Enjoy this traditional Thai combination of tart, salty, sweet, and spicy flavors in your next stir-fry or noodle dish.

Yield:	Prep time:	Serving size:		
about 1⅓ cups	40 minutes	⅓ cup		
Each serving has:				
79 calories	19 g carbohydrates	0 g fat	1 g fiber	2 g protein

¼ cup *tamarind paste*

¾ cup hot water

1 tsp. dried crushed red chiles, or
  1 tsp. cayenne

¼ cup wheat-free tamari

2 TB. fresh lime juice

⅓ cup maple syrup

1. In a medium bowl, combine tamarind paste and hot water until paste is dissolved.

2. Add red chiles, wheat-free tamari, lime juice, and maple syrup, and stir until combined.

3. Transfer to an airtight glass container, and refrigerate for up to 3 weeks.

Variation: Omit the water for a complex dipping sauce that pairs beautifully with collard wraps of cabbage, bean sprouts, mango, and Thai basil or use it as a dip for fresh spring rolls.

DEFINITION

Tamarind paste is made from the fruit of the tamarind tree, a tropical evergreen tree native to Africa and Southeast Asia. Long, brown tamarind pods contain 3 to 12 dark brown seeds surrounded by sticky fruit pulp. When the fruit is ripe, you can make the pulp into a paste by blending the fruit pulp with a bit of water, molding it into a block shape, and sealing it in plastic. Find tamarind paste at your local or online Asian food market or specialty grocer.

Caramelized Fennel and White Bean Sauce

Everyone will think this decadent sauce is full of fat, when in fact, it gets its richness from a base of white beans, sautéed fennel, and a splash of white wine. Enjoy it over pasta, gnocchi, grilled polenta, or braised bitter greens.

Yield:	Prep time:	Cook time:	Serving size:	
about 3 cups	5 minutes	18 minutes	½ cup	
Each serving has:				
61 calories	10 g carbohydrates	1 g fat	3 g fiber	3 g protein

½ cup fennel bulb, thinly sliced

2 large sprigs thyme leaves, minced

¼ small sweet onion, chopped (¼ cup)

2 large cloves garlic

1 TB. virgin coconut oil

¼ cup dry white wine

2 cups vegetable stock

1 cup cooked white beans

1 tsp. sea salt

½ tsp. ground white pepper

1. In a medium skillet over medium heat, sauté fennel, thyme, sweet onion, garlic, and virgin coconut oil for about 15 minutes or until fennel is brown and caramelized.

2. Increase heat to high, and pour in dry white wine. Heat through for about 3 minutes.

3. Transfer fennel mixture to a high-speed blender, and add vegetable stock, white beans, sea salt, and white pepper. Blend on high until completely smooth. Cool for 5 minutes at room temperature.

4. Transfer to an airtight glass container, and refrigerate for up to 3 days.

Variation: Make a satisfying and warming soup by adding 1 or 2 cups more vegetable stock. Blend contents in a high-speed blender for 2 minutes. Transfer to a soup pot, and stir in ½ cup whole white beans. Serve soup sprinkled with parsley and thyme.

Tomato and Lemon-Basil Cream Sauce

Sweet cherry tomatoes pair magnificently with garlic, basil, and lemon in this Italian sauce. Hemp milk and ground seeds provide a silky texture that's perfect over ravioli, noodles, steamed vegetables, zucchini pasta, or spaghetti squash.

Yield:	Prep time:	Serving size:		
about 7 cups	5 minutes	1 cup		
Each serving has:				
80 calories	14 g carbohydrates	0 g fat	5 g fiber	4 g protein

4 cups sweet cherry tomatoes

¼ small sweet onion, minced (¼ cup)

2 medium cloves garlic, minced

¼ cup fresh parsley, minced

1 tsp. sea salt

½ tsp. ground white pepper

¼ cup fresh lemon juice

½ tsp. lemon zest

¾ cup unsweetened hemp milk

1¼ cups cooked Great Northern or cannellini beans

1 cup fresh basil leaves, chopped fine

1. In a food processor fitted with an S blade, combine cherry tomatoes, sweet onion, garlic, parsley, sea salt, and white pepper. Pulse until roughly combined.

2. Add lemon juice, lemon zest, hemp milk, and Great Northern beans, and purée until creamy.

3. Add basil, and pulse until combined. Do not overblend. Cool slightly for 5 minutes at room temperature.

4. Transfer to an airtight glass container, and refrigerate up to 4 days, or freeze for future use.

Variation: Omit the hemp milk and prepare as suggested for a rich and vibrant bruschetta topper. Maybe pulse some black or kalamata olives into the mix for added flavor and texture.

Scallion Hemp Cream Sauce

Cilantro and scallions bring a light and refreshing taste to this sauce perfect for serving alongside a summer succotash of cherry tomatoes, corn, and tomatoes or with a mix of sautéed or grilled mushrooms. It's also wonderful as a spread for nut and bean burgers.

Yield:	Prep time:	Serving size:		
about 2 cups	5 minutes	¼ cup		
Each serving has:				
87 calories	4 g carbohydrates	6 g fat	1 g fiber	5 g protein

½ cup hemp seeds
½ cup unsweetened hemp milk
1 tsp. sea salt
¼ cup fresh lemon juice

7 medium scallions, white and light green parts, chopped
⅛ cup fresh cilantro, minced

1. In a food processor fitted with an S blade, combine hemp seeds, hemp milk, sea salt, and lemon juice. Blend until smooth.

2. Add scallions and cilantro, and blend until combined.

3. Season with additional sea salt and lemon juice as desired.

4. Transfer to an airtight glass container, and refrigerate for up to 3 days.

Variation: Experiment with using other savory herbs such as parsley and basil, and try sweet onions or shallots instead of scallions for a milder and sweeter blend. Or for a creamy sauce with Greek flair, use cucumbers instead of scallions and mint in place of cilantro.

FRESH FACT

Hemp is one of the most nutritionally complete foods found in the natural world. It contains all the essential amino acids, plus many others, and also possesses a wide variety of vitamins and phytochemicals. It has the perfect balance of omega-3, -6, and -9 fatty acids, making it an important food for proper brain function and metabolism.

Cilantro White Bean Sauce

This creamy low-fat sauce—blended with an abundance of fresh cilantro, sesame tahini, and lemon juice in a rich base of white beans—is the perfect complement to any Mediterranean dish, such as falafel, tabbouleh, or roasted eggplant.

Yield:	Prep time:	Serving size:		
about 3½ cups	5 minutes	¾ cup		
Each serving has:				
206 calories	20 g carbohydrates	11 g fat	7 g fiber	8 g protein

2 cups cooked Great Northern or white cannellini beans

2 TB. fresh lemon juice

¼ cup tahini

1 cup vegetable stock

1 tsp. sea salt

⅛ tsp. ground white pepper

2 TB. extra-virgin olive oil

1 cup fresh cilantro leaves, chopped

1. In a high-speed blender, combine Great Northern beans, lemon juice, tahini, vegetable stock, sea salt, and white pepper.

2. Blend until smooth.

3. With the blender running on low, add extra-virgin olive oil and cilantro, and blend until just combined.

4. Season with additional sea salt and white pepper as desired.

5. Transfer to an airtight glass container, and refrigerate for up to 4 days, or freeze for future use.

Variation: Omit the vegetable stock, and enjoy as a decadent dip with crisp vegetables such as cucumbers, carrots, and cauliflower, or spread on flax crackers or gluten-free chips.

Tart Tahini Sauce

This tart sauce made from ground sumac and tahini is a welcome addition to fresh vegetables such as tomatoes and cucumber and can be served as a condiment for vegetable burgers and grain bowls.

Yield: about ¾ cup	Prep time: 5 minutes	Serving size: ¼ cup		
Each serving has:				
114 calories	7 g carbohydrates	9 g fat	3 g fiber	4 g protein

3 TB. tahini	1 TB. fresh lemon juice
1 tsp. balsamic vinegar	½ tsp. dried oregano
1 tsp. sumac powder	½ tsp. sea salt
2 small cloves garlic	½ cup water
1 TB. chia seeds	

1. In a high-speed blender, combine tahini, balsamic vinegar, sumac powder, garlic, chia seeds, lemon juice, oregano, sea salt, and water.

2. Blend until completely smooth. Adjust seasoning as desired.

3. Transfer to an airtight glass container, and refrigerate for up to 5 days.

FRESH FACT

Sumac is a shrub that grows abundantly in Africa and the Mediterranean and is often used in Greek and Middle Eastern cuisine. It's generally coarsely ground and sold in international markets. The flavor resembles a lemon—sour and tangy. You can recognize it by its vibrant crimson red color.

Tangy Green Chile Sauce

This vibrant green sauce made with tangy tomatillos and earthy green chiles is medium hot, but you can boost the heat with more jalapeños if you like. Hemp Sour Cream adds silkiness and nicely balances the heat.

Yield:	Prep time:	Cook time:	Serving size:
4½ cups	5 minutes	about 40 minutes	⅓ cup

Each serving has:				
42 calories	4 g carbohydrates	2 g fat	1 g fiber	2 g protein

2 medium hatch or Anaheim chiles	1 TB. ground cumin
1 medium jalapeño or serrano chile, stemmed and chopped	½ tsp. ground black pepper
10 medium tomatillos, husks removed and quartered	2¼ cups vegetable stock
1 cup fresh cilantro, chopped	½ medium yellow onion, chopped (½ cup)
½ tsp. dried Mexican oregano	3 large cloves garlic, peeled
1 tsp. sea salt	¼ cup Hemp Sour Cream (recipe earlier in this chapter)

1. Char hatch chiles by holding stems tightly and rotating them over a flame for about 2 minutes. Or dry-roast them in a cast-iron skillet over medium-high heat for 6 to 8 minutes, turning often to roast evenly. When skin is evenly blackened, transfer to a paper bag or set out on a cutting board to cool. When chiles are cool enough to handle, remove skins, and chop chiles.

2. In a food processor fitted with an S blade, pulse charred chiles, jalapeño, tomatillos, cilantro, Mexican oregano, sea salt, cumin, and black pepper until fine and blended. Set aside.

3. In a medium saucepan over medium heat, heat ¼ cup vegetable stock. Add yellow onion, and cook for about 5 minutes or until translucent.

4. Add garlic, and cook for 1 minute.

5. Add tomatillo-chile mixture, and heat for at least 10 minutes or until sauce is thick and jamlike.

6. Add remaining 2 cups vegetable stock, increase heat to high, and bring to a boil for about 2 minutes. Reduce heat to low, and simmer for 15 minutes.

7. Stir in Hemp Sour Cream, and season with more sea salt and pepper as desired. Cool slightly for 5 minutes at room temperature.

8. Transfer to an airtight glass container, and refrigerate for up to 7 days.

Variation: For a zesty soup, double the vegetable stock, and add some sautéed mushrooms, chopped red bell pepper, corn kernels, and crumbled tofu. Let simmer for 30 minutes, and enjoy with chopped cilantro and a generous squeeze of fresh lime juice.

TASTY TIP

Serve this sauce with polenta, enchiladas, tacos, and tamales, add it to soups and stews (especially white bean chili), or use it as a marinade for tempeh and tofu.

Sea Salt and Lime Cream Sauce

This creamy topper has a balanced blend of saltiness and tang and is delicious served over enchiladas, romaine and butter leaf salads, mushroom tacos, and grilled tofu.

Yield:	Prep time:	Serving size:		
about 1 cup	10 minutes	¼ cup		
Each serving has:				
144 calories	2 g carbohydrates	11 g fat	1 g fiber	9 g protein

½ cup water	¼ tsp. sea salt
½ cup hemp seeds	⅛ cup fresh lime juice

1. In a high-speed blender, combine water, hemp seeds, sea salt, and lime juice.

2. Blend until smooth.

3. Transfer to an airtight glass container, and refrigerate for up to 7 days.

Variation: For a simple hemp cream you can use to pour over milk or add to tea and smoothies, omit the lime juice and sea salt and season to taste with maple syrup and vanilla extract.

Classic Cream Sauce

Every vegan cook should know how to make a simple and rich cream sauce. This silky, low-fat version is a great base for Alfredo, creamy enchiladas, and scalloped potatoes.

Yield:	Prep time:	Cook time:	Serving size:	
about 4 cups	5 minutes	21 minutes	½ cup	
Each serving has:				
135 calories	9 g carbohydrates	11 g fat	1 g fiber	1 g protein

5 TB. virgin coconut oil

4 TB. brown rice flour

4 cups almond milk

2 tsp. sea salt

½ tsp. ground nutmeg

1. In a medium saucepan over medium-low heat, heat virgin coconut oil. Add brown rice flour, and stir until smooth. Increase heat to medium, and cook for about 8 minutes or until mixture turns a light golden brown.

2. In a separate medium sauce pan over medium heat, heat almond milk for about 4 minutes or until just about to boil.

3. Add hot milk to flour mixture, 1 cup at a time, whisking continuously until very smooth. Bring to a boil, reduce heat to medium, and cook, stirring continuously, for 10 more minutes.

4. Remove from heat, and season with sea salt and nutmeg. Cool slightly for 5 minutes at room temperature.

5. Transfer to an airtight glass container, and refrigerate for up to 5 days.

Variation: Customize your classic cream sauce by adding fresh minced herbs and spices such as thyme, tarragon, rosemary, or fennel. Or blend minced onions, garlic, and nutritional yeast into prepared sauce for a simple Alfredo.

Rustic Spanish Red Sauce

Sweet roasted red peppers, pungent garlic, and nutty almond butter blend to create a rich and creamy sauce perfect over spaghetti squash or with quinoa patties, tofu scramble, or grilled vegetables.

Yield:	Prep time:	Cook time:	Serving size:	
about 1½ cups	10 minutes	1 minute	¼ cup	
Each serving has:				
192 calories	9 g carbohydrates	17 g fat	2 g fiber	4 g protein

2 TB. vegetable stock

4 large cloves garlic, chopped

1 cup roasted red peppers

2 tsp. fresh lemon juice

2 TB. aged balsamic vinegar

½ tsp. red chili flakes

½ cup almond butter

1. In a small saucepan over medium heat, warm vegetable stock. Add garlic, and cook for about 1 minute.

2. Transfer to a food processor fitted with an S blade or a high-speed blender. Add roasted red peppers, lemon juice, balsamic vinegar, red chili flakes, and almond butter, and purée for about 2 minutes or until smooth. Cool slightly for 5 minutes at room temperature.

3. Transfer to an airtight glass container, and refrigerate for up to 5 days.

Variation: To make **Red Pepper Tapenade,** blend the same ingredients, but instead of puréeing, pulse to achieve a course texture. Serve with crackers and cheese, atop grilled asparagus, or spread on grilled bread.

Minted Cucumber Sauce

This creamy, tart vegan yogurt sauce is wonderful as a topping for a grain bowl or as a salad dressing. You can also serve it with a variety of vegetables as a party dip, or spread on grain and bean burgers. It's light, refreshing, and very tasty!

Yield:	Prep time:	Serving size:		
about 2⅓ cups	15 minutes	⅓ cup		
Each serving has:				
25 calories	3 g carbohydrates	1 g fat	0 g fiber	2 g protein

⅔ (12-oz.) pkg. soft silken tofu (1 cup)

⅛ cup fresh lemon juice

¼ cup water

1 TB. sea salt

1 tsp. ground black pepper

1 small cucumber, peeled and shredded (1 cup)

¼ cup packed fresh mint leaves, minced

1. In a high-speed blender, combine silken tofu, lemon juice, water, sea salt, and black pepper.

2. Blend until completely smooth.

3. In a medium bowl, combine cucumber, mint, and silken tofu yogurt. Serve atop your favorite dish or with veggie crackers.

4. Transfer to an airtight glass container, and refrigerate for up to 3 days.

Variation: This vegan version of traditional tzatziki is equally wonderful with equal amounts of fresh dill or parsley in place of the mint.

Chia Mole

The sensual blend of chiles and chocolate is decadent, rich, and complex. The richness of this sauce is achieved with the addition of softened corn tortillas, almond butter, chia seeds, and ripe banana. Smoky chipotle chilies add dimension and bold flavor.

Yield:	Prep time:	Cook time:	Serving size:	
about 6 cups	25 minutes	about 35 minutes	¾ cup	
Each serving has:				
169 calories	29 g carbohydrates	10 g fat	6 g fiber	4 g protein

3 dried ancho chiles, halved and seeded

½ cup hot water

3 (4-in.) corn tortillas, chopped fine

¼ cup unsweetened almond milk

1 TB. virgin coconut oil

½ medium sweet onion, chopped (½ cup)

3 chipotle chiles in adobo sauce, chopped

1 TB. adobo sauce from can of chipotle chiles

2 medium-large tomatoes, chopped (1½ cups)

1 (4-oz.) chili-infused dark chocolate bar

1 tsp. sea salt

1 large very ripe banana, peeled and mashed (1 cup)

⅛ cup almond butter

3 TB. chia seeds

1 tsp. ground cinnamon

⅛ tsp. ground nutmeg

⅛ tsp. ground cloves

½ tsp. ground smoked paprika

1 tsp. dried Mexican oregano

¼ tsp. ground black pepper

1 cup vegetable stock

1. In a small bowl, combine dried ancho chiles and hot water, and let rest at room temperature for 20 minutes. Squeeze excess water from chiles, chop finely, and set aside.

2. In another small bowl, combine tortillas and almond milk, and mash into a paste.

3. In a medium saucepan over medium heat, heat virgin coconut oil. Add sweet onion, and sauté for 5 minutes.

4. Add ancho chiles, chipotle chiles, adobo sauce, tomatoes, dark chocolate, and sea salt, and cook for about 15 minutes or until a rich paste forms.

5. Add banana and tortilla paste, and cook for 5 minutes.

6. Reduce heat to low, and add almond butter, chia seeds, cinnamon, nutmeg, cloves, smoked paprika, Mexican oregano, and black pepper. Stir to combine.

7. Pour in vegetable stock, and cook, stirring, for 2 or 3 minutes.

8. Transfer mixture to a high-speed blender or food processor fitted with an S blade, and blend on high for about 2 minutes or until smooth.

9. Return sauce to the saucepan, reduce heat to low, and simmer for at least 15 minutes. Season with more salt and pepper as desired. Cool slightly for 5 minutes at room temperature.

10. Transfer to an airtight container, and refrigerate for up to 4 days.

Variation: Experiment with spices, nuts, seeds, and nut butters you have on hand. Pine nuts, hemp seeds, pumpkinseeds, and cashews all enhance the creaminess of this traditional Mexican sauce, and including different chiles such as poblanos and pasilla further customizes your mole.

Shiitake Mushroom Gravy

If you've ever had stroganoff, you know what this thick, rich gravy tastes like. Its full, smoky flavor has a bit of tang from the addition of Hemp Sour Cream.

Yield:	Prep time:	Cook time:	Serving size:
about 5 cups	10 minutes	27 minutes	½ cup

Each serving has:				
173 calories	12 g carbohydrates	13 g fat	2 g fiber	5 g protein

⅓ cup virgin coconut oil

¼ small yellow onion, chopped (¼ cup)

4 large cloves garlic, minced

¾ cup shiitake mushrooms, sliced

1 TB. wheat-free tamari

½ tsp. liquid smoke

¼ cup sherry

½ cup brown rice flour

2 cups vegetable stock

2 TB. tomato paste

1 TB. nutritional yeast flakes

¼ cup fresh parsley, minced

½ tsp. sea salt

¼ tsp. ground black pepper

⅛ tsp. ground nutmeg

½ cup Hemp Sour Cream (recipe earlier in this chapter)

1. In a medium saucepan over medium-low heat, melt virgin coconut oil. Add yellow onion and garlic, and sauté for about 5 minutes or until translucent.

2. Add shiitake mushrooms, wheat-free tamari, and liquid smoke. Increase heat to high, and add sherry. Bring to a boil, reduce heat to medium, and cook for about 7 minutes or until volume is reduced by ½.

3. Slowly add brown rice flour, stirring constantly until a paste forms.

4. Gradually whisk in vegetable stock, and stir until combined.

5. Add tomato paste, nutritional yeast flakes, parsley, sea salt, black pepper, nutmeg, and Hemp Sour Cream, and cook for 15 minutes.

6. Remove from heat, and season with more sea salt and black pepper as desired. Cool slightly for 5 minutes at room temperature.

7. Transfer to an airtight glass container, and refrigerate for up to 2 days.

Variation: Add an additional 2 cups vegetable stock and 1 bay leaf to make a savory mushroom soup. Simmer the soup on low for at least 30 minutes to allow flavors to thoroughly combine. Be sure to remove the bay leaf before serving.

Gluten-Free Herb Gravy

Knowing how to make rich and savory gravy is a must, especially during the holiday season. The fact that this gravy is low in fat and gluten free is an added bonus.

Yield:	Prep time:	Cook time:	Serving size:
about 5 cups	5 minutes	22 minutes	½ cup

Each serving has:				
104 calories	14 g carbohydrates	5 g fat	1 g fiber	1 g protein

4 cups vegetable stock, warmed	2 TB. Irish Moss Emulsifier (recipe earlier in this chapter)
2 herb vegetable bouillon cubes	1 tsp. sea salt
3 TB. virgin coconut oil	½ tsp. ground black pepper
1 small sweet onion, minced (1 cup)	½ tsp. liquid smoke flavor
¾ cup brown rice flour	½ cup unsweetened almond or hemp milk

1. In a small saucepan over medium heat, combine vegetable stock and herb vegetable bouillon cubes, and stir until bouillon is completely dissolved. Reduce heat to low.

2. In a large saucepan over medium-high heat, melt virgin coconut oil. Add sweet onion, and sauté for about 8 minutes or until translucent.

3. Slowly add brown rice flour, and cook, stirring constantly, for 2 minutes or until mixture forms a paste.

4. Reduce heat to low, and slowly whisk in warmed vegetable stock.

5. Whisk continuously while adding Irish Moss Emulsifier, and cook, stirring, for about 2 minutes or until all stock is blended and sauce thickens.

6. Add sea salt, black pepper, liquid smoke flavor, and almond milk. Reduce heat to low, and simmer, stirring occasionally, for 10 minutes. Cool slightly for 5 minutes at room temperature.

7. Transfer to an airtight glass container, and refrigerate for up to 2 days.

Variation: Experiment using ingredients you have on hand. Chickpea and amaranth flours work well in place of brown rice flour. You can also season your gravy with fresh herbs such as thyme and rosemary.

Thyme Peach Drizzle

Imagine summertime with a bowl full of fruit topped with this sweet and savory syrup. Sugary ripe peaches are blended with savory thyme and a touch of vanilla for a unique dessert drizzle that will have you begging for more.

Yield:	Prep time:	Serving size:		
about 3 cups	5 minutes	½ cup		
Each serving has:				
65 calories	7 g carbohydrates	0 g fat	1 g fiber	1 g protein

3 medium very ripe peaches, peeled, pitted, and chopped (2½ cups)

1 TB. fresh lemon juice

¼ cup maple syrup

⅛ tsp. sea salt

½ tsp. vanilla extract

1 TB. fresh thyme, minced

1. In a food processor fitted with an S blade, blend peaches, lemon juice, maple syrup, sea salt, and vanilla extract until smooth.

2. Transfer to an airtight glass container, and refrigerate for up to 2 weeks.

3. Stir in thyme before serving.

Variation: Change up the fruit and herb pairing in this recipe by using combinations such as strawberries and mint, apples and rosemary, pineapple and basil, or pears and tarragon.

Marvelous Marinades

Originally, the technique of marinating was used to preserve and tenderize tough cuts of meat, but in the vegan world, it's used to add flavor and complexity to soft root vegetables, bitter greens, fruit, and mushrooms.

Store-bought marinades are loaded with refined sugar, salt, and hydrogenated oils. Making your own is a snap, and you can control the quality of the ingredients you use.

The Building Blocks of a Balanced Marinade

Creating a marinade is all about balancing flavors. There are three main components of marinades: oil, acid, and aromatics. You can include these in varying amounts to create a wide variety of marinade flavors that will keep your taste buds tingling.

Let's look at some common blends using these components:

Acid and oil: This marinade adds flavor and a bit of moisture. A little oil goes a long way, so limit the quantity to 1 or 2 tablespoons for your entire dish and combine with an acid or a blend of acids like apple cider vinegar and lemon.

Oil and aromatics: Use just a touch of nutritious oil, such as flax or hemp, in this marinade, and blend with spices, peppercorns, dried or fresh herbs, and salt.

Acid and aromatics: These nonoil marinades are great for grilling, roasting vegetables, and softening the texture of mushrooms. Think lemon-thyme or jalapeño-lime.

Dry rubs: Rubs are composed of salts, sugars, spices, herbs, and sometimes a drizzle of oil. To apply, coat the food with the rub and leave to marinate and absorb the aromatic flavors. You can then cook with the rub on or scrape it off before cooking.

When and What to Marinate

When it comes to vegan dishes, there's no wrong or right amount of time to marinate. Soft vegetables and fruits absorb flavors rather quickly, so you can marinate effectively in as little as 30 minutes. You may need to allow hard vegetables to marinate for a couple hours or even overnight.

For added flavor and a soft texture, and to keep foods from burning while grilling or roasting, try marinating hard and soft vegetables such as eggplant, winter and summer squash, asparagus, beets, mushrooms, beans, artichokes, parsnips, bitter greens, broccoli, and cauliflower. You can also marinate fruits such as plums, apples, pears, berries, nectarines, and peaches.

Brazilian Hot Lime Marinade

Brazilian cuisine is appreciated for its balance of heat, savor, tang, and spice, and this marinade lives up to that standard.

Yield:	Prep time:	Cook time:	Serving size:	
about 2 cups	15 minutes	5 minutes	¼ cup	
Each serving has:				
46 calories	4 g carbohydrates	3 g fat	1 g fiber	1 g protein

1 TB. virgin coconut oil	1 large fresh tomato, chopped (1 cup)
2 medium jalapeños, ribs removed, and chopped	2 TB. chopped fresh cilantro leaves
5 cloves garlic, crushed	¼ cup fresh lime juice
¼ cup fresh lemon juice	¼ cup water
1 medium white or yellow onion, chopped (1 cup)	½ tsp. sea salt
	2 TB. extra-virgin olive oil

1. In a large cast-iron skillet over medium-high heat, heat virgin coconut oil, turning the skillet to coat. Add jalapeños and garlic, and sauté for about 5 minutes or until edges of jalapeños brown slightly.

2. Add lemon juice, stir, and remove pan from heat.

3. Transfer mixture to a high-speed blender and add white onion, tomato, cilantro leaves, lime juice, water, and sea salt.

4. With the blender running on low speed, slowly add extra-virgin olive oil, and blend until thoroughly combined.

5. Transfer to an airtight glass container, and refrigerate for up to 3 days.

6. Use to enhance root vegetables, mushrooms, tempeh, and beans.

Variation: For a chunky **Brazilian Hot Lime Salsa,** instead of blending ingredients, mix them together in a medium bowl, omitting the water and reducing the lime and lemon juices by half.

Smoky Red Pepper Marinade

This marinade adds warmth to your dish with the smoky heat of chipotle peppers. Nutritional yeast adds a tinge of cheesy taste, and a tomato and red pepper base creates a tantalizing red blend.

Yield:	Prep time:	Serving size:		
about 4 cups	10 minutes	½ cup		

Each serving has:				
44 calories	9 g carbohydrates	0 g fat	2 g fiber	2 g protein

1 (28-oz.) can diced tomatoes, with juice

¼ cup roasted red peppers

4 chipotle peppers in adobo sauce, seeded and chopped

1 TB. canned adobo sauce

2 tsp. wheat-free tamari

1 tsp. dried Mexican oregano

4 cloves garlic, chopped

¼ tsp. sea salt

2 TB. nutritional yeast flakes

2 TB. yellow onion, chopped

1. In a food processor fitted with an S blade, combine tomatoes, roasted red peppers, chipotle peppers, adobo sauce, wheat-free tamari, Mexican oregano, garlic, sea salt, nutritional yeast flakes, and yellow onion.

2. Blend until smooth.

3. Transfer to an airtight glass container, and refrigerate for up to 4 days.

4. Use with lentil and black bean patties; as an enchilada sauce; with potatoes; or as a marinade for vegetables, tempeh, mushrooms, or tofu.

Variation: For a **Smoky Red Pepper and Tomato Soup,** roast 3 cups Roma tomatoes in a 375°F oven for 35 minutes. Purée with sauce ingredients, adding 2 or 3 cups vegetable stock to thin the soup and seasoning with sea salt. You can also create a gourmet sauce by blending the ingredients in this recipe with 1 cup Hemp Sour Cream (recipe in Chapter 10).

Spicy Pineapple Marinade

The distinct earthy flavor of achiote paste blended with mildly tangy and acidic pineapple juice provides a balanced and rich marinade.

Yield:	Prep time:	Serving size:		
about 1¾ cups	15 minutes	¼ cup		
Each serving has:				
40 calories	10 g carbohydrates	0 g fat	1 g fiber	1 g protein

6 cloves garlic, chopped

1 tsp. sea salt

2 TB. achiote paste

2 tsp. ground allspice

1 tsp. ground black pepper

1½ tsp. dried Mexican oregano

3 TB. apple cider vinegar

6 TB. fresh lime juice

1½ cups pineapple juice

1. Using a mortar and pestle, mash garlic with sea salt until a paste forms.

2. In a mixing bowl, combine garlic paste, achiote paste, allspice, black pepper, Mexican oregano, apple cider vinegar, lime juice, and pineapple juice.

3. Transfer to an airtight glass container, and refrigerate for up to 3 days.

4. Use with starchy vegetables such as eggplant, chayote squash, yuca, and potatoes.

Variation: Mix with some Hemp Sour Cream (recipe in Chapter 10) for a tangy and tasty sauce to drizzle over grilled squash, sweet potatoes, and beans.

Mayan Marinade

Spicy chiles, aromatic cloves, warming cinnamon, tangy vinegar, and citrus juices blend to make this complex marinade.

Yield:	Prep time:	Serving size:		
about 2 cups	10 minutes	½ cup		
Each serving has:				
62 calories	11 g carbohydrates	1 g fat	4 g fiber	2 g protein

½ cup fresh orange juice

3 TB. chili powder

4 cloves garlic, chopped

2 TB. dried Mexican oregano

1 tsp. smoked paprika

⅓ cup apple cider vinegar

1½ tsp. sea salt

¼ tsp. ground black pepper

½ tsp. ground cinnamon

⅛ tsp. ground cloves

1 large shallot, minced (2 TB.)

2 TB. fresh lime juice

1. In a food processor fitted with an S blade, combine orange juice, chili powder, garlic, Mexican oregano, smoked paprika, apple cider vinegar, sea salt, black pepper, cinnamon, cloves, shallots, and lime juice.

2. Blend until well combined.

3. Transfer to an airtight glass container, and refrigerate for up to 3 days.

4. Use to add complexity to squash or tofu; as a broth for a pot of beans when mixed with equal amounts of vegetable stock; or to soften starchy fruits and vegetables like plantains, potatoes, and eggplant.

Variation: For a **Warming Mayan Rub,** omit the vinegar, orange juice, and lime juice. Blend together remaining ingredients, and use to coat potatoes, yuca, parsnips, or beets before roasting or grilling.

FRESH FACT

The Yucatan peninsula is known for its pristine beaches, Mayan ruins, and scrumptious food. Achiote is a spice that appears in many traditional Yucatecan dishes and comes from the seeds of the annatto tree, native to this region. Achiote paste is a brilliant red, and its flavor is earthy and slightly tart.

Korean BBQ Marinade

Spicy, sweet, tangy, and salty, this marinade is bursting with flavor and yet is quite balanced.

Yield:	Prep time:	Serving size:		
about 1 cup	10 minutes	2 tablespoons		
Each serving has:				
50 calories	7 g carbohydrates	2 g fat	0 g fiber	1 g protein

¼ cup wheat-free tamari

2 large scallions, white and light green parts, chopped (¼ cup)

2 cloves garlic, minced

1 (1-in.) fresh peeled and grated ginger (2 TB.)

¼ cup maple syrup

1 tsp. red chili flakes

1 TB. toasted sesame oil

2 tsp. sesame seeds

¼ tsp. cayenne

¼ tsp. ground black pepper

2 TB. fresh lime juice

1. In a small bowl, combine wheat-free tamari, scallions, garlic, ginger, maple syrup, red chili flakes, toasted sesame oil, sesame seeds, cayenne, black pepper, and lime juice.

2. Transfer to an airtight glass container, and refrigerate for up to 3 days.

3. Use to marinate tofu and hearty mushrooms or add some to a vegetable broth to enhance noodle soups.

Variation: Reduce tamari to 1 tablespoon and enjoy this blend as a dip for grilled tofu sticks, nori rice rolls, or spring rolls, or as a dressing for a crunchy Asian slaw.

Citrus Mojo Marinade

This *mojo* marinade is a staple in Cuban and Caribbean cuisine. You'll love the contrast of intense garlic and sour flavors.

Yield:	Prep time:	Serving size:		
about 1 cup	15 minutes	¼ cup		
Each serving has:				
36 calories	4 g carbohydrates	2 g fat	0 g fiber	0 g protein

6 cloves garlic

½ small yellow onion, chopped (¼ cup)

1 tsp. sea salt

½ tsp. ground black pepper

¼ tsp. ground cumin

½ tsp. dried Mexican oregano

½ cup fresh orange juice

¼ cup fresh lime juice

¼ cup fresh lemon juice

½ tsp. hot sauce

2 TB. extra-virgin olive oil

1. In a food processor fitted with an S blade, pulse garlic, yellow onion, sea salt, black pepper, cumin, and Mexican oregano until combined but still coarse.

2. Add orange juice, lime juice, lemon juice, hot sauce, and extra-virgin olive oil, and blend until thoroughly combined.

3. Transfer to an airtight glass container, and refrigerate for up to 3 days.

4. Use to marinate yuca, plantains, jicama, and mushrooms.

DEFINITION

Mojo (pronounced mo-ho) is often served with Cuban and Caribbean dishes and is traditionally made with large amounts of garlic, orange, and lime juices. It's very tart and provides depth of flavor to yuca and mushrooms.

Sugar 'n' Spice Rub

Sugar and spice makes everything nice in this sweet, peppery, and spicy rub.

Yield:	Prep time:	Serving size:		
about ¼ cup	10 minutes	1 tablespoon		
Each serving has:				
44 calories	11 g carbohydrates	0 g fat	2 g fiber	1 g protein

1 (2-in.) piece fresh ginger, peeled and chopped	1 tsp. black, pink, green, or red peppercorns
1 clove garlic, minced	1 tsp. dried thyme
2 TB. maple sugar	⅛ tsp. cayenne
1 tsp. red chili flakes	½ tsp. cracked black pepper
1 tsp. whole coriander seeds	1½ tsp. sea salt

1. Using a mortar and pestle, mash ginger, garlic, maple sugar, red chili flakes, coriander seeds, black peppercorns, thyme, cayenne, black pepper, and sea salt into a dry paste.

2. Slather on whole artichokes before grilling or rub on sweet potatoes or beets and roast in a 375°F oven until tender and a bit gooey. Let rubbed food rest for at least 10 minutes before preparing.

Variation: For a sugar and spice wet marinade, add ¼ cup apple juice, and blend until thoroughly combined.

Dips, Spreads, and Snacks

In This Chapter

- Delicious low-fat dips
- Sensational vegan spreads
- Super tasty snacks
- Healthy hors d'oeuvres

Having a variety of recipes for healthful dips and spreads on hand is a great way to keep from grabbing unhealthy snack foods when the urge to munch between meals strikes. What's more, these low-fat alternatives are packed with flavor and taste better than their high-fat counterparts!

The dips and spreads in this chapter are perfect on just about anything. Try them with the chips, crackers, and crisps in this chapter. Or serve them alongside your favorite salad, spread on some gluten-free toast, serve with a plate of raw vegetables, or use them as a filling for veggie wraps.

These recipes rely on bold flavors and sumptuous textures to bring you delightful condiments and snack foods, and I assure you won't even notice that they're low in fat.

Spirulina Fruit Dip

This dip is delicious served with assorted fruits for entertaining. Its nuttiness and mild sweetness complements apples, persimmons, pears, and gluten-free pretzels.

Yield:	Prep time:	Serving size:		
about 2 cups	5 minutes	¼ cup		
Each serving has:				
76 calories	8 g carbohydrates	5 g fat	1 g fiber	2 g protein

2 medium ripe bananas, peeled and mashed (1½ cups)

¼ cup almond butter

¼ cup water

2 tsp. spirulina powder

Pinch sea salt

1. In a high-speed blender, combine bananas, almond butter, water, spirulina powder, and sea salt.

2. Blend until creamy and slightly whipped.

3. Transfer to an airtight glass container, and refrigerate for up to 3 days.

Variation: Swap out the almond butter with tahini for a lovely variation that has a subtler flavor profile.

TASTY TIP

This sweet and creamy fruit dip is a way to get the super nutrition of spirulina into the mouths of everyone in your family. In fact, this dip makes a perfect baby food for little ones ages 9 months and up.

Sweet Pea Hummus Dip

This dip has flavors reminiscent of a traditional hummus, yet its sweetness and creamy texture make it a distinct diversion from a chickpea-based hummus.

Yield:	Prep time:	Serving size:		
about 2½ cups	5 minutes	¼ cup		
Each serving has:				
143 calories	8 g carbohydrates	11 g fat	3 g fiber	4 g protein

2 cups fresh or frozen peas	1 tsp. sea salt
¼ cup water	½ cup tahini
¼ cup fresh lemon juice	¼ cup extra-virgin olive oil
2 small cloves garlic	½ tsp. ground black pepper

1. If using frozen peas, place in boiling water for 1 minute or until thoroughly thawed.

2. In a high-speed blender, combine peas, water, lemon juice, garlic, sea salt, tahini, extra-virgin olive oil, and black pepper.

3. Blend until smooth.

4. Transfer to an airtight glass container, and refrigerate for up to 5 days.

Variation: Also try this recipe using cooked white beans in place of peas. You can add ¼ teaspoon white pepper instead of black pepper and ½ cup chopped parsley to this version as well.

Tamarind Dip

This sweet and very tangy dip is perfect served as an accompaniment to your favorite Thai and Indian dishes, or with ultra-sweet fruits or roasted vegetables.

Yield:	Prep time:	Cook time:	Serving size:
1¼ cups	10 minutes	20 minutes	2 tablespoons

Each serving has:				
26 calories	7 g carbohydrates	0 g fat	1 g fiber	0 g protein

¼ cup deseeded whole tamarind or pressed pulp	1 tsp. whole cumin seeds
1 cup water	1 tsp. whole fennel seeds
4 large fresh pitted dates	1 tsp. garam masala powder
	1 tsp. sea salt

1. In a high-speed blender, combine tamarind pulp and water. Pulse for just a few seconds or until tamarind is broken down but not completely smooth.

2. Use the back of a spoon to firmly press tamarind pulp through a sieve. Discard leftover pressed pulp.

3. Return tamarind liquid to blender, add dates, and blend until completely smooth.

4. In a small pan over medium heat, toast cumin seeds and fennel seeds for 2 minutes or until seeds are lightly brown and begin to pop.

5. In a blender, spice mill, or coffee grinder, coarsely grind toasted cumin and fennel.

6. In a small saucepan over medium heat, combine tamarind-date paste, ground cumin seeds and fennel seeds, garam masala powder, and sea salt. Bring to a low boil, reduce heat to medium-low, and simmer for about 15 minutes or until mixture turns dark brown and coats a spoon when dipped.

7. Transfer to an airtight glass container, and refrigerate for up to 3 days.

Variation: Add about 20 finely minced mint leaves to step 6 to give this dip an extra-authentic Indian taste.

HEADS-UP

You can find the pulp of the tamarind fruit pod whole or shelled and pressed into a block. Either way, you have to remove the tough seeds by hand or follow the directions in the preparation steps for blending and pressing the tamarind pulp. If you deseed your tamarind beforehand, you can skip step 2 and advance to step 3, where you add the dates.

Sesame Ginger Dip

Toasted sesame oil lends this dip the classic sesame taste that combines so well with tamari and maple syrup. It's well balanced and perfect paired with an assortment of fresh vegetables.

Yield:	Prep time:	Serving size:		
1 cup	10 minutes	2 tablespoons		
Each serving has:				
71 calories	9 g carbohydrates	4 g fat	0 g fiber	2 g protein

1 TB. toasted sesame oil	1 (2-in.) piece fresh peeled ginger
2 TB. apple cider vinegar	2 TB. tahini
¼ cup maple syrup	¼ cup water
¼ cup wheat-free tamari	

1. In a high-speed blender, combine toasted sesame oil, apple cider vinegar, maple syrup, wheat-free tamari, ginger, tahini, and water.

2. Blend until thoroughly combined.

Variation: Turn this dip into a delicious dressing by adding ¼ cup water and 1 tablespoon fresh lemon juice.

Zesty Black Bean Dip

This slightly spicy, flavorful, and very creamy dip has the zestiness of sour cream and the punch of a salsa picante. Firm, fresh tomatoes and crispy onions add texture.

Yield:	Prep time:	Serving size:		
about 6 cups	15 minutes	½ cup		
Each serving has:				
97 calories	13 g carbohydrates	3 g fat	4 g fiber	5 g protein

3 cups cooked black beans

½ cup water

⅓ cup pumpkinseeds

1 TB. extra-virgin olive oil

¼ cup fresh lemon juice

1 large clove garlic

1 small jalapeño, stem removed

1 TB. ground cumin

1 TB. ground paprika

1 TB. sea salt

1 medium-large tomato, chopped (⅔ cup)

1 small red onion, chopped (⅓ cup)

½ cup packed chopped fresh cilantro

1. In a high-speed blender, combine 2½ cups black beans, water, pumpkinseeds, extra-virgin olive oil, lemon juice, garlic, jalapeño, cumin, paprika, and sea salt.

2. Blend until smooth.

3. Transfer to a bowl, and stir in remaining ½ cup black beans, tomato, red onion, and cilantro.

4. Transfer to an airtight glass container, and refrigerate for up to 5 days.

Variation: Make a quick-and-easy black bean burger by adding an additional 1 cup whole black beans during step 3. Work mixture into 10 (2×½-inch-thick) patties, and bake at 350°F for 20 minutes. Or brown lightly in a large skillet over medium heat for 6 minutes per side.

Raw Cheesy Hemp Spread

This delicious spread tastes oh-so-close to processed cheese dips. Bell peppers and a bit of nutritional yeast combine to mimic a cheesy flavor and provide that familiar orange color, too.

Yield:	Prep time:	Chill time:	Serving size:	
3½ cups	10 minutes	3 hours	¼ cup	
Each serving has:				
124 calories	5 g carbohydrates	10 g fat	2 g fiber	8 g protein

1 cup hemp seeds	⅛ cup fresh lemon juice
½ cup water	¼ cup virgin coconut oil
1 medium zucchini, chopped (1 cup)	1 medium clove garlic
½ medium red bell pepper, ribs and seeds removed, and diced (¼ cup)	¼ cup nutritional yeast flakes
	2 tsp. sea salt

1. In a high-speed blender, combine hemp seeds, water, zucchini, red bell pepper, lemon juice, virgin coconut oil, garlic, nutritional yeast flakes, and sea salt.

2. Blend until completely smooth.

3. Transfer to an airtight glass container, and refrigerate for 3 hours or until set. It should have a slightly firm spreadable texture.

4. Store in the refrigerator for up to 5 days.

Variation: If you ever have nostalgic cravings for macaroni and cheese, omit the virgin coconut oil, garlic, and ½ cup zucchini, and add an extra ½ cup water to this recipe to make a **Smooth and Creamy Cheese Sauce.** Mix with some cooked macaroni, and satisfy that craving.

TASTY TIP

This low-fat vegan cheesy dip is great for serving vegan and nonvegan guests. Plus, it's the perfect snack to serve kids who don't like "health food." It's super spreadable, so serve it with some crackers and a little spreading knife for a delightful treat.

Artichoke Spinach Spread

This healthy dip is wonderfully smooth and creamy yet also pleasantly chunky. Pungent spices and fresh basil give this artichoke dip that extra something special.

Yield:	Prep time:	Cook time:	Serving size:	
about 8 cups	10 minutes	20 minutes	½ cup	
Each serving has:				
70 calories	10 g carbohydrates	2 g fat	3 g fiber	4 g protein

2 cups cooked chickpeas

⅓ cup water

1 TB. fresh lemon juice

3 TB. nutritional yeast flakes

1 tsp. sea salt

6 fresh basil leaves

⅛ tsp. cayenne

¼ tsp. ground black pepper

2 TB. virgin coconut oil

1 medium yellow onion, chopped (1 cup)

3 medium cloves garlic, minced

4 cups packed fresh spinach, chopped

1 (16-oz.) can artichoke hearts, drained, and finely chopped (1½ cups)

1. In a food processor fitted with an S blade, pulse chickpeas, water, lemon juice, nutritional yeast flakes, sea salt, basil, cayenne, and black pepper until well combined but still somewhat chunky.

2. In a large saucepan over medium-high heat, heat virgin coconut oil. Add yellow onion and garlic, and cook for 6 minutes or until onions are translucent.

3. Reduce heat to low, add spinach and artichoke hearts, and cook for 3 minutes or until spinach wilts.

4. Remove from heat, add chickpea mixture, and stir to combine.

5. Transfer to an airtight glass container, and refrigerate for up to 3 days.

Variation: For a smoother dip, blend step 1's ingredients until smooth. Give this dip a bit of smoky flavor by replacing the cayenne with ¼ teaspoon chipotle powder or liquid smoke.

FRESH FACT

Artichokes are one of the highest vegetable sources of antioxidants. They're a member of the thistle family, which is renowned for the antioxidant silymarin, known to regenerate liver cells. Artichoke leaves also contain compounds reputed to reduce cancer cells.

Simple Mayonnaise Spread

This creamy spread is so close to the real thing, you might convert even the most devoted mayo fans. It's slightly tart and mildly sweet, and it complements practically anything.

Yield:	Prep time:	Chill time:	Serving size:	
about 1½ cups	10 minutes	30 minutes	2 tablespoons	
Each serving has:				
64 calories	3 g carbohydrates	5 g fat	0 g fiber	2 g protein

⅓ cup hemp seeds

2 TB. virgin coconut oil

½ cup Irish Moss Emulsifier (recipe in Chapter 10)

1 cup water

1 TB. apple cider vinegar

1 TB. fresh lemon juice

2 TB. Dijon mustard

½ TB. sea salt

1 TB. coconut or date sugar

1. In a high-speed blender, combine hemp seeds, virgin coconut oil, Irish Moss Emulsifier, water, apple cider vinegar, lemon juice, Dijon mustard, sea salt, and coconut sugar.

2. Blend until completely smooth.

3. Transfer to an airtight container, and refrigerate for 30 minutes to set.

4. Refrigerate for up to 1 week.

Variation: A basic mayo is the perfect base for creating other more flavorful spreads. You can add 2 teaspoons chipotle powder and about 12 fresh basil leaves or a mélange of herbs such as fresh oregano, rosemary, and thyme.

TASTY TIP

Coconut oil becomes solid at room temperature but melts when warmed, so it's great for use as a thickener. In this recipe, blending coconut oil with the other ingredients for several minutes melts the oil sufficiently, and the mayonnaise becomes thick and spreadable when refrigerated.

Zucchini Spread

Zucchini makes a perfect substitute for chickpeas in this fresh twist on traditional hummus. It's a bit thinner than many hummus blends, but it's thick with Middle Eastern flair and flavor.

Yield:	Prep time:	Serving size:		
about 3 cups	10 minutes	¼ cup		
Each serving has:				
149 calories	9 g carbohydrates	12 g fat	2 g fiber	4 g protein

3 large zucchinis, chopped (2½ cups)	⅓ cup fresh parsley, chopped
½ cup fresh lemon juice	1 tsp. sea salt
½ cup tahini	2 tsp. ground cumin
⅛ cup extra-virgin olive oil	¼ tsp. cayenne

1. In a food processor fitted with an S blade, combine zucchinis, lemon juice, tahini, extra-virgin olive oil, parsley, sea salt, cumin, and cayenne.

2. Process until smooth.

3. Transfer to an airtight glass container, and refrigerate for up to 5 days.

Variation: Add some white beans to this spread for extra thickness. You also could omit the lemon juice and opt instead for 1 tablespoon balsamic vinegar and 2 tablespoons sumac powder for a shocking pink spread.

FRESH FACT

It's a bit of a misnomer to call this recipe a *hummus* even though the taste and texture is similar to it. The term *hummus* usually refers to the familiar Middle Eastern dish that combines chickpeas with tahini and lemon juice.

Salt and Vinegar Kale Chips

Kale chips are all the rage lately. These crispy kale chips have a potent salty-sour taste reminiscent of traditional salt and vinegar potato chips.

Yield:	Prep time:	Bake time:	Serving size:	
32 chips	10 minutes	15 minutes	8 chips	
Each serving has:				
324 calories	21 g carbohydrates	21 g fat	2 g fiber	19 g protein

1 cup hemp seeds or Brazil nuts	Pinch cayenne
⅛ cup fresh lemon juice	1 small clove garlic
¼ cup apple cider vinegar	2 tsp. sea salt
⅓ cup water	⅛ small red onion, chopped (2 TB.)
1 tsp. maple syrup	2 large heads curly kale, stems removed and torn into 2- to 4-in. pieces

1. Preheat the oven to 350°F. Line a baking sheet with parchment paper.

2. In a high-speed blender, combine hemp seeds, lemon juice, apple cider vinegar, water, maple syrup, cayenne, garlic, sea salt, and red onion.

3. Blend until completely smooth.

4. Place curly kale leaves into a large bowl. Add dressing, and using your hands, massage dressing into kale until completely covered.

5. Arrange kale leaves on the prepared baking sheet, and bake for about 15 minutes.

Variation: To make raw kale chips, dehydrate at 105°F for about 4 hours on one side, flip, and dehydrate for 4 more hours. For **Ranch Kale Chips,** add an additional clove garlic, ½ cup chopped green bell pepper, ¼ teaspoon white pepper, and ½ cup chopped fresh parsley to the blender in step 2. You should also reduce apple cider vinegar to ⅛ cup and omit the cayenne. For **Cheesy Kale Chips,** massage Cheesy Hemp Spread (recipe earlier in this chapter) into the chopped kale before baking or dehydrating.

Spicy Kelp Chips

If you like roasted seaweed snacks, this is a chip for you! Rehydrating the kelp before preparing these chips gives them an extra crunch. The spicy, sweet sauce is the perfect thing to complement the strong flavor of kelp.

Yield:	Prep time:	Bake time:	Serving size:	
20 chips	10 minutes	2 hours	4 chips	
Each serving has:				
80 calories	11 g carbohydrates	3 g fat	1 g fiber	3 g protein

¼ cup pumpkinseeds

⅓ cup water

⅛ cup wheat-free tamari

⅛ cup maple syrup

½ tsp. cayenne

20 kelp strips, rehydrated according to package directions

1. Preheat the oven to 200°F. Line a baking sheet with parchment paper.

2. In a high-speed blender, combine pumpkinseeds, water, wheat-free tamari, maple syrup, and cayenne.

3. In a medium bowl, combine pumpkinseed sauce and kelp strips, and toss to coat evenly.

4. Lay kelp strips flat on the prepared baking sheet, and drizzle any leftover sauce over top.

5. Bake for 1 hour, flip, and bake for 1 more hour or until crisp.

Variation: You can dehydrate kelp chips at 105°F for about 4 hours. You can also make these chips using smaller bits of rehydrated wakame. Grind all ingredients together to make a paté, which you can spread onto or dehydrate into chips.

FRESH FACT

Kelp is a great natural source of thyroid-protective iodine. It also has been shown to help heal the digestive tract and protect against health issues associated with radiation exposure. It's often eaten in soups or seaweed salads, but dehydrating it makes it crispy and crunchy and takes away the sometimes slimy texture it can have when served in a soup.

Curry Quinoa Crisps

These savory little crisps have a similar crunch to rice crackers but have *way* more flavor. Curry powder gives them just a touch of heat and the slight sweetness of lemon rounds out the flavors perfectly.

Yield:	Prep time:	Bake time:	Serving size:	
18 crisps	15 minutes	4 hours	6 crisps	
Each serving has:				
212 calories	32 g carbohydrates	7 g fat	5 g fiber	8 g protein

2 cups cooked quinoa	2 tsp. coarsely ground black pepper
¼ cup wheat-free tamari	1 TB. fresh lemon juice
⅛ cup coconut sugar	1 tsp. sea salt
1 TB. curry powder	¼ cup sesame seeds
2 tsp. ground cumin	

1. Preheat the oven to 200°F. Line a rimless baking sheet with parchment paper.

2. In a high-speed blender, combine quinoa, wheat-free tamari, coconut sugar, curry powder, cumin, black pepper, lemon juice, and sea salt. Blend on high for about 2 minutes or until smooth.

3. Stir in sesame seeds.

4. Place ½ of batter on the prepared baking sheet, and roll to ½ inch thickness. Cut rolled batter into 2-inch squares.

5. Bake for 2 hours, flip, and bake for 2 more hours or until crisp.

Variation: Make a batch of savory **Caraway Quinoa Crisps** by omitting the curry powder, black pepper, and lemon juice and adding 2 teaspoons caraway seeds, 1 teaspoon anise seeds, 1 teaspoon ground sage, and 6 sun-dried tomatoes, rehydrated in warm water for 20 minutes, to the blended quinoa mixture.

HEADS-UP

There's no specific recipe for curry, although a few popular brands seem to be more common. Some of these blends are very spicy, though. If you're not familiar with different curry combinations, err on the side of caution and do a taste test before using curry in this recipe.

Italian Veggie Crackers

These crispy little delights have a wonderful Italian-inspired flavor and you could easily top them with some Cheesy Hemp Spread to make miniature vegan pizza snacks.

Yield:	Prep time:	Bake time:	Serving size:	
40 crackers	20 minutes	4 hours	8 crackers	
Each serving has:				
74 calories	8 g carbohydrates	4 g fat	4 g fiber	3 g protein

2 medium zucchini, chopped (2 cups)

1 medium tomato, chopped (½ cup)

1 large red bell pepper, ribs and seeds removed, and chopped (1 cup)

6 medium stalks celery, chopped (2 cups)

½ small sweet onion, chopped (¼ cup)

7 sun-dried tomatoes, rehydrated in warm water for 20 minutes, drained, and squeezed

1 TB. fresh rosemary leaves

2 tsp. fresh thyme leaves

2 tsp. sea salt

1 cup ground flaxseeds

1. Preheat the oven to 200°F. Line a baking sheet with parchment paper.

2. In a high-speed blender, combine zucchini, tomato, red bell pepper, celery, sweet onion, sun-dried tomatoes, rosemary, thyme, and sea salt. Blend for 2 minutes or until smooth.

3. In a large bowl, combine blended vegetable mixture and ground flaxseeds.

4. Use a dessert spoon to scoop generous dollops of vegetable-flaxseed mixture onto the prepared baking sheet. Using the back of the spoon, spread dollops into small circles about ½ inch thick.

5. Bake for about 2 hours, flip, and bake for 2 more hours or until dry and crispy.

Variation: Create a raw cracker by dehydrating them at 105°F for about 6 hours. Flip and dehydrate 4 to 6 more hours. To make **Sour Cream and Onion Veggie Crackers,** omit the sun-dried tomatoes, rosemary, and thyme. Add ⅓ cup hemp seeds, another ¼ cup sweet onion, and 1 tablespoon dried dill to the blended mixture, and stir in 2 tablespoons minced chives.

Super Green Popcorn

This spicy popcorn is a nutritious treat with a slightly cheesy taste.

Yield:	Prep time:	Cook time:	Serving size:	
about 4 cups	10 minutes	5 minutes	1 cup	
Each serving has:				
70 calories	10 g carbohydrates	1 g fat	4 g fiber	8 g protein

3 TB. nutritional yeast flakes

1 TB. spirulina powder

⅛ tsp. cayenne

⅛ tsp. granulated garlic

½ tsp. sea salt

4 cups freshly air-popped popcorn

1. In a small bowl, combine nutritional yeast flakes, spirulina powder, cayenne, granulated garlic, and sea salt.

2. While popcorn is still hot, sprinkle on spice blend and toss to coat.

Variation: Make **Sweet Chipotle Popcorn** by omitting the spirulina and adding ¼ teaspoon chipotle powder instead. Drizzle popcorn with 2 tablespoons maple syrup and toss to coat before adding your spice blend.

Sumptuous Suppertime

If you're craving something you can really sink your teeth into, you'll find it here! In Part 5, I provide many vibrant veggie entrées to satisfy any appetite. No longer will relatives mock you for eating nothing but side dishes when you fill their plates with these incredible creations sure to please any palate.

Bursting with exotic flavors, toothsome textures, wholesome goodness, and soul-soothing vegetables, the hearty stews and spicy chilies in Part 5 are sure to become comfort food favorites.

You'll love the versatile array of side dishes I present in this part. They're the perfect complement to any of the entrée recipes, or you can combine a number of them for a complete multicourse meal that puts the traditional meat-and-potatoes dinner to shame.

Vibrant Veggie Entrées

In This Chapter

- Hearty and warming noodle dishes
- Creative twists on common comfort foods
- Flavorful, vegetable-packed main dishes
- Robust grains and legumes for satisfying meals

Some people claim you've got to have meat to make a filling main dish, but nothing could be further from the truth. The low-fat vegan entrées in this chapter are far more satisfying than any meat-based meal, and all these vibrant vegetable dishes offer far more nutrition!

In this chapter, I share some time-tested recipes with a vegan twist and some cutting-edge entrées that will bring some refreshing new flavor combinations to your dinner table.

Tofu Pad Thai

This warm, flavorful, and aromatic concoction of comforting noodles, hot chiles, sour tamarind, tart lime, and a touch of sweetness will surely become an instant favorite.

Yield:	Prep time:	Cook time:	Serving size:	
6 cups	10 minutes	30 minutes	1½ cups	
Each serving has:				
424 calories	57 g carbohydrates	17 g fat	4 g fiber	17 g protein

4 cups water

6 oz. pad thai rice noodles

2 TB. virgin coconut oil

2 medium shallots, thinly sliced (¼ cup)

2 small cloves garlic, minced (1 TB.)

16 oz. extra-firm tofu, drained and cut into ½-in. cubes

1 cup Pad Thai Sauce (recipe in Chapter 10)

1 large head broccoli, cut into small florets (1 cup)

1 cup mung bean sprouts

4 large green onions, whites and light green parts only, thinly sliced (⅓ cup)

¼ cup fresh cilantro leaves, chopped

¼ cup crushed almonds

4 lime wedges

1. In a large saucepan over high heat, bring water to a boil. Add pad thai noodles, and return to a boil. Remove from heat, cover, and let stand for 15 minutes.

2. Meanwhile, in a large skillet over high heat, melt virgin coconut oil. When very hot, add shallots and garlic, and cook for 1 minute. Remove shallots and garlic from the skillet, and set aside.

3. Add tofu to the skillet, and cook for 6 to 8 minutes or until tofu is lightly browned.

4. Add Pad Thai Sauce, pad thai rice noodles, and broccoli, and stir-fry for 3 minutes or until broccoli is tender and noodles are relaxed and have absorbed ½ of sauce.

5. Divide among 4 plates, and top each with ¼ cup mung bean sprouts, 1 tablespoon green onions, 1 tablespoon cilantro, 1 tablespoon almonds, and 1 lime wedge.

Variation: Make a soothing ramen-style soup by adding cooked rice noodles to a bowl of warm vegetable stock, stir in some of the Pad Thai Sauce, add cooked broccoli and tofu, and top off your bowl of steaming noodles with bean sprouts, green onions, cilantro, crushed almonds, and a lime wedge.

Tuscan Squash and Pesto

Spaghetti squash is a delicious alternative to glutinous pasta. Squash noodles are a tad sweet, crunchy, and surprisingly filling for a food that's fat free, low in calories, and fiber rich. The pesto with peppery arugula and nutty pumpkinseeds complements the noodle's texture, taste, and color.

Yield:	Prep time:	Cook time:	Serving size:	
about 6 cups	15 minutes	35 minutes	1½ cups	
Each serving has:				
199 calories	18 g carbohydrates	14 g fat	5 g fiber	8 g protein

1 medium (about 4-lb.) spaghetti squash, halved lengthwise, and seeds removed

1 tsp. virgin coconut oil

1 small red onion, thinly sliced (½ cup)

1 cup Arugula and Pumpkinseed Pesto (recipe in Chapter 10)

12 cherry tomatoes, halved

2 TB. chopped fresh basil

1. Preheat the oven to 350°F. Line a baking sheet with parchment paper.

2. Place cut side of spaghetti squash face down on parchment paper, and bake for 30 minutes. Remove from the oven and let cool to room temperature before handling.

3. Using a large spoon or fork, scoop stringy flesh out of squash halves and transfer to a large bowl.

4. In a medium saucepan over medium-high heat, heat virgin coconut oil. Add red onion, and cook for 3 minutes.

5. Add Arugula and Pumpkinseed Pesto, and heat until warm. Transfer Arugula and Pumpkinseed Pesto and onion to squash noodles, and toss to coat.

6. Divide among bowls, top each serving with 6 cherry tomato halves and 2 teaspoons basil, and serve.

Variation: Make a unique breakfast meal using squash noodles. Follow instructions for baking and removing flesh, and divide among cereal bowls. Sprinkle each bowl with ⅛ teaspoon cinnamon and nutmeg, and add 1 tablespoon maple syrup, 1 tablespoon raisins, 2 teaspoons shredded coconut, and 1 tablespoon ground flaxseeds. Top off with 2 tablespoons hemp milk, and you have a hearty and low-fat morning meal.

Caribbean-Style Yuca Pie

This casserole has a delightfully chewy and slightly crispy crust made from whipped yuca. The rich and savory sautéed vegetable filling is enhanced with Caribbean flavors of lime, garlic, salt, orange, and chiles.

Yield:	Prep time:	Cook time:	Serving size:	
9 slices	30 minutes	2¼ hours	1 slice	
Each serving has:				
272 calories	46 g carbohydrates	7 g fat	4 g fiber	3 g protein

8 cups water	3 cups mixed mushrooms, chopped fine
2 tsp. sea salt	2 TB. vegan Worcestershire sauce
1 bay leaf	2 medium carrots, peeled and diced (1 cup)
2 large cloves garlic	½ cup frozen peas, thawed
2 medium yuca roots, peeled, center core discarded, and cut into 2-in. cubes (4 cups)	½ (16-oz.) can unsalted diced tomatoes, with juice (1 cup)
¾ cup unsweetened almond milk	¾ tsp. ground cumin
4 TB. plus 1 tsp. virgin coconut oil, melted	2 cups Citrus Mojo Marinade (recipe in Chapter 11)
1 medium sweet onion, diced (1 cup)	¼ cup fresh cilantro, chopped
2 small jalapeños, stems and seeds removed, and minced	Pinch black pepper

1. In a large saucepan over medium-high heat, bring water, 1 teaspoon sea salt, bay leaf, and garlic to a boil. Add yuca root, reduce heat to low, and simmer for 1 hour, 15 minutes. Check yuca for uneven white spots. If it is evenly pale yellow, it is finished cooking; drain water and transfer yuca to a food processor fitted with an S blade.

2. Add ½ cup almond milk to yuca, and purée until smooth. With the motor running, add 4 tablespoons virgin coconut oil and ½ teaspoon sea salt, and blend until smooth and creamy. Add more of remaining ¼ cup almond milk if needed to get a spreadable texture. Set aside.

3. In a large skillet over medium heat, heat remaining 1 teaspoon virgin coconut oil. Add sweet onion, remaining ½ teaspoon sea salt, and jalapeños, and cook for about 6 minutes or until tender. Using a slotted spoon, remove onions and jalapeños from the skillet, and set aside.

4. Add mushrooms and vegan Worcestershire sauce to remaining coconut oil in the skillet, and cook for 5 minutes.

5. Add carrots, and cook for about 8 minutes or until tender.

6. Stir in peas, tomatoes, cooked onions and jalapeños, cumin, and Citrus Mojo Marinade. Cook for 10 minutes to let flavors combine.

7. Stir in cilantro, and remove from heat.

8. Preheat the oven to 375°F. Lightly grease a 9×11 casserole dish.

9. Pour vegetable mixture into the prepared casserole dish, and spread into an even layer. Using a greased spoon, drop 1-inch spoonfuls of yuca dough in rows over top of vegetables. Finish with a sprinkling of black pepper.

10. Bake on the middle rack for 30 minutes. Transfer to top rack, turn heat to broil, and bake for 10 more minutes or until yuca crust is browned. Remove from the oven, let sit for 5 to 10 minutes, and serve.

Variation: You can make yuca pockets similar to Indian samosas by rolling yuca dough into 3-inch balls and then creating a large dent in the middle. Drop 3 table-spoons vegetable blend into the dent, and close yuca dough around the mixture. Place pockets on a baking sheet, brush the top of each pocket with melted coconut oil, and bake in a 375°F oven for 35 to 40 minutes. Move the baking sheet to the top rack for the last 10 minutes of baking to brown the tops.

FRESH FACT

Yuca, also known as cassava, is a root vegetable that's sometimes compared to white potatoes. It's stickier and denser, however, making it excellent for use in crusts or as a thickener in soups and stews. Tapioca flour is made from cassava and used as a thickening agent in many baked goods, desserts, and packaged foods. Look for fresh yuca that's long and cylindrical and has a brown skin, or frozen and prepared yuca in the freezer section of South American and Asian food markets.

Braised Rapini and Squash

Slightly bitter rapini mellows when cooked, and its crunch pairs perfectly with the smooth texture of delicata squash. Finished with shallots, pungent garlic, spicy chili flakes, and sweet and tangy dried currants, this dish is filling and simply fabulous in the fall.

Yield:	Prep time:	Cook time:	Serving size:
about 6 cups	10 minutes	30 minutes	1½ cups

Each serving has:				
346 calories	51 g carbohydrates	12 g fat	6 g fiber	11 g protein

4 qt. water	½ tsp. red chili flakes
6 oz. uncooked quinoa spaghetti	½ tsp. sea salt
1 large bunch rapini, ends trimmed	2 TB. fresh lemon juice
2 medium delicata squash, peeled and cut into 1-in. cubes (2 cups)	¼ cup vegetable stock, warmed
	¼ cup chopped fresh parsley
2 TB. virgin coconut oil	¼ cup dried currants
1 large shallot, thinly sliced (2 TB.)	2 TB. pine nuts
3 medium cloves garlic, thinly sliced	Pinch ground black pepper

1. In a large saucepan over high heat, bring water to a boil. Add quinoa spaghetti, and return to a boil. Cook, stirring often, for 6 to 9 minutes. Drain and set aside.

2. Meanwhile, in a vegetable steamer over high heat, bring 2 inches water to a boil. Add rapini and delicata squash, cover, and steam for 3 minutes.

3. Remove rapini from the pan, chop into bite-size pieces, and set aside. Let squash steam for 10 more minutes.

4. In a large skillet over medium-high heat, heat virgin coconut oil. Add shallot and garlic, and sauté for 2 minutes.

5. Add squash, rapini, red chili flakes, sea salt, lemon juice, and vegetable stock, and cook for 4 minutes. Remove from heat.

6. Stir in parsley, currants, and pine nuts, and season with black pepper. Serve atop quinoa spaghetti.

Variation: If rapini isn't in season, you can use broccoli florets instead. Also experiment with replacing the currants with other dried fruits like chopped figs, raisins, or cranberries.

TASTY TIP

Nutritious quinoa noodles are made with a blend of corn and quinoa, and therefore are gluten free.

Summer Succotash

This fresh succotash salad has a vibrant and crunchy blend of asparagus, sweet corn, zucchini, hearty greens, lentils, and a tangy Dijon vinaigrette.

Yield:	Prep time:	Cook time:	Serving size:	
6 cups	15 minutes	35 minutes	1½ cups	
Each serving has:				
332 calories	50 g carbohydrates	9 g fat	19 g fiber	17 g protein

2 cups water

1 cup small French green lentils

2 medium cloves garlic

1 bay leaf

2 sprigs thyme

¾ tsp. sea salt

14 large asparagus stalks, cut into ½-in. pieces (1 cup)

1 TB. virgin coconut oil

Kernels from 1 ear fresh corn (1 cup)

1 medium zucchini, small diced (⅔ cup)

2 medium kale leaves, chopped into bite-size pieces (2 cups)

½ small red onion, thinly sliced (¼ cup)

½ cup Zippy Dijon Dressing (recipe in Chapter 8)

1 cup fresh spinach leaves

Pinch ground black pepper

Pinch sea salt

1. In a medium saucepan over medium-high heat, bring water, French green lentils, garlic, bay leaf, thyme, and sea salt to a boil. Reduce heat to low, and simmer for 15 minutes.

2. Add asparagus, and cook for 5 more minutes. Drain and reserve lentils and asparagus. Discard bay leaf.

3. In a large skillet over medium-high heat, heat virgin coconut oil. When hot, add corn, and cook, stirring frequently, for 8 minutes.

4. Add zucchini, cooked lentils and asparagus, kale leaves, and red onion, and cook for 4 minutes.

5. Stir in Zippy Dijon Dressing, spinach leaves, and black pepper. Warm for 1 minute. Season with sea salt, and serve.

Warm Carrot Noodles

Raw carrots are peeled into long ribbons and tossed with a traditional Indian spice blend of turmeric, cumin, coriander, and ginger. Buttery chickpeas, raisins, and shredded coconut marry perfectly with the sweet carrot noodles for a bold-flavored fat-free dish.

Yield:	Prep time:	Cook time:	Serving size:	
about 4 cups	15 minutes	10 minutes	1 cup	
Each serving has:				
193 calories	38 g carbohydrates	3 g fat	8 g fiber	6 g protein

½ tsp. sea salt

⅛ tsp. coriander seed

⅛ tsp. whole cumin seeds

¼ tsp. ground black pepper

2 tsp. sesame seeds

¼ tsp. ground turmeric

1 medium clove garlic

1 (1-in.) piece fresh peeled and minced ginger

½ cup vegetable stock

½ tsp. vanilla extract

2 tsp. maple syrup

8 medium carrots, peeled into long ribbons

1 cup cooked chickpeas

2 tsp. shredded or flaked unsweetened coconut

¼ cup raisins

½ cup fresh cilantro leaves, chopped

1. Using a mortar and pestle, mash sea salt, coriander seed, cumin seeds, black pepper, sesame seeds, turmeric, garlic, and ginger into a fine powder. Transfer to a small bowl.

2. Add vegetable stock, vanilla extract, and maple syrup to seasoning powder, and stir to combine.

3. In a large skillet over medium heat, heat sauce until just boiling. Reduce heat to low, add carrots and chickpeas, and cook for 5 minutes.

4. Stir in coconut and raisins, and cook for 1 more minute.

5. Divide carrots among bowls, and top with ¼ cup cilantro leaves.

Variation: Carrot noodles are also delicious served cold. Combine with Tart Tahini Sauce (recipe in Chapter 10), and toss with fresh vegetables and 1 tablespoon seeds such as hemp or pumpkinseeds.

Chilled Edamame and Soba

Edamame and soba go together perfectly, and in this dish, they're tossed with a traditional Asian dressing of garlic, tamari, rice vinegar, maple syrup, and a touch of sesame oil for a salty-sweet flavor you'll love.

Yield:	Prep time:	Cook time:	Serving size:	
about 6 cups	10 minutes	10 minutes	1½ cups	
Each serving has:				
247 calories	27 g carbohydrates	11 g fat	4 g fiber	7 g protein

7 cups water

½ tsp. sea salt

6 oz. uncooked soba noodles

1 cup frozen shelled edamame

2 medium carrots, peeled and julienned (1 cup)

1 (3-in.) piece peeled daikon radish, julienned

1 tsp. chili-garlic sauce

2 TB. rice vinegar

1 TB. maple syrup

1 cup Toasted Sesame and Soy Dressing (recipe in Chapter 8)

4 tsp. black sesame seeds

Pinch toasted nori seasoning

Pinch dulse flakes

1. In a medium saucepan over high heat, bring 4 cups water and sea salt to a boil. Add soba noodles, and cook for 9 minutes. Drain, rinse noodles in cold water, and transfer to a large bowl.

2. Meanwhile, in a small saucepan over high heat, bring remaining 3 cups water to a boil. Add edamame, and boil for 3 minutes. Drain and set aside.

3. In a medium bowl, combine carrots, daikon radish, chili-garlic sauce, rice vinegar, and maple syrup. Let sit for 15 minutes.

4. Add edamame and Toasted Sesame and Soy Dressing to noodles, and toss to coat evenly.

5. Divide among 4 serving bowls, and top each with ¼ of carrot-daikon mix, 1 teaspoon black sesame seeds, 1 pinch toasted nori seasoning, and 1 pinch dulse flakes.

Variation: For a hot meal, pour 2 cups hot vegetable stock over the noodles and vegetables and enjoy slurping up your noodles.

Zero-Fat Raw Zucchini Pasta

Zucchini noodles are an extremely versatile vegan food. This decadent pasta dish combines raw zucchini noodles with fresh carrots and spinach, all tossed with a scrumptious fat-free Tomato and Lemon-Basil Cream Sauce.

Yield:	Prep time:	Serving size:		
about 15 cups	30 minutes	3 cups		
Each serving has:				
84 calories	16 g carbohydrates	0 g fat	5 g fiber	5 g protein

3 medium zucchinis	2 medium peeled carrots, diced (1½ cups)
3 cups Tomato and Lemon-Basil Cream Sauce (recipe in Chapter 10)	4 cups fresh spinach leaves

1. Cut zucchinis in ½ through the middle. Using a *spiral slicer* or vegetable peeler, cut zucchinis into long noodles, and transfer to a large mixing bowl.

2. Pour in Tomato and Lemon-Basil Cream Sauce, add carrots and spinach leaves, and toss to coat evenly. Divide among 4 plates, and serve.

Variation: Make an entirely raw dish by using pine nuts or hemp seeds in place of the cooked beans when making the Tomato and Lemon-Basil Cream Sauce.

DEFINITION

A **spiral slicer,** or *spiralizer,* is a must-have tool for any vegan cook. This simple device has small, mandoline-like blades and can turn daikon radishes, raw potatoes, beets, carrots, squash, and zucchini into beautiful, long and crunchy spiral noodles.

Maple-Grilled Tempeh

Even if you've never taken a liking to tempeh, this dish may make you a fan. Maple syrup, liquid smoke, vinegar, and Dijon mustard glaze the tempeh to add sweetness and a bold, zippy flavor. It's tossed with wilted kale and served atop nutty quinoa for a satisfying meal.

Yield:	Prep time:	Cook time:	Serving size:	
about 6 cups	10 minutes	25 minutes	1½ cups	
Each serving has:				
564 calories	73 g carbohydrates	20 g fat	6 g fiber	31 g protein

2 cups water

½ tsp. sea salt

1 cup uncooked quinoa, rinsed

4 TB. wheat-free tamari

½ cup maple syrup

1 tsp. Dijon mustard

1 tsp. apple cider vinegar

1 tsp. liquid smoke

1 tsp. virgin coconut oil

1 small red onion, thinly sliced (½ cup)

2 small cloves garlic, thinly sliced

16 oz. tempeh, cut into ½-in. strips

½ tsp. red chili flakes

6 medium lacinato kale leaves, cut into bite-size pieces (3 cups)

1½ TB. sesame seeds

1. In a medium saucepan over high heat, bring water and sea salt to a boil. Add quinoa, and bring to a boil. Reduce heat to low, cover, and simmer for 12 minutes. Remove from heat, fluff with fork, and set aside.

2. Meanwhile, in a small bowl, combine wheat-free tamari, maple syrup, Dijon mustard, apple cider vinegar, and liquid smoke.

3. In a large skillet over medium-high heat, heat virgin coconut oil. Add red onion, and cook for 5 minutes.

4. Add garlic, and cook for 1 minute.

5. Add tempeh, sauce, and red chili flakes. Reduce heat to medium, and cook for 5 minutes.

6. Reduce heat to low, add kale leaves, and simmer for 5 more minutes.

7. Divide cooked quinoa among 4 bowls, and top each with ¾ cup tempeh and kale mixture and 1 pinch sesame seeds.

Variation: For a sweet and savory on-the-go protein snack, marinate tempeh in maple syrup blend from recipe for at least 1 hour and bake in a 350°F oven for 20 minutes. Omit the remaining ingredients.

FRESH FACT

Originally from Indonesia, tempeh is a cultured soy product that has a wonderfully nutty flavor and a firm texture. It crumbles easily, too, making it an ideal alternative to tofu in casseroles, stir-fries, chilies, and burgers and as a topper for grain salads and bowls. Note that tempeh is often made with the addition of barley and other grains and may not be a gluten-free food depending on the brand. Look for prepared tempeh in the refrigerated section at your local natural foods market.

Steamy Stews, Chilies, and Grain Bowls

14

In This Chapter

- Hearty and warming vegetable stews
- Filling chilies
- Bold-flavored grain bowls
- Vegan twists on traditional international fare

There's nothing better than a hot bowl of healthy, hearty vegetables to fill your belly and warm you to the core. The exotic flavors, classic combinations, and decidedly dense nutrition of the steaming stews and chilies in this chapter are perfect for one-pot meals.

Right alongside them, you'll find their perfect counterparts: grain bowls with tons of flavor and texture. Each stew or grain bowl is a meal on its own, but they can also be served together for a more dynamic meal.

Chilean Zucchini Stew

Earthy zucchini and sweet corn blend harmoniously in this chunky and spicy stew. Chickpeas add texture and protein, and loads of herbs and spices give this dish its signature flavor.

Yield:	Prep time:	Cook time:	Serving size:
about 6 cups	15 minutes	35 minutes	1½ cups

Each serving has:				
229 calories	41 g carbohydrates	6 g fat	9 g fiber	9 g protein

1 TB. virgin coconut oil	½ tsp. cayenne
1 medium yellow onion, diced (1 cup)	½ tsp. dried marjoram
3 large cloves garlic, minced	2 tsp. dried Mexican oregano
2 medium-large zucchini, sliced into ½ moons (3 cups)	½ tsp. ground paprika
	1 TB. ground cumin
1 cup frozen sweet corn kernels	1 tsp. sea salt
1 (28-oz.) can diced tomatoes, with juice	½ tsp. ground black pepper
	1 cup cooked chickpeas
2 cups vegetable stock	2 TB. fresh lemon juice
½ tsp. dried thyme	½ cup fresh cilantro, chopped
1 TB. chili powder	

1. In a large cast-iron skillet over medium-high heat, heat virgin coconut oil, turning the skillet to coat. Add yellow onion and garlic, and sauté for 4 minutes.

2. Add zucchini, and sauté for 4 more minutes.

3. Stir in sweet corn, tomatoes, vegetable stock, thyme, chili powder, cayenne, marjoram, Mexican oregano, paprika, cumin, sea salt, and black pepper. Increase heat to high, and bring to a boil.

4. Add chickpeas, reduce heat to low, and simmer for 15 minutes.

5. Stir in lemon juice and cilantro, and serve.

Variation: For **Zucchini Chutney,** a traditional Chilean hors d'oeuvre, reduce the vegetable stock to ½ cup and omit the chickpeas. Serve at room temperature alongside gluten-free crackers or toast.

Japanese Pumpkin Stew

Kabocha squash, or Japanese pumpkin, is sweet and rich and balances perfectly with warming spices and buttery chickpeas, making it the perfect hearty stew for a cold winter day.

Yield:	Prep time:	Cook time:	Serving size:	
about 6 cups	10 minutes	40 minutes	1½ cups	
Each serving has:				
297 calories	49 g carbohydrates	9 g fat	9 g fiber	8 g protein

2 TB. virgin coconut oil

3 large shallots, minced (½ cup)

3 small cloves garlic, minced

1 large celery stalk, diced (½ cup)

2 medium carrots, peeled and diced (1½ cups)

1 small kabocha squash, peeled, seeds removed, and cut into 1-in. cubes (4 cups)

3 cups vegetable stock

½ tsp. ground cinnamon

¼ tsp. ground nutmeg

½ tsp. ground turmeric

½ tsp. cayenne

2 TB. maple syrup

1 tsp. sea salt

1½ cups cooked chickpeas

½ cup unsweetened almond milk

1. In a large sauce pot over medium heat, heat virgin coconut oil. Add shallots, and cook for 1 minute.

2. Add garlic, and cook for 1 more minute.

3. Add celery, carrots, and kabocha squash, and sauté for 4 minutes.

4. Add vegetable stock, cinnamon, nutmeg, turmeric, cayenne, maple syrup, and sea salt. Bring to a boil, reduce heat to low, cover, and simmer for 25 minutes.

5. Add chickpeas and almond milk, and warm, uncovered, for 10 more minutes.

Variation: For **Japanese Pumpkin Casserole,** layer this stew over 3 cups cooked quinoa in a 9×11 baking dish. Sprinkle with 2 cups shredded vegan cheese, and bake in a 375°F oven for 20 minutes.

Spanish Cacao Chili

Not too long ago, chocolatiers began infusing their dark chocolate with pasilla and ancho chiles. That's precisely what you'll find in this robust bean chili made of a blend of pinto beans, chiles, spices, cacao powder, and a touch of almond butter.

Yield:	Prep time:	Cook time:	Serving size:
about 8 cups	10 minutes	40 minutes	2 cups

Each serving has:				
288 calories	46 g carbohydrates	8 g fat	14 g fiber	13 g protein

2 TB. virgin coconut oil

1 small red onion, diced (½ cup)

1 small red bell pepper, ribs and seeds removed, and diced (¾ cup)

4 medium cloves garlic, minced

1 jalapeño, stem and seeds removed, and minced

2 large tomatoes, peeled and crushed (2 cups)

2 cups vegetable stock

5 tsp. chili powder

2 TB. maple syrup

1 TB. ground cumin

¼ to 2 tsp. cayenne

1 tsp. ground paprika

1 tsp. dried marjoram

½ tsp. fresh thyme

½ tsp. ground cinnamon

Pinch ground nutmeg

2 tsp. sea salt

1 tsp. ground black pepper

4 TB. raw cacao powder

1 TB. almond butter

1 TB. vegan Worcestershire sauce

1 tsp. aged balsamic vinegar

1 tsp. liquid smoke

1 bay leaf

2 cups cooked black beans

2 cups cooked pinto beans

1. In a large soup pot over medium heat, heat virgin coconut oil. Add red onion, red bell pepper, garlic, and jalapeño, and cook for about 5 minutes or until tender.

2. Add tomatoes, vegetable stock, chili powder, maple syrup, cumin, cayenne, paprika, marjoram, thyme, cinnamon, nutmeg, sea salt, black pepper, raw cacao powder, almond butter, vegan Worcestershire sauce, aged balsamic vinegar, and liquid smoke, and bring to a boil.

3. Add bay leaf, cover, reduce heat to low, and simmer for 25 minutes.

4. Add black beans and pinto beans, cover, and simmer for 10 more minutes. Remove bay leaf.

5. Divide chili among 4 bowls, and serve.

Variation: For a **Southwestern Vegan Sloppy Joe,** reduce the vegetable stock to 1 cup, add 1 cup crumbled tofu, and spoon a generous serving of this chili onto a toasted gluten-free bun. Sprinkle on some shredded vegan cheese, grab a handful of napkins, and dig in!

FRESH FACT

Raw cacao is actually good for you and you can eat it every day without the negative effects associated with processed chocolate, such as weight gain. Consuming 1 ounce pure cacao daily increases your consumption of precious antioxidants, the good mood–enhancing amino acid tryptophan, and healthful omega-6. You also get a healthy dose of magnesium, a mineral lacking greatly in the American diet. To maximize the benefits associated with cacao, add it in during the last step to minimize its exposure to heat.

White and Green Chili

Full of tangy tomatillos, lime, mildly hot green chiles, creamy tofu, and white beans, this protein-rich chili is a simple and comforting staple for a main meal.

Yield:	Prep time:	Cooke time:	Serving size:	
about 8 cups	10 minutes	40 minutes	1½ cups	
Each serving has:				
326 calories	37 g carbohydrates	13 g fat	12 g fiber	19 g protein

2 medium cloves garlic

1 tsp. sea salt

2 TB. virgin coconut oil

16 oz. extra-firm tofu, crumbled

1 medium-small yellow onion, diced (¾ cup)

½ medium green bell pepper, ribs and seeds removed, and diced (½ cup)

3 cups Tangy Green Chile Sauce (recipe in Chapter 10)

2 cups vegetable stock

1 TB. maple syrup

2 tsp. ground cumin

1 tsp. dried oregano

½ tsp. ground coriander

½ tsp. ground black pepper

2 TB. fresh lime juice

3 cups cooked white beans

¼ cup fresh cilantro, chopped

1. Using a mortar and pestle, mash garlic and sea salt together into a paste.

2. In a large saucepan over medium-high heat, heat virgin coconut oil. Add tofu, and cook for about 10 minutes or until it browns.

3. Add yellow onion, green bell pepper, and garlic paste, and cook for about 5 minutes or until bell pepper is tender.

4. Add Tangy Green Chile Sauce, vegetable stock, maple syrup, cumin, oregano, coriander, and black pepper. Increase heat to high, and bring to a boil. Reduce heat to low, cover, and simmer 15 minutes.

5. Add lime juice and white beans, cover, and cook for 10 more minutes.

6. Divide among 5 serving bowls, and top with about 1 tablespoon chopped cilantro.

Variation: Use this chili as a filling for tacos or enchiladas. Top with extra Tangy Green Chile Sauce, Hemp Sour Cream (recipe in Chapter 10), and vegan jack cheese for a decadent Mexican meal.

Red Lentil Dahl

Warm your core with this traditional Indian dish that's hot hot hot, thanks to three layers of spicy chiles and warming herbs like turmeric, coriander, ginger, and cumin. The red lentils cook down to the consistency of a thick soup and pair happily with a bowl of fluffy rice.

Yield:	Prep time:	Cook time:	Serving size:	
about 4 cups	10 minutes	40 minutes	1 cup	
Each serving has:				
280 calories	41 g carbohydrates	8 g fat	7 g fiber	14 g protein

2 TB. virgin coconut oil	2 cups water
2 TB. fresh peeled and grated ginger	1 tsp. sea salt
6 medium cloves garlic, chopped fine	¼ cup fresh lemon juice
1 tsp. chili powder	3 dried red chiles
2 tsp. ground coriander	1 medium white onion, chopped fine (¾ cup)
2 small green chiles, stems removed, and minced	2 tsp. whole cumin seeds
1 tsp. ground turmeric	1 tsp. ground cumin
1 cup red lentils	¼ cup fresh cilantro, chopped

1. In a large cast-iron skillet over medium-high heat, heat 1 teaspoon virgin coconut oil, turning the skillet to coat. Add ginger, 3 cloves chopped garlic, chili powder, 1 teaspoon coriander, green chiles, and turmeric. Add red lentils and water, and bring to boil. Reduce heat to low, cover, and simmer for 20 minutes.

2. Uncover, increase heat to medium, and add sea salt and lemon juice.

3. In a separate small saucepan over medium heat, heat remaining 1 tablespoon virgin coconut oil. Add remaining 3 cloves chopped garlic, dried red chiles, white onion, and cumin seeds. Cook for 2 minutes.

4. Add remaining 1 teaspoon coriander and cumin, and stir to combine.

5. Pour spice blend into lentils, add cilantro, and stir to combine.

Variation: Use this as a filling for stuffed bell peppers. Cut off the tops of 4 large bell peppers, and hollow out the insides. Fill with dahl, top each with 2 tablespoons gluten-free breadcrumbs, and bake, uncovered, in a 350°F oven for 35 to 40 minutes or until bell peppers are tender. Sprinkle each with 1 tablespoon fresh chopped cilantro, and drizzle with Tart Tahini Sauce (recipe in Chapter 10) before serving.

Green Goddess Curry

You get a hit of heat from the fresh Thai chiles, the savor of cumin and coriander, plus a whopping waft of the fresh cilantro, lemongrass, and lime zest synonymous with Thai food. Blend all this with fresh green veggies, and you get a dish worthy of being served to a goddess.

Yield:	Prep time:	Cook time:	Serving size:	
about 6 cups	20 minutes	20 minutes	1½ cups	
Each serving has:				
171 calories	23 g carbohydrates	9 g fat	4 g fiber	3 g protein

1 tsp. whole cumin seeds	1 TB. fresh lime juice
1 tsp. whole coriander seeds	1 TB. virgin coconut oil
3 Thai green bird chiles	1 small yellow onion, thinly sliced (½ cup)
3 small cloves garlic, chopped	1 cup fresh green beans, chopped
1 tsp. sea salt	10 medium asparagus spears, chopped (1 cup)
1 (1-in.) piece fresh peeled and chopped ginger	½ large green bell pepper, ribs and seeds removed, and diced (½ cup)
2 medium lemongrass stalks, soft insides only, chopped	1 cup unsweetened almond milk
½ tsp. lime zest	1 cup lite coconut milk
2 TB. maple syrup	1 medium bok choy, chopped (1 cup)
1 cup fresh cilantro leaves	

1. Using a mortar and pestle, grind together cumin seeds, coriander seeds, Thai green bird chiles, garlic, sea salt, ginger, lemongrass, and lime zest. Transfer paste to a food processor fitted with an S blade.

2. Add maple syrup, cilantro, and lime juice to the food processor, and purée until thoroughly combined.

3. In a large skillet over medium heat, heat virgin coconut oil. Add yellow onion, and sauté for 5 minutes.

4. Add green beans, asparagus, and green bell pepper, and sauté for 3 minutes.

5. Add curry paste to vegetables, and pour in almond milk and coconut milk. Reduce heat to low, and simmer for 10 minutes.

6. Add bok choy, and heat for 3 minutes. Serve with cooked rice or quinoa.

Variation: Not in the mood for green? Make a red curry paste grinding together red bird chiles, 3 cloves garlic, 1 teaspoon sea salt, 2 small minced shallots, ½ teaspoon turmeric, ½ teaspoon ground coriander, ½ teaspoon ground cumin, and the same amounts of lemongrass, ginger, lime zest, and juice from the recipe. Then use red bell pepper instead of green and carrots and pumpkin instead of green beans, bok choy, and asparagus.

> **HEADS-UP**
>
> Working with lemongrass can be tricky. Fresh stalks are very rigid, and you must remove the outer layers to get to the soft middle. Before chopping, pound out the soft flesh with a kitchen mallet to soften and then chop or mince. If fresh lemongrass isn't available, look for packaged lemongrass in a squeezable tube or lemongrass powder. Just 1 or 2 teaspoons of either is sufficient to create the flavor and aroma of the fresh herb.

Mushroom Millet Risotto

Get the richness and texture of traditional mushroom risotto while reaping the benefits of fiber-rich millet. Nutritional yeast gives this dish a cheesy flavor that perfectly complements the earthiness of mixed mushrooms.

Yield:	Prep time:	Cook time:	Serving size:	
about 5 cups	10 minutes	20 minutes	1 cup	
Each serving has:				
468 calories	49 g carbohydrates	25 g fat	8 g fiber	16 g protein

1 TB. virgin coconut oil

1⅓ cups uncooked millet

1 medium yellow onion, diced (1 cup)

2 small cloves garlic, minced

1 tsp. sea salt

6 cups vegetable stock, warm

2 cups mixed shiitake, chanterelle, or porcini mushrooms, diced

½ cup hemp milk

¼ cup fresh parsley, minced

3 TB. nutritional yeast flakes

2 TB. fresh lemon juice

2 TB. pine nuts (optional)

1. In a large skillet over medium heat, heat virgin coconut oil. Add millet, and toast for about 8 minutes or until golden brown.

2. Add yellow onion, garlic, and sea salt, and sauté for 5 minutes.

3. Increase heat to medium-high, and begin adding vegetable stock, ½ cup at a time, stirring continuously until all liquid is absorbed into millet. Repeat in ½-cup increments until all liquid is used and absorbed and millet is moist and tender but still has a bit of bite to it.

4. Stir in mixed mushrooms, hemp milk, parsley, nutritional yeast flakes, and lemon juice, and cook for 1 minute.

5. Divide among 5 bowls, and top each with 2 teaspoons pine nuts (if using).

Variation: For a fun party treat, scoop hot risotto into 1-inch balls, roll in ground hemp seeds, and sauté in a large skillet over medium-high heat with a small amount of coconut oil. Remove from the pan and serve immediately with Rustic Spanish Red Sauce (recipe in Chapter 10).

TASTY TIP

The secret to making a creamy—and not mushy—vegan risotto is to first toast the grains for a few minutes. Pour the preheated vegetable stock over the grain ¼ cup or less at a time and ensure all the liquid is absorbed by the millet before adding more. It's also essential to stir continuously while adding the liquid.

Fried Red Rice

A unique twist on fried rice, this dish includes robust *red rice* and gets its creamy texture from a touch of rich coconut milk. The satisfying crunch, savory Asian flare, and vibrant color make it enjoyable as a meal on its own or as a side dish.

Yield:	Prep time:	Cook time:	Serving size:	
about 6 cups	15 minutes	35 minutes	1½ cups	
Each serving has:				
526 calories	93 g carbohydrates	16 g fat	9 g fiber	11 g protein

3½ cups water

2 cups red rice, rinsed and soaked for 30 minutes

2 TB. virgin coconut oil

1 medium yellow onion, diced (1 cup)

4 small cloves garlic, minced

1 tsp. red chile flakes

1 (1-in.) piece fresh peeled and grated ginger

2 tsp. ground coriander

2 large carrots, peeled and thinly sliced (about 1½ cups)

1 cup fresh green beans, chopped

¼ tsp. sea salt

1 cup lite coconut milk

¼ cup wheat-free tamari

1 TB. maple syrup

½ cup fresh Thai or regular basil leaves, torn

2 TB. lime juice

¼ cup crushed Brazil nuts

1. In a medium saucepan over high heat, bring water to a boil. Add red rice, reduce heat to low, and simmer, covered, for 35 minutes. Let stand, covered, for 10 minutes. Fluff with a fork, and set aside.

2. In a large skillet over medium-high heat, heat virgin coconut oil. Add yellow onion, garlic, red chile flakes, ginger, coriander, carrots, green beans, and sea salt, and stir-fry for 6 minutes or until vegetables are slightly tender.

3. Add coconut milk, wheat-free tamari, and maple syrup. Bring to a boil, and cook for 3 minutes.

4. Add rice, Thai basil, lime juice, and Brazil nuts. Heat for 2 minutes and serve.

Variation: Slice an acorn squash in half lengthwise, scoop out the seeds, and fill both halves with cooked fried rice. Place filled squash in a baking dish with ½ inch water, cover, and bake at 350°F for 40 to 50 minutes.

> **DEFINITION**
>
> **Red rice,** also known as Bhutanese rice, is a medium-grain rice grown in the Himalayas. When cooked, it takes on a slightly sticky texture and has a nutty flavor. It's partially milled, which means it has more bran left intact than brown rice and, thus, more fiber. It also contains B vitamins, calcium, iron, and the red-pigmented antioxidant anthocyanin, known as a cancer inhibitor. Find red rice in the bulk or specialty foods sections at your natural food store.

Quinoa Tabbouleh

One of my favorite meals is a plate of Sweet Pea Hummus Dip (recipe in Chapter 12), Tart Tahini Sauce (recipe in Chapter 10), and a generous serving of this light and simple tabbouleh. Abundant amounts of parsley and lemon juice give this dish its fresh-from-the-garden flavor.

Yield:	Prep time:	Cook time:	Serving size:	
about 4 cups	5 minutes	15 minutes	1 cup	
Each serving has:				
507 calories	49 g carbohydrates	31 g fat	6 g fiber	11 g protein

3 cups water

1½ cup uncooked quinoa, rinsed

1 tsp. sea salt

2 small cloves garlic

4 to 6 TB. fresh lemon juice

½ cup extra-virgin olive oil

1 large tomato, seeds removed and diced (1 cup)

1 small white onion, diced small (½ cup)

2 cups fresh parsley, minced

1. In a medium saucepan over high heat, bring water to a boil. Add quinoa, reduce heat to low, cover, and simmer for 12 minutes. Set aside and let rest, covered, for 5 minutes. Fluff with a fork, transfer to a large bowl, and cool completely.

2. Using a mortar and pestle, mash sea salt and garlic together into a paste. Transfer to a small bowl.

3. Stir lemon juice into garlic paste, and slowly whisk in extra-virgin olive oil until thoroughly combined.

4. Add tomato, white onion, and parsley to quinoa. Pour in dressing, and toss to combine.

Variation: In a small bowl, combine 2 tablespoons flax meal and 6 tablespoons water into a gel, and mix into tabbouleh ingredients. Form tabbouleh into 2-inch balls, and flatten into ½-inch-thick patties. Sauté tabbouleh patties in batches in 1 tablespoon coconut oil per batch in a medium skillet over medium-high heat. Serve warm with a drizzle of Garlic Tahini Dressing (recipe in Chapter 8).

Chilean Quinoa Bowl

Prepare to be bowled over by this rich and hearty quinoa dish full of pungent spices, vegetables, and beans and served with steamed kale and a creamy Garlic Tahini Dressing.

Yield:	Prep time:	Cook time:	Serving size:
about 8 cups	15 minutes	45 minutes	2 cups

Each serving has:				
387 calories	58 g carbohydrates	8 g fat	10 g fiber	14 g protein

2 cups water

1 cup uncooked quinoa

½ tsp. sea salt

2 medium kale leaves, chopped (2 cups)

3 cups Chilean Zucchini Stew (recipe earlier in this chapter)

¼ cup Garlic Tahini Dressing (recipe in Chapter 8)

3 large green onions, white and light green parts only, thinly sliced (½ cup)

¼ cup fresh cilantro, chopped

1. In a medium saucepan over high heat, bring water to a boil. Add quinoa and sea salt, reduce heat to low, and simmer, covered, for 12 minutes. Remove from heat, and let sit, covered, for 5 minutes. Fluff with a fork, and set aside.

2. Meanwhile, in a steamer pan over high heat, bring 2 inches of water to a boil. Add kale leaves to the steamer pan, cover, and steam for 30 seconds.

3. Divide quinoa among 4 bowls, and top each with ¾ cup Chilean Zucchini Stew, ½ cup steamed kale, and 2 tablespoons Garlic Tahini Dressing. Sprinkle each with 2 tablespoons green onions and 1 tablespoon cilantro, and serve.

Variation: The best thing about bowls is the freedom for experimentation they provide. Use rice or millet in place of the quinoa, or add cooked beans like adzuki or white beans instead. Top with steamed or raw veggies, try a red sauce like Drunken Tomato Marinara Sauce (recipe in Chapter 10), and you have a completely different dish.

Tempting Tapas and Super Sides

In This Chapter

- Simple sides that pack entrée punch
- Protein-rich grain and legume burgers
- Veggie-packed tapas plates
- Tasty twists on traditional Italian dishes

In many cultures, it's common to eat several smaller meals throughout the day rather than sit down for three large meals in the morning, afternoon, and evening. In Spain, in fact, *tapas*, or "small plates," are served in place of large portions and are available all day at cafés and restaurants. Proponents of this relaxed eating style claim it helps keep your metabolism burning strong and keeps you thinner than if you eat until you're stuffed.

Of course, if you're sitting down for a staple meal, one of the best ways to keep your menu lively and enjoyable is to get some healthy variety by pairing several small dishes or by combining a side dish, a soup, and a salad. These small meals also make great food to take with you on the go and are terrific as snacks with one of the spreads or dips from Chapter 12.

Getting Creative

With the recipes in this chapter, you can build a meal as simple or complex as you desire and use a variety of ingredients for your every whim. I like to use bases made of brown rice, like in the case of the Margarita Mochi Pizza, and gluten-free buns for legume and grain patties and Sloppy Tofu Burgers. When I make tostadas, I use blue corn crusts for extra flair and color, and sometimes I make a quick veggie lasagna by layering thin slices of zucchini, beets, and tomatoes with creamy layers of a bean sauce and sautéed mushrooms.

In this chapter, you'll also see how spices and herbs enhance beans, grains, potatoes, and veggies to provide the essence of a complete entrée.

Sloppy Tofu Burgers

Get ready for a messy meal with this vegan sloppy joe! Crumbled tofu is simmered in a tomato-based sauce that's rich in vinegar and spice, and all is topped with sweet pickles and spicy jalapeños for extra flair.

Yield:	Prep time:	Cook time:	Serving size:	
8 burgers	10 minutes	30 minutes	1 burger	
Each serving has:				
303 calories	52 g carbohydrates	6 g fat	3 g fiber	11 g protein

1 TB. virgin coconut oil	½ tsp. sea salt
1 small sweet onion, diced (½ cup)	3 cups Kansas City Barbecue Sauce (recipe in Chapter 10)
½ medium green bell pepper, ribs and seeds removed, and diced (½ cup)	8 gluten-free burger buns
2 small cloves garlic, minced	16 jarred thin sweet pickle slices
16 oz. extra-firm tofu, crumbled (2 cups)	16 canned pickled jalapeño slices

1. In a large skillet over medium heat, heat virgin coconut oil. Add sweet onion and green bell pepper, and sauté for about 6 minutes or until tender.

2. Add garlic, and cook for 1 minute. Remove vegetables from the pan, and set aside.

3. In the same skillet, sauté tofu and sea salt for about 8 minutes or until browned.

4. Add cooked onions, bell peppers, and garlic to the pan, and pour in Kansas City Barbecue Sauce. Stir to combine, reduce heat to low, and simmer for 15 minutes.

5. Divide tofu mixture among 8 gluten-free burger buns, and top each with 2 slices sweet pickle and 2 slices jalapeño.

Variation: For a soy-free dish, dice 3 medium portobello mushrooms and use in place of the tofu.

Carrot-Millet Burgers

Toothsome millet is nicely complemented by softened sweet carrots and Indian spices and topped with creamy and cool Minted Cucumber Sauce.

Yield:	Prep time:	Cook time:	Serving size:
10 burgers	15 minutes	about 1 hour	1 burger

Each serving has:				
259 calories	45 g carbohydrates	4 g fat	7 g fiber	11 g protein

1½ cups water

½ cup millet, soaked overnight and rinsed

1 TB. virgin coconut oil

1 medium sweet onion, minced (1 cup)

2 large cloves garlic, minced

2 medium kale leaves, chopped (2 cups)

⅛ cup vegetable stock

1 TB. ground cumin

½ tsp. ground cinnamon

1½ tsp. sea salt

½ tsp. ground black pepper

1 tsp. ground turmeric

2 TB. wheat-free tamari

4 large carrots, peeled and grated (3 cups)

⅛ cup ground flaxseed

⅛ cup nutritional yeast flakes

¾ cup chickpea flour

10 gluten-free burger buns

¼ cup Minted Cucumber Sauce (recipe in Chapter 10)

1½ cups fresh arugula leaves

1 medium cucumber, sliced into 20 thin slices

1. In a medium saucepan over high heat, bring water to a boil. Add millet, reduce heat to low, cover, and simmer for 20 minutes.

2. Meanwhile, preheat the oven to 350°F. Lightly coat a large baking sheet with nonstick cooking spray.

3. In a large skillet over medium heat, heat virgin coconut oil. Add sweet onion, and cook for about 8 minutes or until translucent.

4. Add garlic, and stir for 1 minute.

5. Add kale leaves and vegetable stock, and cook for about 5 minutes or until kale softens.

6. Stir in cumin, cinnamon, sea salt, black pepper, turmeric, and wheat-free tamari. Reduce heat to medium, and cook for 5 minutes.

7. Transfer cooked vegetables to a food processor fitted with an S blade. Add 1 cup cooked millet and carrots, and pulse until mixture is blended but still has some texture.

8. Transfer mixture to a large bowl, and mix in remaining ½ cup cooked millet, ground flaxseed, nutritional yeast flakes, and chickpea flour. Form mixture into 10 (⅓-cup) burgers, place on the prepared baking sheet, and bake for 40 minutes, turning once halfway through the bake time.

9. Divide patties among gluten-free burger buns, and top each with 1 or 2 teaspoons Minted Cucumber Sauce, ⅛ cup arugula leaves, and 2 cucumber slices.

Variation: Make a yummy salad by crumbling cooked patties over a bowl of mixed greens, shredded carrots, radishes, and spouts. Serve with Tart Tahini Sauce (recipe in Chapter 10).

TASTY TIP

Delicate and nutty millet is a hard grain, and therefore takes longer to prepare than other gluten-free grains such as quinoa, rice, or buckwheat. To reduce its cook time, I soak millet in water overnight and then thoroughly rinse off the soaking water before cooking.

Hemp Lentil Burgers

Nutty hemp seeds blend with earthy lentils for a hearty soy- and nut-free burger that's rich in protein and fiber and that'll serve as a satisfying lunch or dinner meal.

Yield:	Prep time:	Cook time:	Serving size:	
10 burgers	15 minutes	1 hour	1 burger	
Each serving has:				
277 calories	30 g carbohydrates	12 g fat	12 g fiber	15 g protein

1½ cups brown lentils

3 cups plus 6 TB. water

1½ tsp. sea salt

½ cup chickpea flour

½ medium sweet onion, minced (½ cup)

4 medium carrots, peeled and grated (2 cups)

¼ cup wheat-free tamari

½ cup hemp seeds

2 TB. Italian seasoning

2 tsp. chili powder

2 tsp. ground cumin

¼ tsp. cayenne

2 TB. fresh parsley, minced

2 large cloves garlic, minced

1 (½-in.) piece fresh peeled and minced ginger

¼ cup fresh cilantro, minced

2 small celery stalks, finely chopped (½ cup)

2 TB. ground flaxseed

2 TB. virgin coconut oil

10 large romaine leaves

½ cup Simple Mayonnaise Spread (recipe in Chapter 12)

½ cup sunflower sprouts

10 small tomatoes, sliced

1. In a medium saucepan over high heat, combine brown lentils, 3 cups water, and ½ teaspoon sea salt. Bring to a boil, reduce heat to low, cover, and simmer for 30 minutes.

2. Meanwhile, preheat the oven to 375°F. Lightly coat a large baking sheet with nonstick cooking spray.

3. In a food processor fitted with an S blade, blend chickpea flour, sweet onions, carrots, wheat-free tamari, hemp seeds, Italian seasoning, chili powder, cumin, cayenne, parsley, garlic, ginger, cilantro, and celery until a smooth paste forms.

4. In a small saucepan over medium heat, heat remaining 6 tablespoons water. Add ground flaxseed, and stir until it reaches a gooey and gel-like consistency.

5. Transfer blended vegetables to a large bowl, and stir in lentils and flaxseed mixture. Form mixture into 10 (⅓-cup) burgers, place on the prepared baking sheet, and bake for 30 minutes. Remove from the oven.

6. In a large saucepan over medium-high heat, heat virgin coconut oil. Add burgers, and sauté for 4 minutes per side or until lightly browned.

7. Divide patties among romaine leaves, and top each with 2 teaspoons Simple Mayonnaise Spread, 5 or 6 sunflower sprouts, and 1 tomato slice.

Variation: For a burger with more texture and density, add 1 cup chopped shiitake mushrooms to the blended vegetable mixture. Serve with cabbage leaves, radish sprouts, daikon radishes, and Creamy Ginger Miso Dressing (recipe in Chapter 8).

Margarita Mochi Pizza

Puffed brown rice *mochi* has a lightly crispy, dense, and chewy texture, which is a perfect base for a pizza with gooey and crunchy toppings. This simple Italian recipe is made using fresh tomatoes, torn basil, and vegan mozzarella piled atop a thin layer of a Tomato and Lemon-Basil Cream Sauce.

Yield:	Prep time:	Cook time:	Serving size:	
about 6 slices	5 minutes	20 minutes	2 slices	
Each serving has:				
391 calories	68 g carbohydrates	12 g fat	5 g fiber	9 g protein

1 (10-oz.) pkg. mochi, cut through center lengthwise into 2 large, thin rectangles	1½ cups Tomato and Lemon-Basil Cream Sauce (recipe in Chapter 10)
½ tsp. sea salt	1 cup shredded vegan mozzarella cheese
	2 plum tomatoes, cut into thin slices (1 cup)
	1 cup fresh basil leaves, torn

1. Preheat the oven to 450°F. Lightly coat a baking sheet with nonstick cooking spray.

2. Lay both mochi rectangles on the prepared baking sheet, sprinkle each with sea salt, and bake for 12 minutes.

3. Top each mochi half with ¾ cup Tomato and Lemon-Basil Cream Sauce, ½ cup mozzarella cheese, ½ cup plum tomatoes, and ½ cup basil.

4. Bake for 5 to 7 more minutes or until cheese melts. Cut each rectangle into 3 equal slices, and serve.

Variation: This mochi pizza recipe is so easy to customize. Use toppings like sun-dried tomatoes, artichoke hearts, caramelized onions, and kale. Experiment with sauces like Rustic Spanish Red Sauce, Tart Tahini Sauce, or Kansas City Barbecue Sauce (recipes in Chapter 10).

DEFINITION

If you've never had **mochi,** you're in for a treat. This brown rice dough is gluten free, and when baked, it puffs nicely, providing an airy, slightly sweet, and chewy base for desserts, bread puddings, and pizzas.

Sweet Peppercorn–Crusted Artichokes

Artichokes have a distinct earthy flavor profile and are raised to decadent heights with this sweet, spicy, and savory crusting of herbs, sugar, and spice. Cooked to soften and then grilled to perfection, these artichokes are the perfect accompaniment to a summer barbecue.

Yield:	Prep time:	Cook time:	Serving size:
4 artichoke halves	5 minutes	1 hour	1 artichoke half

Each serving has:				
93 calories	15 g carbohydrates	4 g fat	5 g fiber	2 g protein

2 large artichokes	½ tsp. sea salt
½ tsp. whole coriander seeds	1 tsp. dried oregano
½ tsp. red or green peppercorns	1 tsp. dried thyme
1 TB. fresh peeled and grated ginger	2 TB. maple syrup
2 small cloves garlic, chopped	1 TB. virgin coconut oil, melted

1. Trim spiny ends of all leaves from artichokes. Cut artichokes through middle lengthwise and remove hairs surrounding the heart.

2. Fill a large pot with water, and bring to a boil over high heat. Add artichoke halves, and cook for 30 minutes. Transfer to a bowl, and set aside.

3. Preheat the grill to medium-high.

4. Using a mortar and pestle, mash together coriander seeds, red peppercorns, ginger, garlic, sea salt, oregano, and thyme. Transfer to a small bowl.

5. Add maple syrup and melted virgin coconut oil, and stir to combine.

6. Using your hands, coat all sides of artichokes with spice paste.

7. Place artichokes cut side down on the heated grill, and cook for 12 minutes. Turn over and cook for 12 more minutes. Serve hot.

Variation: Add south-of-the-border flair to this succulent side dish by adding ¼ teaspoon cayenne, ¼ teaspoon chili powder, and 2 tablespoons fresh lime juice to the mix. Omit the ginger and thyme.

TASTY TIP

Artichokes are one of the most gourmet foods all on their own, but it never hurts to dress them up a bit! This recipe is the perfect way to bring some spice to your life while reaping the huge health benefits of the artichokes themselves.

Indian-Spiced Yams

Creamy and sweet roasted yams are enhanced with the warming spices of India. Enjoy as a side dish or main course when paired with a side of Cayenne-Crusted Chickpeas (recipe later in this chapter).

Yield:	Prep time:	Cook time:	Serving size:	
about 4 cups	5 minutes	40 minutes	1 cup	
Each serving has:				
229 calories	40 g carbohydrates	7 g fat	6 g fiber	2 g protein

2 large peeled yams, cut into 1-in. chunks (about 4 cups)	1 TB. fresh peeled and minced ginger
2 TB. virgin coconut oil, melted	1 small clove garlic, minced
1 TB. ground cumin	¼ tsp. ground cinnamon
½ tsp. ground coriander	⅛ tsp. ground nutmeg
1 tsp. dried mint	½ tsp. sea salt
2 tsp. ground turmeric	½ tsp. vanilla extract

1. Preheat the oven to 375°F. Lightly coat a large rimmed baking sheet with non-stick cooking spray.

2. In a large bowl, toss yams, melted virgin coconut oil, cumin, coriander, mint, turmeric, ginger, garlic, cinnamon, nutmeg, sea salt, and vanilla extract to coat.

3. Turn out yams onto the prepared baking sheet, and roast for 40 minutes, turning yams occasionally to ensure even browning.

Variation: For a fall-inspired roasted vegetable dish, omit the cumin, coriander, mint, and turmeric, and replace with 1 tablespoon pumpkin pie spice and ¼ cup maple syrup.

Cayenne-Crusted Chickpeas

Move over nuts and olives; there's a new starter in town. These tart and spicy roasted chickpeas are simple to prepare and perfect for premeal noshing.

Yield:	Prep time:	Cook time:	Serving size:	
about 2 cups	5 minutes	40 minutes	½ cup	
Each serving has:				
200 calories	24 g carbohydrates	9 g fat	6 g fiber	7 g protein

½ tsp. cayenne	½ tsp. ground ginger
2 TB. virgin coconut oil, melted	2 small cloves garlic, minced
2 tsp. sumac seasoning	2 TB. fresh lemon juice
1 tsp. sea salt	2 cups cooked chickpeas
¼ tsp. ground white pepper	

1. Preheat the oven to 400°F.

2. In a small bowl, combine cayenne, melted virgin coconut oil, sumac seasoning, sea salt, white pepper, ginger, garlic, and lemon juice.

3. Transfer sauce to a medium bowl, add chickpeas, and toss to coat.

4. Turn out chickpeas onto a baking sheet, and roast for 40 minutes, shaking the pan occasionally to ensure even roasting.

Variation: Make a **Fresh and Tangy Bean Salad** by skipping the roasting step and instead tossing the cooked chickpeas and seasoning blend with 1 tablespoon apple cider vinegar, 2 tablespoons chopped kalamata olives, 4 tablespoons diced tomatoes, and 2 tablespoons fresh minced parsley.

FRESH FACT

Sumac has been used medicinally in Native American cultures for centuries. The roots of the shrub are often eaten raw, or are cooked to make a traditional health tonic or tea. Research has demonstrated sumac is beneficial in treating diabetes and some cancers. It also has antiseptic, astringent, and diuretic properties. It's often used in South America, Africa, and India to treat mouth sores, sore throats, urinary infections, asthma, and inflammation.

Chipotle Corn

Sweet corn on the cob comes to vibrant life with a caramelized glaze of smoky chipotle peppers, tangy lime juice, sea salt, and agave nectar.

Yield:	Prep time:	Cook time:	Serving size:
4 ears corn	5 minutes	15 minutes	1 ear corn

Each serving has:				
169 calories	37 g carbohydrates	3 g fat	3 g fiber	5 g protein

2 TB. fresh lime juice	1 small clove garlic, minced
1 TB. hemp seeds	½ tsp. sea salt
2 canned chipotle peppers in adobo sauce, seeds removed, and chopped	¼ tsp. ground black pepper
	2 TB. agave nectar
1 TB. adobo sauce from canned chipotles	4 medium ears fresh sweet corn

1. Preheat the grill to medium.

2. In a small food processor fitted with an S blade, combine lime juice, hemp seeds, chipotle peppers, adobo sauce, garlic, sea salt, black pepper, and agave nectar.

3. Using your hands, thoroughly coat ears of corn with chipotle mixture.

4. Place ears of corn directly over the flame, and cook for 10 to 15 minutes or until kernels are tender and browned and chipotle blend has caramelized on corn.

Variation: Make a **Spicy Summer Corn Salad** by cooking corn in boiling water for 8 minutes and then removing the kernels with a sharp blade. Transfer kernels to a medium bowl, and toss with chipotle blend. Add fresh chopped green onions and cilantro to taste.

Lemony Gnocchi

A light and refreshing twist on traditional gnocchi, these plump pillows of potato dough are tossed with a scrumptious sauce of tangy lemon, savory thyme, pungent garlic, and creamy blended hemp seeds.

Yield:	Prep time:	Cook time:	Serving size:	
about 6 cups	20 minutes	1 hour	1½ cups	
Each serving has:				
527 calories	67 g carbohydrates	22 g fat	8 g fiber	18 g protein

4 large russet potatoes	4 small cloves garlic, minced
3¾ tsp. sea salt	1 tsp. lemon zest
2 cups amaranth flour	2 TB. fresh thyme leaves, minced
¼ cup hemp seeds	¼ cup fresh parsley, minced
¼ cup extra-virgin olive oil	2 tsp. apple cider vinegar
⅓ cup fresh lemon juice	

1. Preheat the oven to 400°F.

2. Wrap russet potatoes in aluminum foil, place directly on the middle oven rack, and cook for 1 hour.

3. Bring a large pot of water and 3 teaspoons sea salt to a boil over high heat.

4. Set out a large platter, and cover with ½ cup amaranth flour.

5. In a food processor fitted with an S blade, pulse hemp seeds, extra-virgin olive oil, lemon juice, garlic, lemon zest, remaining ¾ teaspoon sea salt, thyme, parsley, and apple cider vinegar until combined but not completely smooth. Transfer mixture to medium serving bowl.

6. Remove potatoes from the oven, peel immediately, and mash through a ricer onto a large tray or cutting board. Let cool for 15 minutes.

7. Sprinkle 1 cup amaranth flour over riced potatoes, and using your hands, massage flour and potatoes together. Continue to add flour 2 tablespoons at a time and massage gently until you have a nice pillow of dough that's not sticky and doesn't separate or crumble.

8. Roll dough into 3 (½-inch-thick) cords, and using a sharp knife, cut the cords into 1-inch-long pieces, being sure not to mash the pieces as you cut. Dust each piece with flour on the plate, and while holding a fork in one hand, use the other hand to roll each piece of gnocchi across the fork's prongs, using gentle pressure, to create horizontal lines across gnocchi. Be sure not to mash gnocchi onto the fork. You want each piece to stay in a nice plump pillow shape.

9. Place gnocchi in boiling water for 1 or 2 minutes, and as gnocchi rise to the surface, gently remove with a slotted spoon and transfer to a bowl of sauce. Gently toss to coat gnocchi with sauce, and divide among 4 plates.

Variation: Make a sweet gnocchi using yams or sweet potatoes in place of russets. Or for a fun and brilliant presentation, use purple potatoes. For either variation, toss the cooked gnocchi with Caramelized Fennel and White Bean Sauce (recipe in Chapter 10).

HEADS-UP

The key to plump gnocchi with a traditional "bite" is to use very dry cooked potatoes like a russet and avoid those with more moisture such as a red or purple potato. Be sure you bake the potatoes as opposed to cooking the potatoes in water because the oven's heat will dry them out. Also, while adding flour to the cooked potatoes and working them together, be sure not to overwork the dough into a completely uniform texture.

Sweets and Sippers

If you're looking for that extra something special to satisfy a sweet tooth, look no further. Part 6 offers many alternatives to rich, sugar-laden, fat-heavy desserts that are still bursting with fantastic flavor and rich textures—and are low in fat! You'll find fresh takes on some classic desserts as well as new and exciting treats that are sure to become favorites.

Part 6 wraps up with a chapter full of delightful drinks. When you settle in for the evening, why not try a tasty tonic as the perfect nightcap? In the morning, begin your day with a soul-warming, satisfying drink that will put pep in your step. And for the mixologist, there are a few very special virgin cocktails you can easily turn into the perfect mixed drink.

Indulgent Delights

In This Chapter

- Sweet-tooth tamers
- Indulging without guilt
- Superfoods make super desserts
- Low-fat vegan sweet treats

Desserts are usually the first thing to go when you embark on any kind of diet or make a commitment to eating healthy foods. It's easy to fall off the wagon, though, especially if you start feeling deprived of the foods you enjoy most. Having a sweet treat can be emotionally soothing, but it can also contribute to a negative cycle of weakened will-power and disappointment.

Fortunately, the healthy sweet treats in this chapter are completely nutritious and will fit in perfectly with your long-term health goals!

Guilt-Free Pleasures

You simply can't live on cakes and ice cream without serious adverse health reactions, but that doesn't mean sweets can't play a part in your healthy relationship with food. It's important for your self-esteem and for the success of long-term weight-management goals to feel like you can indulge from time to time. Of course, it's even better to indulge without going into a downward spiral by finding nutritious treats that taste amazing.

Not every bite of a pie or nibble of a cookie has to be a guilty little pleasure. With the recipes in this chapter, you can boast about creating and enjoying decadent desserts while showing off your trim waistline. Also, you can finally give your kids the sweets they beg for without feeling like you'll have to deal with their sugar crash later.

Super Healthy Sweets

How often have you heard someone say you should finish your dessert because it's good for you? Not very often. But that's about to change.

Desserts made from whole foods and unprocessed ingredients add necessary fiber to your diet in addition to an array of vitamins, minerals, and phytonutrients. Many low-fat sweets also have impressive amounts of protein, too.

On top of that, you can also add a variety of nutritionally dense foods that will further enhance both the taste and health benefits of your treats. Superfoods like chia seeds, spirulina, and hemp are perfect add-ins for many desserts. They work behind the scenes to improve the texture, taste, and nutrition of your sweets and can be snuck into almost anything! The minerals and phytonutrients you gain by adding superfoods to your desserts also help you to digest them more slowly and prevent spikes in blood sugar.

The bottom line: finish your dessert because it's good for you!

Lavender Tea Cookies

These mildly sweet cookies have the subtle aroma of lavender, which pairs perfectly with a hint of lemon zest. They're light and crispy and are perfect for dunking into a hot cup of Earl Grey tea.

Yield:	Prep time:	Bake time:	Serving size:	
36 cookies	20 minutes	8 minutes	2 cookies	
Each serving has:				
214 calories	26 g carbohydrates	13 g fat	0 g fiber	1 g protein

2 cups white rice flour

½ cup tapioca starch

¾ cup coconut sugar, powdered in a blender

1 tsp. sea salt

2 tsp. crushed lavender flowers

1 cup solid virgin coconut oil

2 TB. fresh lemon juice

1 tsp. lemon zest

3 drops lavender essential oil (optional)

1 tsp. vanilla extract

1. Preheat the oven to 325°F. Line a baking sheet with parchment paper.

2. In a large bowl, combine white rice flour, tapioca starch, powdered coconut sugar, sea salt, and lavender flowers.

3. Add solid virgin coconut oil, lemon juice, lemon zest, lavender essential oil (if using), and vanilla extract, and using an electric mixer on low speed, thoroughly combine.

4. Scoop 2 tablespoons of cookie dough, roll into a ball, and flatten slightly. Or roll dough to about ¼ inch thick and use a cookie cutter to create desired shapes. Place cookies on the prepared baking sheet, and repeat with remaining dough.

5. Bake for about 8 minutes or until edges are light brown. Remove from the oven, and transfer to wire racks to cool before serving.

HEADS-UP

If you use the lavender essential oil, be sure to use an essential oil clearly labeled "therapeutic grade." Many essential oils are labeled "food grade," but these are often cut with synthetic oils, solvents, and other carrier oils that can cause allergic reactions. They can also contain concentrated amounts of pesticides. Unlabeled oils are even lower quality and should be avoided. Therapeutic-grade essential oils are the only oils made completely from plant distillates.

Superfruit Hemp Treats

These little fruit-filled bites are a big hit with kids. They're very sweet and just a tad tart, similar to the flavor of fruit leather but with lots more nutrition!

Yield:	Prep time:	Serving size:		
22 treats	10 minutes	2 treats		
Each serving has:				
140 calories	30 g carbohydrates	2 g fat	4 g fiber	4 g protein

12 dried pitted apricots, chopped (1 cup)

6 dried figs, chopped (½ cup)

½ cup dried goji berries

½ cup dried Incan berries

¼ cup hemp seeds

2 TB. *superfruit powder* (optional)

1. In a food processor fitted with an S blade, combine apricots, figs, goji berries, Incan berries, hemp seeds, and superfruit powder (if using).

2. Roll 2 tablespoons of mixture into a ball, and place in an airtight container. Repeat with remaining mixture.

3. Refrigerate for up to 3 weeks.

Variation: To make your own fruit leather, blend the ingredients in a high-speed blender with about 2 cups water. Pour the fruit liquid onto a dehydrator tray, and dehydrate about 6 hours at 105°F. Flip over and dehydrate for 3 more hours or until chewy. Store in a sealed container in a cool, dark place for up to 1 week.

DEFINITION

Superfruit powder is a dehydrated, powdered blend of some of the most antioxidant-rich fruits on the planet. It often includes an array of added probiotics and enzymes in addition to the amazing vitamin and mineral profile of the fruits themselves. Many different brands are available (see Appendix B).

Raw Cacao-Nut Bites

These rich and chocolaty brownie-textured treats are similar in flavor to a German chocolate cake. They'll melt in your mouth!

Yield:	Prep time:	Chill time:	Serving size:	
about 12 bites	10 minutes	3 hours	1 bite	
Each serving has:				
250 calories	21 g carbohydrates	20 g fat	6 g fiber	2 g protein

½ cup ground flaxseed

¼ cup warm water

½ cup coconut butter

¼ cup raw cacao powder

1½ cups large medjool or deglet noor pitted dates

2 tsp. vanilla extract

½ tsp. sea salt

1 cup shredded coconut

1. In a large bowl, combine ground flaxseed and warm water. Let stand 15 minutes.

2. In a food processor fitted with an S blade, pulse flaxseed mixture, coconut butter, raw cacao powder, medjool dates, vanilla extract, and sea salt until coconut butter is melted and mixture begins to roll into a ball.

3. Add coconut, and pulse again until thoroughly combined.

4. Divide mixture among the squares of an ice-cube tray, and press. Refrigerate for at least 3 hours.

5. When ready to eat, remove squares from ice-cube trays, and serve.

Variation: For a spicy twist on this chocolate treat, omit the coconut, and add 2 teaspoons orange zest, 1 teaspoon ground cinnamon, and ¼ teaspoon cayenne.

Maqui Berry Bites

These nutty bites are extremely tasty, and they're fun to serve to kids and friends because their bright purple color brings about quite a reaction! They're sweet, a tad tart, and full of antioxidants and powerful nutrition.

Yield:	Prep time:	Bake time:	Serving size:	
36 bites	10 minutes	20 minutes	2 bites	
Each serving has:				
239 calories	24 g carbohydrates	12 g fat	6 g fiber	11 g protein

1½ cups hemp pulp, leftover from making hemp milk

1 cup coconut flour

2 TB. tahini

5 large pitted dates

1 TB. *maqui powder*

½ tsp. vanilla extract

½ tsp. sea salt

¼ cup maple syrup

½ cup hemp milk

1. Preheat the oven to 325°F. Line a baking sheet with parchment paper.

2. In a food processor fitted with an S blade, blend hemp pulp, coconut flour, tahini, dates, maqui powder, vanilla extract, sea salt, maple syrup, and hemp milk until a loose dough forms.

3. Roll 2 tablespoons of mixture into balls, and place on the prepared baking sheet.

4. Bake for 20 minutes. Remove and cool to room temperature before serving or storing in an airtight container.

DEFINITION

Maqui powder is made from dehydrated, ground maqui berries, a supreme superfruit with one of the highest-known antioxidant profiles. You can often find the berries in the raw foods section of your natural foods store or online (see Appendix B).

Pumpkin Chia Pudding

This pudding re-creates the nostalgic flavors of a holiday pumpkin pie and takes the creamy, rich texture to the next level of deliciousness.

Yield:	Prep time:	Chill time:	Serving size:	
about 3 cups	10 minutes	30 minutes	½ cup	
Each serving has:				
132 calories	19 g carbohydrates	5 g fat	7 g fiber	3 g protein

1 cup cooked pumpkin purée	¼ cup maple syrup
⅓ cup chia seeds	2 tsp. pumpkin pie spice
1½ cup almond milk	1 tsp. vanilla extract

1. In a high-speed blender, combine pumpkin purée, chia seeds, almond milk, maple syrup, pumpkin pie spice, and vanilla extract.

2. Transfer to an airtight container, and refrigerate for 30 minutes to set.

Variation: Make a power breakfast that will jump-start your day or sufficiently support a morning workout by adding ½ cup mashed banana and 3 chopped and pitted dates to the blender. Allow to set and then stir in 2 tablespoons rolled oats and top with a pinch of ground cinnamon.

Raw Choco-Maca Pudding

This simple and nutritious pudding has an almost tapioca-like texture that makes it very appealing. Nutty maca powder enhances the rich flavors of chocolate and vanilla.

Yield:	Prep time:	Chill time:	Serving size:	
about 3 cups	10 minutes	30 minutes	¾ cup	
Each serving has:				
216 calories	28 g carbohydrates	11 g fat	12 g fiber	5 g protein

2 cups vanilla almond milk

⅛ cup raw cacao powder

¼ cup maple syrup

1 tsp. vanilla extract

1 TB. maca powder

¼ tsp. sea salt

½ cup chia seeds

1. In a large bowl, whisk together vanilla almond milk, raw cacao powder, maple syrup, vanilla extract, maca powder, and sea salt.

2. Whisk in chia seeds until all seeds are coated with liquid.

3. Refrigerate for at least 30 minutes to set.

Variation: You may also blend, rather than stir, chia seeds into the other ingredients to yield a smooth and silky consistency.

Raw Caramel Flan

This incredible dessert has the rich custard texture of traditional flan combined with the mouthwatering flavor of salted caramel.

Yield:	Prep time:	Chill time:	Serving size:
6 flans	15 minutes	3 hours	1 flan

Each serving has:				
201 calories	48 g carbohydrates	3 g fat	5 g fiber	2 g protein

2 cups almond milk	14 large pitted medjool or deglet noor dates
1 cup Irish Moss Emulsifier (recipe in Chapter 10)	2 tsp. sea salt
Meat from 1 small young coconut (⅓ cup)	1 tsp. vanilla extract
	1 cup water

1. In a high-speed blender, blend 1½ cups almond milk, Irish Moss Emulsifier, young coconut meat, 7 medjool dates, 1 teaspoon sea salt, and vanilla extract until completely smooth.

2. Pour into 6 individual custard dishes, and refrigerate for about 3 hours or until flan is gelatinous and well set.

3. In a high-speed blender, combine remaining ½ cup almond milk, remaining 7 medjool dates, remaining 1 teaspoon sea salt, and water until completely smooth. Set aside.

4. When flan is set, turn custard dishes upside down, and turn out flan onto dessert plates. Drizzle about ¼ cup caramel topping over each flan, and serve.

Variation: Make a **Raw Cheesecake** by omitting the ingredients for the caramel sauce and the vanilla extract and reducing the sea salt to ¼ teaspoon. Add ¼ cup fresh lemon juice, and pour over a crust made from 1 cup ground flaxseeds and 1 cup dates processed and pressed into a spring-form pan. Refrigerate at least 3 hours before serving.

TASTY TIP

If you have access to lucuma powder, you can significantly increase the caramel flavor by adding 2 tablespoons into the topping blend. This low-glycemic sweetener is made from the fruit of the lucuma tree native to Peru, and its flavor is naturally reminiscent of caramel. Look for lucuma powder in the raw foods or sweeteners section of your natural foods store or online (see Appendix B).

Raw Key Lime Tart

Wonderfully tart Key lime juice gives this sweet and creamy tart filling that exciting zing Key lime pies are famous for. A subtle flax crust makes a wonderful base for this mouthwatering dessert.

Yield:	Prep time:	Chill time:	Serving size:	
6 (4-inch) tarts	20 minutes	4 hours	1 tart	
Each serving has:				
601 calories	90 g carbohydrates	26 g fat	26 g fiber	13 g protein

1 cup ground flaxseed	¼ medium avocado, peeled, seeded, and mashed (¼ cup)
1 cup coconut flour	½ tsp. spirulina powder
½ cup almond milk	2 cups water
17 large pitted dates	⅓ cup virgin coconut oil
½ tsp. sea salt	1 cup Irish Moss Emulsifier (recipe in Chapter 10)
1 tsp. Key lime zest	
1 cup fresh Key lime juice or regular lime juice	

1. In a food processor fitted with an S blade, process ground flaxseed, coconut flour, almond milk, 7 dates, and sea salt until fully combined and doughlike.

2. Press flaxseed mixture into 4 (4-inch) tart pans to form a thin and flat crust.

3. In a high-speed blender, blend remaining 10 dates, Key lime zest, Key lime juice, avocado, spirulina powder, water, virgin coconut oil, and Irish Moss Emulsifier until coconut oil is melted and mixture is completely smooth.

4. Pour Key lime liquid into tart crusts, and refrigerate for about 4 hours or until tarts are set and somewhat firm to touch.

Variation: Make a **Lemon Tart** by replacing the Key lime juice and zest with lemon juice and zest. Omit the avocado and spirulina, and add ½ teaspoon turmeric powder instead.

FRESH FACT

Key limes differ from common limes in several ways. They're notably smaller than the common lime, but they're also more tart and have a distinct taste and smell. Common limes are fine to use in this recipe, but a Key lime will make it extra special. If you have leftover Key lime liquid, pour it into ice-cube trays or Popsicle molds, and freeze.

Rosemary Sweet Potato Pie

This sweet and savory pie has a real down-home taste. The play of flavors between pungent rosemary and warming spices like cloves and cinnamon are dynamic and subtle but makes this traditional holiday dessert a bit more interesting.

Yield:	Prep time:	Bake time:	Serving size:	
6 (4-inch) pies	10 minutes	50 minutes	1 pie	
Each serving has:				
453 calories	63 g carbohydrates	23 g fat	5 g fiber	4 g protein

1 cup white rice flour

1⅛ cups tapioca starch

2 tsp. fresh rosemary leaves, finely minced

1½ tsp. sea salt

½ tsp. cracked black pepper

½ cup virgin coconut oil

2 medium orange sweet potatoes, cooked, peeled, and mashed (2 cups)

⅓ cup unsweetened almond milk

⅛ cup maple syrup

Pinch nutmeg

2 tsp. ground cinnamon

½ tsp. ground cloves

2 TB. toasted shredded coconut

1. Preheat the oven to 350°F.

2. In a large bowl, combine white rice flour, 1 cup tapioca starch, rosemary, ½ teaspoon sea salt, and black pepper. Scoop virgin coconut oil into flour mixture, and pinch together until thoroughly combined.

3. Press dough into 4 (4-inch) tart pans to about ¼ inch thickness, and poke several times with a fork.

4. Bake for about 15 minutes or until lightly toasted.

5. Meanwhile, in a high-speed blender, combine orange sweet potatoes, almond milk, maple syrup, remaining ⅛ cup tapioca starch, nutmeg, cinnamon, cloves, and remaining 1 teaspoon sea salt.

6. Pour sweet potato mixture into piecrusts, and top each with ½ tablespoon toasted shredded coconut.

7. Bake pies for about 40 minutes or until a knife or toothpick inserted into the center comes out clean. Remove from the oven, and allow to cool before serving.

Variation: Make a delicious holiday soup with these ingredients. Omit the flour and tapioca starch, and follow the blending instructions. Add 2 or 3 cups vegetable stock, too, depending on desired consistency. You also can add an additional 1 cup almond milk to enhance creaminess. Top soup with shredded coconut.

Frozen Blueberries 'n' Cream

Blueberries have a delicate flavor that pairs perfectly with earthy vanilla. Young coconut makes this frozen dessert a creamy and delightful treat that will help you combat cravings for ice cream or other high-fat alternatives.

Yield:	Prep time:	Freeze time:	Serving size:	
4 cups	10 minutes	5 hours	½ cup	
Each serving has:				
115 calories	23 g carbohydrates	3 g fat	3 g fiber	1 g protein

2 cups fresh or frozen blueberries	Meat from young coconut (½ cup)
Water from 1 large young coconut (1½ cups)	7 large pitted dates
	1 tsp. vanilla extract

1. In a high-speed blender, combine blueberries, young coconut water, young coconut meat, dates, and vanilla extract.

2. Transfer to a freezer-safe container, and freeze for at least 5 hours to set. Just before serving, process through a champion juicer for a soft-serve consistency.

Variation: For a **Raspberry Sherbet,** omit the blueberries and add ¼ cup fresh lemon juice and ½ cup fresh or frozen raspberries.

HEADS-UP

Young coconuts can be difficult to hack into without a cleaver, and using a smaller knife may create lots of small pieces of coconut shell to loosen or that remain in the poured-off coconut water or coconut meat. Save yourself from biting into a piece of hard shell by straining your coconut milk as you pour it out of the coconut. Also, using a large serrated knife to saw through the top of the coconut works very well for me.

Berry-Chia Popsicles

These delicious sweet treats are the perfect replacement for Popsicles filled with high-fructose corn syrup and sugar. They're every bit as fruity, sweet, and tart as store-bought frozen treats but pack a superior nutritional punch!

Yield:	Prep time:	Freeze time:	Serving size:	
12 Popsicles	10 minutes	4 hours	1 Popsicle	
Each serving has:				
123 calories	20 g carbohydrates	4 g fat	7 g fiber	3 g protein

2 cups frozen pineapple chunks

2 cups frozen mixed berries

⅔ cups chia seeds

1 cup fresh orange juice

½ cup water

1. In a high-speed blender, combine pineapple, mixed berries, chia seeds, orange juice, and water.

2. Pour liquid into ice-cube trays or Popsicle molds, and insert sticks to use as handles.

3. Freeze for at least 4 hours or until completely frozen.

Variation: Make a tropical frozen treat by replacing the mixed berries with equal amounts of frozen or fresh ripe mango.

TASTY TIP

Homemade frozen desserts have a tendency to become very icy unless processed in an ice-cream maker prior to storage. If you forego the Popsicle molds and decide to indulge in this dessert as a sorbet, you can improve its texture by freezing the mixture in ice-cube trays and then pressing the cubes through a champion juicer or processing them in your high-speed blender. This will make your frozen desserts far more enjoyable than eating them straight from the freezer.

Decadent Drinks

In This Chapter

- Energizing hot drinks
- Tonic teas for wellness
- Cooling frozen mixes
- Fabulous fresh fruit drinks

It's always nice to have the perfect beverage for your every whim and every need. In this chapter, I share several recipes that will warm you up on a cold day, get you up and running in the morning, and keep the common cold at bay. A few double as healthy fruit drinks or mixers, too.

No matter the occasion, you can find a drink to suit the moment in this chapter's drink menu.

Vanilla-Maca Hot Chocolate

Warm vanilla and comforting chocolate make an ideal base for high-powered maca.
This earthy take on a hot chocolate will rock you into action even on the coldest,
snuggle-up day!

Yield:	Prep time:	Cook time:	Serving size:	
1½ cups	10 minutes	5 minutes	1½ cups	
Each serving has:				
224 calories	45 g carbohydrates	6 g fat	2 g fiber	2 g protein

1½ cups almond milk   ½ tsp. vanilla extract

1½ tsp. raw cacao powder   3 TB. maple syrup

1½ tsp. maca powder

1. In a small saucepan over medium heat, whisk together almond milk, raw cacao
   powder, maca powder, vanilla extract, and maple syrup.

2. Heat for 5 minutes or until warm but not boiling. Serve immediately.

Variation: There's nothing quite like a spiced hot chocolate to warm you on a
particularly cold day. A pinch of cayenne and ½ teaspoon cinnamon added to this hot
chocolate will warm you all the way through.

Matcha Steamer

Matcha is the richest-tasting form of green tea. It has the familiar earthy and astringent flavor of traditional green tea, but it lends itself to slightly more decadent creations as well. This steamy, frothy cup of green goodness will give you a boost of energy and antioxidants.

Yield:	Prep time:	Cook time:	Serving size:	
about 1 cup	10 minutes	10 minutes	1 cup	
Each serving has:				
217 calories	33 g carbohydrates	7 g fat	1 g fiber	5 g protein

1 cup hemp milk   1½ tsp. matcha powder
2 TB. maple syrup

1. In a small saucepan over medium heat, warm ⅔ cup hemp milk and maple syrup for 8 minutes or until hot but not boiling.

2. For a layered presentation, pour hot sweetened hemp milk into a clear, heat-proof glass mug, and froth using a whisk or handheld frother.

3. In a small bowl or wide teacup, whisk together remaining ⅓ cup hemp milk and matcha powder until thoroughly combined.

4. Slowly pour matcha hemp milk through the froth of the warmed, sweetened hemp milk. You should have a layer of green liquid on the bottom topped by a layer of white hemp milk and a layer of foam. Stir just before drinking.

Variation: Matcha has a wonderful flavor all its own, but peppermint complements it in a very exciting way. For a **Matcha Mint Freeze,** add 1 cup ice cubes, 2 drops therapeutic-grade peppermint essential oil, 1 cup hemp milk, 3 tablespoons maple syrup, and 1½ teaspoons matcha powder. Blend until smooth.

DEFINITION

Matcha powder is made from the finely ground leaves of shade-grown tencha green tea leaves. It has a dark green color due to its high chlorophyll content and is a bit sweeter than other green teas. It's traditionally mixed with hot water in a small bowl and whisked with a bamboo brush to make a brilliant green tea. Modern recipes utilizing matcha powder include green tea cakes, ice creams, and a variety of specialty drinks.

House Chai

The sweet spices in this chai blend are warming and toning to the digestive system. It's a perfect after-dinner drink, thanks to its dessertlike flavor, and it will bring ease to your full belly.

Yield:	Prep time:	Cook time:	Serving size:	
6 cups	5 minutes	25 minutes	1½ cups	
Each serving has:				
113 calories	22 g carbohydrates	4 g fat	4 g fiber	2 g protein

3½ cups water

5 (3-in.) cinnamon sticks

1 TB. black peppercorns

2 TB. whole cardamom pods

2 TB. whole cloves

1 (3-in.) piece fresh grated ginger

¼ cup maple syrup

1 tsp. vanilla extract

3 cups unsweetened vanilla almond milk

1. In a medium saucepan over medium-high heat, bring water to a boil. Add cinnamon sticks, black peppercorns, cardamom pods, cloves, and ginger. Cover, reduce heat to low, and simmer for 20 minutes.

2. Strain out spices, and return tea to the saucepan.

3. Add maple syrup, vanilla extract, and almond milk, and stir. Divide among 4 mugs, and serve.

Variation: For **Extra-Warming Chocolate Chai,** add ½ teaspoon cayenne during step 1 and whisk in ⅓ cup raw cacao powder during step 3.

Yerba Maté Latte

Yerba maté has a pleasant earthy taste reminiscent of green tea, and vanilla almond milk perfectly accompanies it in a way that will easily replace your morning latte. You won't even miss the coffee!

Yield:	Prep time:	Cook time:	Serving size:	
about 2 cups	5 minutes	15 minutes	1 cup	
Each serving has:				
56 calories	8 g carbohydrates	3 g fat	1 g fiber	1 g protein

½ cup water

3 TB. yerba maté leaves and stems

1½ cups vanilla almond milk

1 TB. maple syrup

1. In a small saucepan over medium-high heat, bring water to a boil. Add yerba maté leaves and stems, and remove pan from heat. Cover, and allow tea to steep for about 5 minutes.

2. Meanwhile, in a small saucepan over medium heat, warm vanilla almond milk and maple syrup for 8 minutes or until hot but not boiling.

3. Strain yerba maté leaves from tea, and add tea to sweetened almond milk. Using a whisk or handheld frother, whip maté until light foam forms.

Variation: If you're trying to avoid coffee but miss the taste, add 1 tablespoon coffee substitute made from roasted chicory and dandelion root to mimic the flavor of coffee and get the morning pick-me-up without the coffee crash and burn. Find grain coffee substitutes in the coffee section of your health food store or online (see Appendix B).

FRESH FACT

People who can't tolerate the caffeine in green tea often do well with yerba maté. This may be due in part to the levels of theobromine, also found in chocolate, compared to the caffeine it contains. The specific chemical composition of maté metabolizes differently from other caffeinated beverages and has a less exciting effect on the body. Its taste is similar to green tea, but it has a slightly more bitter and earthy flavor.

Elderberry Elixir

Elderberries are naturally very tart and taste somewhat similar to unripe blueberries. This concentrated tea elixir is sweetened to perfection to offset the tartness of the berries.

Yield:	Prep time:	Cook time:	Steep time:	Serving size:
about 1 cup	10 minutes	30 minutes	12 hours	¼ cup

Each serving has:				
79 calories	20 g carbohydrates	0 g fat	2 g fiber	0 g protein

2 cups water
½ cup dried elderberries
¼ cup elder flowers

¼ cup maple syrup
1 TB. lemon juice

1. In a small saucepan over medium-high heat, combine water, elderberries, and elder flowers. Bring to a boil, reduce heat to low, and simmer, covered, for 10 minutes.

2. Remove from heat, and refrigerate for 12 hours. Remove from the refrigerator, and mash berries to further extract their juices.

3. Return the saucepan to medium heat, and simmer for 20 minutes.

4. Strain out herbs, and stir in maple syrup and lemon juice. Divide among 4 glasses, or refrigerate in an airtight glass container for up to 1 month.

FRESH FACT

Elderberries and elder flowers are well documented as a folk remedy for immune system support and for preventing and treating illnesses caused by viruses. Some research suggests that elderberries are also anti-inflammatory and suppress the growth of cancer cells. Elder flowers are known to reduce inflammation in mucous membranes, making them helpful for respiratory distress, nagging coughs, and sinus swelling.

Belly Balancer Tea

This comforting drink has the best of both warming and cooling herbs and spices, which are all reputed to ease tummy troubles. It's both mildly spicy and refreshingly cool-tasting.

Yield:	Prep time:	Cook time:	Serving size:	
3 cups	5 minutes	20 minutes	1½ cup	
Each serving has:				
33 calories	8 g carbohydrates	0 g fat	2 g fiber	1 g protein

3 cups water

1 TB. whole fennel seeds

1 (3-in.) cinnamon stick

2 TB. dried chamomile flowers

1 tsp. black peppercorns

2 TB. dried peppermint leaves

¼ cup maple syrup

1. In a small saucepan over medium-high heat, combine water, fennel seeds, cinnamon stick, chamomile flowers, black peppercorns, and peppermint leaves. Bring to a boil, and immediately reduce heat to medium-low. Simmer for about 20 minutes, adding water if tea begins to evaporate.

2. Strain out herbs, and serve with maple syrup to sweeten.

Variation: This warming tummy tea is soothing on its own, but you can also add 1 tablespoon dried ginger to the herb mix for extra relief.

Cold Calm Tea

This spicy, sweet, minty, and lemony tea is perfect for soothing cold symptoms and helps boost your immune system at the same time.

Yield:	Prep time:	Cook time:	Serving size:	
about 4 cups	5 minutes	20 minutes	1 cup	
Each serving has:				
39 calories	10 g carbohydrates	0 g fat	0 g fiber	0 g protein

3 cups water	1 TB. dried lemongrass
1 (2-in.) piece fresh peeled ginger	Pinch cayenne
2 TB. dried mullein leaves	2 TB. fresh lemon juice
2 tsp. dried thyme	2 TB. maple syrup
3 TB. dried peppermint leaves	

1. In a small saucepan over medium-high heat, bring water to a boil. Add ginger, mullein leaves, thyme, peppermint leaves, lemongrass, and cayenne. Reduce heat to low, and simmer, covered, for about 15 minutes.

2. Strain out herbs, and stir in lemon juice and maple syrup. Divide among 4 cups, or refrigerate and then reheat on the stove for 5 minutes if you want to sip 1 cup at a time.

Variation: This tea is great for both a sore throat and a cough. If you want to focus on the cough-relieving properties, omit the lemon juice and cayenne, and add 1 tablespoon dried licorice and 2 teaspoons dried elecampane root to aid decongestion and soothe breathing.

TASTY TIP

Mullein leaves are excellent in healing respiratory diseases because they help loosen and expel mucus from the body. They are also a natural painkiller and help reduce swelling of the glandular system. Purchase loose mullein leaves from a local tea shop, in the loose tea section of your health food store, or online (see Appendix B).

Frozen Kiwi Tini

This frozen treat has a wonderfully tart tinge and a dreamy sweet finish.

Yield:	Prep time:	Serving size:		
about 2 cups	5 minutes	1 cup		
Each serving has:				
97 calories	26 g carbohydrates	0 g fat	1.5 g fiber	0 g protein

½ small honeydew melon, peeled
   and chopped (1 cup)

1 large kiwi, peeled and chopped
   (¼ cup)

1 cup ice cubes

2 TB. coconut sugar

1. In a high-speed blender, combine honeydew melon, kiwi, ice cubes, and coconut sugar.

2. Blend until completely smooth.

Variation: For a spirited version, frost the rim of 2 martini glasses with coconut sugar. Pour ⅛ cup vodka and blended fruits into a cocktail shaker, shake vigorously, and pour into the martini glasses. Top with a very thin slice of fresh kiwi.

Blackberry Peach Sangria

Lush blackberries blend perfectly with succulent peaches to create a refreshing fruit beverage that's delicious served alongside leafy green salads and Mexican fare.

Yield:	Prep time:	Serving size:		
about 3½ cups	10 minutes	¾ cup		
Each serving has:				
103 calories	26 g carbohydrates	0 g fat	3 g fiber	1 g protein

1 cup water	1 cup seltzer water
2 medium peaches, sliced	1 TB. fresh lemon juice
¾ cup fresh or frozen blackberries	1 small orange, peeled and cut into thin slices
¼ cup maple syrup	

1. In a high-speed blender, combine water, 1 peach, and ½ cup blackberries. Blend until completely smooth.

2. Strain liquid through a fine-mesh strainer or cheesecloth, and reserve fruit purée for a dessert or breakfast topper.

3. In a pitcher, combine blended blackberry and peach juice, maple syrup, seltzer water, and lemon juice.

4. Add remaining 1 peach, remaining ¼ cup blackberries, and orange slices, and stir well.

Variation: To make a traditional sangria, replace the water with 1 cup red wine and add ½ cup peach or blackberry brandy.

HEADS-UP

Sangria is a traditional Spanish libation made from red or sometimes white wine, a fresh juice blend, and fresh citrus and other fruits, which marinate in the wine. The drink is thin and pourable, just like freshly squeezed juice. To achieve a smooth and refreshing texture, be sure to strain the blackberry seeds from your juice blend.

Coco Water Colada

Pure pineapple perfection and creamy coconut deliver amazing nutrition and terrific taste in this classic frozen delight.

Yield:	Prep time:	Serving size:		
about 3 cups	5 minutes	¾ cup		
Each serving has:				
183 calories	37 g carbohydrates	5 g fat	4 g fiber	2 g protein

Water from 1 large young coconut (1½ cups)

Meat from 1 young coconut (⅓ cup)

1 cup frozen pineapple bits

4 large pitted medjool or deglet noor dates

1 TB. shredded coconut

1. In a high-speed blender, combine young coconut water, young coconut meat, pineapple, and medjool dates.

2. Blend until completely smooth.

3. Serve in 2 glasses sprinkled with shredded coconut.

Variation: You can blend up an alcoholic version of this virgin colada by adding ¼ cup of your favorite rum during step 1.

Blood Orange Mojito

Sweet and sour citrus, a hint of mint, and bubbly seltzer water combine into a simple drink that will keep you cool on a hot summer day.

Yield:	Prep time:	Serving size:		
about 2 cups	10 minutes	½ cup		
Each serving has:				
45 calories	12 g carbohydrates	0 g fat	0 g fiber	0 g protein

3 medium blood oranges, juiced
   (½ cup)

¼ cup fresh lime juice

⅛ cup maple syrup

⅓ cup seltzer water

⅛ cup bruised and slivered mint leaves

½ cup crushed ice

3 thin blood orange slices, skin intact

3 thin lime slices

1. In a high-speed blender, combine blood orange juice, lime juice, maple syrup, and seltzer water.

2. Blend until completely smooth.

3. Pour into a pitcher, add mint leaves and crushed ice, stir well, and garnish with blood orange and lime slices.

Variation: Add ¼ cup white rum during step 1 for an adult version of this drink.

FRESH FACT

Blood oranges are the only type of citrus that contain anthocyanin pigments, which also give blueberries their classic blue-purple hue. Anthocyanin adds to their antioxidant value and tinges the oranges with an almost berrylike flavor and flesh color distinctly different from other orange varieties.

Liquid Garden

This savory and spicy tomato-based veggie cocktail has a similar flavor to other well-known vegetable blends, but it has 12 delectable and juicy vegetables for a bit more *umph*.

Yield:	Prep time:	Serving size:		
about 3 cups	20 minutes	1 cup		
Each serving has:				
22 calories	5 g carbohydrates	0 g fat	2 g fiber	1 g protein

1 large tomato, chopped (1 cup)

½ medium green bell pepper, ribs and seeds removed, and chopped (½ cup)

2 medium celery stalks, diced (⅓ cup)

1 small jalapeño, chopped (1 TB.)

⅛ small head purple cabbage, chopped (¼ cup)

¼ cup fresh parsley, chopped

1 medium chard leaf

1 medium clove garlic

1 medium carrot, juiced (⅛ cup)

½ small red beet, juiced (⅛ cup)

1 TB. fresh lemon juice

1 (½-in.) piece fresh peeled and grated horseradish (½ tsp.)

½ tsp. sea salt

¼ tsp. ground black pepper

3 medium celery stalks

1. In a high-speed blender, combine tomato, green bell pepper, celery, jalapeño, purple cabbage, parsley, chard, garlic, carrot juice, red beet juice, lemon juice, horseradish, sea salt, and black pepper.

2. Blend until completely smooth.

3. Divide among 3 glasses, and serve each with 1 fresh celery stalk.

Variation: For a brunch-worthy **Bloody Mary Cocktail,** frost the rim of a tall glass with celery salt. Add ¼ cup vodka to the tomato mix, shake, and pour into the prepared glass. Garnish each with 1 celery stalk, 1 pickled green bean, 2 green olives, and a scant shaving of fresh horseradish.

Nut or Seed Milk

I use plant milks in soups, in smoothies, poured over granola, and in desserts. This recipe allows for customization depending on the type of nut or seed you prefer. I normally opt for sweeter almonds, Brazil nuts, or even coconut.

Yield:	Prep time:	Soak time:	Chill time:	Serving size:
about 4 cups	10 minutes	12 hours	2 hours	1 cup
Each serving has:				
105 calories	7 g carbohydrates	4 g fat	1 g fiber	3 g protein

1½ cups raw almonds, Brazil nuts, cashews, coconut meat, or hemp seeds

7 cups water

1 tsp. vanilla extract

¼ tsp. fine sea salt

2 tsp. agave nectar

1. Soak raw almonds for 12 hours in 3 cups water in the refrigerator. If using cashews or hemp seeds, soak for 6 hours. When using coconut meat, soaking is not needed.

2. Strain and rinse nuts or seeds and transfer to a high-speed blender. Add remaining 4 cups water, and blend on high for 2 minutes.

3. Using a nut milk bag, strain milk into a large glass container. Freeze pulp for future use.

4. Transfer nut milk back into the rinsed blender, add vanilla extract, sea salt, and agave nectar, and blend on high for 30 seconds.

5. Store milk in an airtight glass container, and chill for at least 2 hours and up to 5 days.

Variation: Customize your milk with strawberries or cacao by blending in either ¾ cup strawberry or ¼ cup raw cacao during step 4. In both cases, increase the quantity of agave nectar to 2 tablespoons.

Glossary

Appendix

A

80-10-10   The ideal macronutrient balance of an optimal low-fat vegan diet: 80 percent complex carbohydrates, 10 percent protein, and 10 percent fat.

acid-forming food   Food such as meat, eggs, milk, cheese, grains, and beans that lowers the body's pH, creating an acidic environment. Acid-forming foods can increase the risk of osteoporosis, asthma, and kidney problems.

AFA blue-green algae   A type of cyanobacteria properly known as aphanizomenon flos-aquae (AFA), this algae is an abundant source of vitamins, minerals, essential fatty acids, and amino acids. AFA is the only concentrated vegan food source of DHA and EPA fatty acids.

agave nectar   A natural sweetener extracted from the agave plant that mostly consists of fructose sugars and should be used in moderation because it may cause sudden changes in blood sugar levels. It was once thought of as being low glycemic but has since been updated to high glycemic status.

al dente   Italian for "against the teeth," this term refers to pasta or rice that's neither soft nor hard but just slightly firm against the teeth.

alkaline-forming food   Plant food such as fruits and vegetables that raises the body's pH toward its ideal level of 7.4 pH.

allspice   A spice named for its flavor echoes of several spices (cinnamon, cloves, nutmeg) used in many desserts and in rich marinades and stews.

amaranth   A South American food plant whose edible seeds and greens are a good source of protein, fiber, calcium, iron, phosphorus, and vitamins A, C, and E.

amino acid   Molecules that are the building blocks of protein. Essential amino acids are those the body needs to make protein but cannot produce, so one must obtain them from his or her diet. Nonessential amino acids are those the human body can produce.

antioxidant   A protective phytochemical that blocks the harmful effects of oxidation on cells. Numerous plant substances, including vitamins and phenols, have antioxidant properties.

arborio rice   A plump Italian rice used for, among other purposes, risotto.

artichoke heart   The center part of the artichoke flower, often found canned or frozen in grocery stores.

arugula   A spicy-peppery green with leaves that resemble a dandelion and have a distinctive and very sharp flavor.

B vitamins   A family of eight vitamins including thiamin, riboflavin, niacin, and folic acid, we require for metabolism, healing, and a healthy nervous system.

bake   To cook in a dry oven. Dry-heat cooking often results in a crisping of the exterior of the food being cooked. Moist-heat cooking, through methods such as steaming, poaching, etc., brings a much different, moist quality to the food.

baking powder   A dry ingredient used to increase volume and lighten or leaven baked goods.

balsamic vinegar   Vinegar produced primarily in Italy from a specific type of grape and aged in wooden barrels. It's heavier, darker, and sweeter than most vinegars.

basil   A flavorful, almost sweet, resinous herb delicious with tomatoes and used in all kinds of Italian- and Mediterranean-style dishes.

baste   To keep foods moist during cooking by spooning, brushing, or drizzling with a liquid.

beat   To quickly mix substances.

Belgian endive   *See* endive.

bile   A substance produced by the liver the body uses to break down dietary fats so they can be digested.

blacken   To cook something quickly in a very hot skillet over high heat, usually with a seasoning mixture.

blanch   To place a food in boiling water for about 1 minute or less to partially cook the exterior and then submerge in or rinse with cold water to halt the cooking.

blend To completely mix something, usually with a blender or food processor, slower than beating.

boil To heat a liquid to the point where water is forced to turn into steam, causing the liquid to bubble. To boil something is to insert it into boiling water. A rapid boil is when a lot of bubbles form on the surface of the liquid.

bok choy A member of the cabbage family with thick stems, a crisp texture, and a fresh flavor. It's perfect for stir-frying.

bouillon Dried essence of stock from vegetables or other ingredients. It's a popular starting ingredient for soups because it adds natural flavor.

braise To cook with the introduction of some liquid, usually over an extended period of time.

broil To cook in a dry oven under the overhead high-heat element.

broth *See* stock.

brown To cook in a skillet, turning, until the food's surface is seared and brown in color, to lock in the juices.

brown rice A whole-grain rice, including the germ, with a characteristic pale brown or tan color. It's more nutritious and flavorful than white rice.

bruschetta (or **crostini**) Slices of toasted or grilled bread with garlic and olive oil, often with other toppings.

buckwheat A seed, related to the sorrel family, that's high in protein and fiber and heart-protecting flavonoids. Buckwheat flour can be used to make gluten-free baked goods and is used in Japanese soba noodles. It is also a popular pancake ingredient.

canapé A bite-size hors d'oeuvre usually served on a small piece of bread or toast.

capsaicin The heat-giving phenolic compound in chiles. It's used as a topical pain reliever for diseases such as arthritis and has metabolism-boosting and antioxidant properties.

caramelize To cook sugar over low heat until it develops a sweet caramel flavor, or to cook vegetables (especially onions) in oil over low heat until they soften, sweeten, and develop a caramel color.

caraway   A distinctive spicy seed, often used for bread and cabbage dishes. It's known to reduce stomach upset, which is why it's often paired with foods like sauerkraut.

cardamom   An intense, sweet-smelling spice used in baking and coffee and common in Indian cooking.

carob   A tropical tree that produces long pods from which the dried, baked, and powdered flesh—carob powder—is used in baking. The flavor is sweet and reminiscent of chocolate.

carotenoid   A class of plant compounds characterized by its orange pigment. Carotenoids are powerful antioxidants and an excellent source of vitamin A.

cayenne   A fiery spice made from hot chile peppers, especially the cayenne chile, a slender, red, and very hot pepper.

chia seed   An ancient seed originating in South America that has a unique, energy-giving composition of 31 grams of fat, 38 grams of fiber, and 16 grams of protein per 100 grams.

chickpea (or **garbanzo bean**)   A roundish yellow-gold bean used as the base ingredient in hummus. Chickpeas are high in fiber and low in fat.

chile (or **chili**)   Any one of many different "hot" peppers, ranging in intensity from the relatively mild ancho pepper to the blisteringly hot habañero.

chili powder   A warm, rich seasoning blend that includes chile pepper, cumin, garlic, and oregano.

Chinese five-spice powder   A pungent mixture of equal parts cinnamon, cloves, fennel seed, anise, and Szechuan peppercorns.

chive   A member of the onion family, chives grow in bunches of long leaves that resemble tall grass or the green tops of onions and offer a light onion flavor.

chlorella   A type of single-celled algae cultivated for its beneficial health properties. It's a rich source of protein, vitamins, minerals, and essential fatty acids.

cholesterol   A substance found exclusively in animal foods such as eggs, meat, and dairy. High cholesterol levels are linked to increased risk of heart disease.

chop   To cut into pieces, usually qualified by an adverb such as *"coarsely* chopped" or by a size measurement such as "chopped into ½-inch pieces." "Finely chopped" is much closer to mince.

chutney   A thick condiment often served with Indian curries made with fruits and/ or vegetables with vinegar, sugar, and spices.

cider vinegar   A vinegar produced from apple cider, popular in North America.

cilantro   A member of the parsley family used in Mexican dishes (especially salsa) and some Asian dishes. Use in moderation because the flavor can overwhelm. The seed of the cilantro plant is the spice coriander.

cinnamon   A rich, aromatic spice commonly used in baking or desserts. Cinnamon can also be used for delicious and interesting entrées.

clove   A sweet, strong, almost wintergreen-flavor spice used in baking.

coconut sugar   A low-glycemic sweetener made from the dehydrated sap of the coconut tree. Also called palm sugar.

complex carbohydrate   A starch your body must convert to glucose for fuel. Complex carbohydrates are typically found in vegetables and whole grains.

compote   A chilled dish of fresh or dried fruit that's slowly cooked in a sugary syrup made of liquid, spices, and fruit bits.

conventional   Refers to food products and/or methods of growth and production that use pesticides, herbicides, antibiotics, and other artificial chemicals.

coriander   A rich, warm, spicy seed used in all types of recipes, from African to South American, from entrées to desserts.

cortisol   A hormone produced by the body in response to fear or stress. It's linked to increased abdominal fat and elevated risk of illnesses like heart disease, diabetes, and stroke.

cream   To beat an ingredient or fat, often with other spices and sweeteners.

crimini mushroom   A relative of the white button mushroom that's brown in color and has a richer flavor. The larger, fully grown version is the portobello. *See also* portobello mushroom.

crudité   Fresh vegetables served as an appetizer, often all together on one tray.

cumin   A savory, almost smoky-tasting spice popular in Middle Eastern, Mexican, and Indian dishes. Cumin is a seed; ground cumin seed is the most common form used in cooking.

curry   Rich, spicy, Indian-style sauces and the dishes prepared with them. A curry uses curry powder as its base seasoning.

curry powder   A ground blend of rich and flavorful spices used as a basis for curry and many other Indian-influenced dishes. Common ingredients include hot pepper, nutmeg, cumin, cinnamon, pepper, and turmeric. Some curry can also be found in paste form.

dash   A few drops, usually of a liquid, released by a quick shake.

denatured protein   A protein that contains all its original amino acids but in which the chemical bonds are partially broken down, supposedly making them easier to digest. When denatured, enzymes are destroyed and many proteins may coagulate into indigestible protein bonds.

dice   To cut into small cubes about ¼-inch square.

Dijon mustard   A hearty, spicy mustard made in the style of the Dijon region of France.

dill   A pungent herb that pairs wonderfully with a bit of lemon and makes a wonderful addition to dressings and salads.

dollop   A spoonful of something creamy and thick, generally as a topping or finish.

double boiler   A set of two pots designed to nest together, one inside the other, and provide consistent, moist heat for foods that need delicate treatment. The bottom pot holds water (not quite touching the bottom of the top pot); the top pot holds the food you want to heat.

drizzle   To lightly sprinkle drops of a liquid over food, often as the finishing touch to a dish.

edamame   Fresh, plump, pale green soybeans, similar in appearance to lima beans, often served steamed and either shelled or still in their protective pods.

electrolyte   Essential minerals including calcium, magnesium, sodium, and potassium the body requires to regulate cellular communication and water transfer and to maintain muscle function.

emulsifier   A food or additive that prevents the separation of its water and fat content. For example, emulsifiers are commonly used in margarine or puddings to maintain a creamy, consistent texture.

endive   A green that resembles a small, elongated, tightly packed head of romaine lettuce. The thick, crunchy leaves can be broken off and used with dips and spreads.

endocannabinoid   An appetite-enhancing neurochemical released in response to consumption of fatty foods.

entrée   The main dish in a meal.

essential amino acids   The nine amino acids—histidine, leucine, phenylalanine, threonine, tryptophan, valine, isoleucine, lysine, and methionine—the body needs to build protein but cannot produce and so must be obtained from food.

essential fatty acid (EFA)   Fat such as omega-3 and omega-6 that are necessary to human health but the body cannot produce, so they must be obtained from food.

extra-virgin olive oil   *See* olive oil.

extract   A concentrated flavoring derived from foods or plants through evaporation or distillation that imparts a powerful flavor without altering the volume or texture of a dish.

fat-soluble vitamin   The vitamins A, D, K, and E, which are stored in fat and the liver and support hormone production.

fennel   In seed form, a fragrant, licorice-tasting herb. The bulbs have a mild flavor and a celery-like crunch and are used as a vegetable in salads or cooked recipes.

fiber   The nondigestible substance in the cell walls of plants that acts as a cleansing agent in the body, promoting good digestion and encouraging detoxification.

flavonoid   A group of phytochemicals found in plants such as broccoli, beans, hops, and citrus fruits. They're powerful antioxidants and blood builders.

flour   Grains ground into a meal. Wheat is perhaps the most common flour, but oats, rye, buckwheat, millet, quinoa, chickpeas, etc. can also be used.

folate   A naturally occurring B vitamin found in hazelnuts that's essential for proper fetal development. It protects against neural tube defects such as spina bifida.

fold   To combine a dense and light mixture with a circular action from the middle of the bowl.

free radical   A toxic atom containing unpaired electrons that attacks and damages human cells. They promote heart disease and inflammatory illnesses such as arthritis and Alzheimer's disease.

fry   *See* sauté.

garlic   A member of the onion family, a pungent and flavorful vegetable used in many savory dishes. A garlic bulb contains multiple cloves. Each clove, when chopped, provides about 1 teaspoon of garlic.

genetically modified (GMO)   Designation for plants whose genes have been artificially altered to induce certain characteristics, such as disease or drought resistance. The long-term effects of genetic modification on human health are unknown, so these foods are best avoided. Most American-grown conventional soybeans are genetically modified, so it's best to eat organic soy products.

ginger   A flavorful root available fresh or dried and ground that adds a pungent, sweet, and spicy quality to a dish.

globular protein   Simple, easily digested protein structures that form enzymes, regulate cellular respiration, form the basis for hormones, and transport molecules throughout the body (i.e., hemoglobin transporting oxygen).

glycemic index (GI)   A measure of how a food affects the body's blood sugar levels. High-GI foods include sugars and simple carbohydrates that cause abrupt rises in blood sugar; low-GI foods such as protein and complex carbohydrates are broken down slowly, causing a steady release of sugar for energy.

handful   An unscientific measurement, it's the amount of an ingredient you can hold in your hand.

hemp seed   The highly nutritious seed of the hemp plant. Hemp seeds are made up of 44 grams fat, 7 grams fiber, and 33 grams protein per 100 grams and contain a beneficial 3:1 ratio of omega-6 to omega-3 fatty acids.

herbes de Provence A seasoning mix of basil, fennel, marjoram, rosemary, sage, and thyme, common in the south of France.

hors d'oeuvre French for "outside of work" (the "work" being the main meal), an hors d'oeuvre can be any dish served as a starter before a meal.

horseradish A potent, spicy root that forms the flavor base in tangy mustards. Pure horseradish should be used sparingly, as its flavor can be overpowering.

hummus A thick, Middle Eastern dip or spread made of puréed chickpeas, lemon juice, olive oil, garlic, and often tahini.

inflammatory disease An illness such as arthritis, asthma, blindness, and dementia caused by inflammation of body tissues.

infusion A liquid in which flavorful ingredients such as herbs have been soaked or steeped to extract their flavor into the liquid.

insulin A hormone produced by the pancreas that regulates blood sugar levels and helps control metabolism. High sugar intake results in the rapid release of insulin. Over time, this cycle can lead to insulin resistance.

insulin resistance A condition in which the body loses its ability to control blood sugar due to long-term excess sugar intake and a variety of other factors. Long-term insulin resistance means the pancreas can no longer produce enough insulin to manage the body's glucose levels, and diabetes can develop as a result.

Irish moss A red marine algae from which carrageenan is derived. It may be purchased fresh or dried and is used to thicken both raw and cooked foods.

isoflavone A type of phytochemical, most commonly found in soy products, that's linked to reducing the risk of heart disease, breast cancer, osteoporosis, and the symptoms of menopause.

Italian seasoning A blend of dried herbs, including basil, oregano, rosemary, and thyme.

jicama A juicy, crunchy, sweet, large, round Central American vegetable. If you can't find jicama, try substituting sliced water chestnuts.

julienne A French word meaning "to slice into very thin pieces."

kalamata olive   Traditionally from Greece, a medium-small, long black olive with a rich, smoky flavor.

Key lime   A very small lime grown primarily in Florida known for its tart and pleasing taste.

knead   To work dough by hand to make it pliable.

kosher salt   A coarse-grained salt made without any additives or iodine.

lecithin   Fat-based compounds that regulate nutrient flow in living cells. They occur naturally in plants and animals and are also isolated from foods such as soy, sunflower seeds, hemp seeds, grains, and beans. They may be used as a food supplement or emulsifier.

lentil   A tiny lens-shape pulse used in European, Middle Eastern, and Indian cuisines.

lignan   A type of phenol found in high concentration in flaxseeds. It's a strong antioxidant thought to protect against cancer and heart disease.

low-fat seed   A group of seeds relatively low in fat and high in carbohydrates, meaning they can be used as grain substitutes. Some examples are quinoa, amaranth, millet, and buckwheat.

lutein   A carotenoid essential for healthy eyes and skin. Pistachio nuts and blueberries are especially good sources of lutein.

macronutrients   The main energy-providing components (calories) of human nutrition: carbohydrates, protein, and fat.

mandoline   A slicing tool used to achieve very thin slices and speed preparation work.

maqui berry   A small purple-black berry with an impressive antioxidant content—one of the highest levels known. The polyphenols in these berries carry a variety of antioxidant and cancer-fighting benefits.

marinate   To soak a food in a seasoned sauce, a marinade, that's high in acid content.

marjoram   A sweet herb, cousin of and similar to oregano, popular in Greek, Spanish, and Italian dishes.

masa harina   A dried, powdered corn flour used in traditional Central and South American cuisine.

matcha powder   A fine powder made from ground shade-grown tencha green tea leaves. It has a high chlorophyll content, which yields a striking green color.

medium-chain fatty acid   A type of fat found in coconut oil, which the body treats as a carbohydrate, meaning the body burns it rather than storing it. Foods containing medium-chain fatty acids are popular with endurance athletes. Unlike other saturated fats, medium-chain fatty acids are known to protect against heart disease.

meld   To allow flavors to blend and spread over time. Melding is often why recipes call for overnight refrigeration and why some dishes taste better as leftovers.

mesclun   Mixed salad greens, usually containing lettuce and other assorted greens such as arugula, cress, and endive.

micronutrients   The component part of macronutrients that provide noncaloric nutrients—e.g., vitamins, minerals, enzymes, and phytonutrients.

millet   A tiny, round, yellow-colored, nutty-flavored grain often used as a replacement for couscous.

mince   To cut into very small pieces, smaller than diced, about ⅛ inch or smaller.

miso   A fermented, flavorful soybean paste, key in many Japanese dishes.

mitochondria   An internal component of living cells that supplies energy to the rest of the cell. Mitochondria produce the substance adenosine triphosphate (ATP), which powers cellular function.

mochi   A cultured, cooked, glutinous rice cake that's dense and hard until baked, when it puffs up and becomes chewy and crispy.

mortar and pestle   A tool set, usually made from stone or wood, used to crush spices and herbs and turn grains into flour.

mouthfeel   The overall sensation in the mouth resulting from a combination of the temperature, taste, smell, and texture of a food.

nutmeg   A sweet, fragrant, musky spice used primarily in baking.

nutritional yeast   A type of yeast typically grown on molasses used as an addition to dressings, sauces, soups, dips, spreads, and so on because of its slightly cheesy flavor.

olive   The fruit of the olive tree commonly grown on all sides of the Mediterranean. Black olives are also called ripe olives. Green olives are immature, although they're also widely eaten. *See also* kalamata olive.

olive oil   A fragrant liquid produced by crushing or pressing olives. Extra-virgin olive oil—the most flavorful and highest quality—is produced from the first pressing of a batch of olives; oil is also produced from later pressings.

omega-3 fatty acid   A group of fatty acids (ALA, EPA, and DHA) the body cannot manufacture. They're important for brain development and health, cardiovascular health, and immune function.

oregano   A fragrant, slightly astringent herb used in Greek, Spanish, and Italian dishes.

organic   Foods produced without the use of artificially manufactured pesticides, herbicides, and fungicides.

oxidation   The browning of fruit flesh that happens over time with exposure to air. Minimize oxidation by rubbing the cut surfaces with lemon juice.

oxidative damage   The damage caused to cells and DNA by free radicals as a result of oxygen exposure.

paprika   A rich, red, warm, earthy spice that lends a rich red color to many dishes.

parboil   To partially cook in boiling water or broth.

parsley   A fresh-tasting green, leafy herb, often used as a garnish.

pâté   A savory loaf, in this case made from ground nuts and vegetables, served cold and spread or sliced on crusty bread or crackers.

phenols or **phenolic acid**   Aromatic compounds found in plants such as vanilla, ginger, cacao, tea, and coffee. Plants produce and use phenols for reproduction, growth, and repair. They are antioxidants and help combat cancer, heart disease, and strokes.

phytic acid   A compound found in unfermented soy products that impedes the body's ability to absorb minerals like calcium, magnesium, and zinc.

phytoestrogen   A plant compound that mimics the hormone estrogen. Soybeans are especially rich in phytoestrogens, which may disrupt healthy hormone production if eaten in excess.

phytonutrients   Chemical compounds found in fruit and vegetables plants produce to protect themselves that are also beneficial to human health. They include carotenoids, flavonoids, sulphides, isoflavones, capsaicin, and lycopene.

pinch   An unscientific measurement for the amount of an ingredient—typically, a dry, granular substance such as an herb or seasoning—you can hold between your finger and thumb.

pine nut   A nut that's rich (high in fat), flavorful, and a bit pine-y. Pine nuts are a traditional ingredient in pesto and add a hearty crunch to many other recipes.

polenta   A mush made from cornmeal that can be eaten hot or cooked until firm and cut into squares.

porcini mushroom   A rich and flavorful mushroom used in rice and Italian-style dishes.

portobello mushroom   A mature and larger form of the smaller crimini mushroom. Brown, chewy, and flavorful, portobellos are often served as whole caps, grilled, or as thin sautéed slices. *See also* crimini mushroom.

preheat   To turn on an oven, broiler, or other cooking appliance in advance of cooking so the temperature will be at the desired level when the assembled dish is ready for cooking.

probiotics   Beneficial bacteria that break down food particles in our digestive systems. Probiotics are initially acquired through the process of birth and breastfeeding and may be replenished later in life by consuming unwashed produce and fermented foods, and via supplementation.

purée   To reduce a food to a thick, creamy texture, typically using a blender or food processor.

quinoa   A flavorful grainlike seed that's extremely high in protein and calcium.

red rice   Generally refers to a nonglutinous, medium-grain rice that may also be called Bhutanese rice. It has more fiber and more antioxidant activity than brown rice.

reduce   To boil or simmer a broth or sauce to remove some of the water content, resulting in more concentrated flavor and color.

refined fat   A fat that's extracted and processed into a filtered, heated, deodorized, or otherwise heavily altered form of oil. Refined fats are heavily oxidized and indigestible. Avoid them if you can.

reserve   To hold a specified ingredient for another use later in the recipe.

rice vinegar   Vinegar produced from fermented rice or rice wine, popular in Asian-style dishes. (It's not the same thing as rice wine vinegar.)

ricer   A handled kitchen tool with a medium chamber, big enough for an average potato, that has small holes on the bottom. It's used to press vegetables like potatoes into a ricelike shape.

risotto   A popular Italian rice dish made by toasting arborio rice in oil and then slowly adding liquid to cook the rice, resulting in a creamy texture.

roast   To cook something uncovered in an oven, usually without additional liquid.

rosemary   A pungent, sweet herb. A little goes a long way.

roux   A mixture of a fat and flour used to thicken sauces and soups.

saffron   An expensive spice made from the stamens of crocus flowers. Saffron lends a dramatic yellow color and distinctive flavor to a dish. Use only tiny amounts.

sage   An herb with a musty yet fruity, lemon-rind scent and "sunny" flavor.

saponin   A phytochemical common to beans and peas known to have cancer-fighting properties. They have a soapy quality, which you may notice while rinsing certain grains and legumes.

saturated fat   Mostly found in animal products such as butter, milk, and cheese, saturated fats are solid at room temperature. High intake of some saturated fats is linked to greater risk of heart disease. The saturated fat in coconuts is an exception to this generality.

sauté   To pan-cook over heat at a lower temperature than what's used for frying.

savory   A popular herb with a fresh, woody taste. Can also describe the flavor of food.

scant   An ingredient measurement directive not to add any extra, perhaps even leaving the measurement a tad short.

sear   To quickly brown the exterior of a food over high heat, sealing in its flavor.

seitan   A soy-free meat substitute composed of wheat gluten. It was originally made by Buddhist monks and is a popular alternative to tofu. It has a very high gluten content.

selenium   A mineral found in Brazil nuts that fights cancer, neurological diseases, and infections and is important for proper thyroid function.

sesame oil   An oil made from pressing sesame seeds. It's tasteless if clear and aromatic and flavorful if brown.

shallot   A member of the onion family that grows in a bulb somewhat like garlic but has a milder onion flavor. When a recipe calls for shallot, use the entire bulb.

shiitake mushroom   A large, dark brown mushroom with a hearty, meaty flavor. It can be used fresh or dried, grilled, as a component in other recipes, and as a flavoring source for broth.

short-grain rice   A starchy rice popular in Asian-style dishes because it readily clumps, making it perfect for eating with chopsticks.

simmer   To boil gently so the liquid barely bubbles.

simple carbohydrate   A sugar such as fructose (fruit sugar), lactose (milk sugar), sucrose, and glucose that's rapidly absorbed by the body and may lead to swift increases in blood sugar levels.

skillet (also **frying pan**)   A generally heavy, flat-bottomed, metal pan with a handle designed to cook food over heat on a stovetop or campfire.

skim   To remove fat or other material from the top of a liquid.

spiral slicer   A spiral slicer is a kitchen tool shaped like a dome with a crank on the top. It can mandoline slice and shred vegetables into long, thin noodles.

spirulina   A type of algaelike cyanobacteria popularly used as a dietary supplement because it's rich in protein; minerals such as zinc, iron, and copper; B vitamins; and gamma linolenic acid, a type of essential fatty acid.

standard American diet (SAD)   The relatively high-fat, high-calorie diet common in America, characterized by consumption of large amounts of animal protein, processed foods, refined carbohydrates, and sugar. It is associated with increased risk of heart disease, cancer, degenerative illnesses, and diabetes.

steam   To suspend a food over boiling water and allow the heat of the steam (water vapor) to cook the food. This quick-cooking method preserves a food's flavor and texture.

steep   To let sit in hot water, as in steeping tea in hot water for 10 minutes.

stew   To slowly cook pieces of food submerged in a liquid. Also, a dish prepared by this method.

stir-fry   To cook small pieces of food in a wok or skillet over high heat, moving and turning the food quickly to cook all sides.

stock   A flavorful broth made by cooking vegetables with seasonings until the liquid absorbs these flavors. The liquid is strained and the solids are discarded. Stock can be eaten alone or used as a base for soups, stews, etc.

super-greens powder   A high-quality blend of different powdered grasses like wheatgrass or barley grass that may also contain various herbs like nettle or horsetail. Some super-greens powders also contain probiotics and enzymes.

superfruit powder   A diverse combination of many different fruits with high antioxidant activity. Many superfruit powders may also contain herbs, enzymes, and probiotics.

tahini   A paste made from sesame seeds used to flavor many Middle Eastern recipes.

tamari   A wheat- and gluten-free soy sauce made of fermented soybeans.

tamarind   A sweet, pungent, flavorful fruit used in Indian-style sauces and curries.

tapas   A Spanish term meaning "small plate" that describes individual-size appetizers and snacks served cold or warm.

tarragon   A sweet, rich-smelling herb perfect with vegetables, especially asparagus.

tempeh   An Indonesian food made by culturing and fermenting soybeans into a cake, sometimes mixed with grains or vegetables. It's high in protein and fiber.

teriyaki   A Japanese-style sauce composed of soy sauce, rice wine, ginger, and sugar.

thyme   A minty, zesty herb.

tofu   A cheeselike substance made from soybeans and soy milk.

tomatillo   A popular Latin American food that's a member of the gooseberry family—although it tastes more like a green tomato—used in savory dishes and salsas. Its husk resembles a paper lantern.

trans-fat   A hydrogenated fat that's solid at room temperature, such as margarine. Trans-fats are stable and have a long shelf life, so they're often used in processed foods. They raise the levels of low-density lipid (LDL) cholesterol, which is bad for your heart.

triglyceride   A type of fat your body stores in the blood. Excess triglycerides can lead to health problems such as heart disease and stroke. Eating large quantities of simple carbohydrates, such as sugar, is linked to increased amounts of triglycerides in the blood.

turmeric   A spicy, pungent yellow root used in many dishes, especially Indian cuisine, for color and flavor. Turmeric has tremendous anti-inflammatory properties and is the source of the yellow color in many prepared mustards.

unsaturated fat   A mostly plant-based fat that's liquid at room temperature. Unsaturated fats include olive oil, avocado oil, sunflower oil, and the fat in many nuts and seeds.

vegan   Refers to a plant-based diet free of animal and animal-derived foods such as meat, fish, eggs, dairy, honey, gelatin, and rennet. Many vegans abstain from wearing leather, silk, or wool and avoid using products tested on animals.

vegetable steamer   An insert with tiny holes in the bottom designed to fit on or in another pot to hold food to be steamed above boiling water. *See also* steam.

vinegar   An acidic liquid widely used as a dressing and seasoning, often made from fermented grapes, apples, or rice. *See also* balsamic vinegar; cider vinegar; rice vinegar; white vinegar; wine vinegar.

wasabi   Japanese horseradish, a fiery, pungent condiment used with many Japanese-style dishes. It's most often sold as a powder to which you add water to create a paste.

water chestnut   A white, crunchy, and juicy tuber popular in many Asian dishes. It holds its texture whether cool or hot.

whisk   To rapidly mix, introducing air to the mixture.

white mushroom   A button mushroom. When fresh, white mushrooms have an earthy smell and an appealing soft crunch.

white vinegar   The most common type of vinegar, produced from grain.

whole grain   A grain derived from the seeds of grasses, including rice, oats, rye, wheat, wild rice, quinoa, barley, buckwheat, bulgur, corn, millet, amaranth, and sorghum.

wild rice   Not a rice at all, this seed of a grass has a rich, nutty flavor and serves as a nutritious main or side dish.

wine vinegar   Vinegar produced from red or white wine.

zest   Small slivers of peel, usually from a citrus fruit such as a lemon, lime, or orange.

Resources

Information is a powerful tool! In this appendix, I've assembled a list of books and websites to help you further your journey to a healthy low-fat vegan diet.

Vegan, Low-Fat Vegan, and Healthy Healing Books

Barnard, Neal, MD. *Breaking the Food Seduction.* New York, NY: St. Martin's Press, 2003.

Burroughs, Stanley. *The Master Cleanser.* Reno, NV: Burroughs Books, 1976.

Campbell, Colin T., and Thomas M. Campbell II. *The China Study: The Most Comprehensive Study of Nutrition Ever Conducted and the Startling Implications for Diet, Weight Loss, and Long-Term Health.* Dallas, TX: Benbella Books, 2006.

Cousens, Gabriel. *Conscious Eating.* Berkeley, CA: North Atlantic Books, 2000.

Esselstyn, Caldwell. *Prevent and Reverse Heart Disease.* New York, NY: Avery Trade, 2007.

Graham, Dr. Douglas N. *The 80/10/10 Diet.* Key Largo, FL: FoodnSport Press, 2006.

Klein, David. *Self Healing Colitis and Crohn's.* Sebastopol, CA: Colitis and Crohn's Health Recovery Center, 2006.

Marcus, Erik. *Vegan: The New Ethics of Eating.* Ithaca, NY: McBooks Press, 2001.

Ornish, Dean. *Dr. Ornish's Program for Reversing Heart Disease: The Only System Scientifically Proven to Reverse Heart Disease Without Drugs or Surgery.* New York, NY: Ivy Books, 1995.

Reinfeld, Mark, and Bo Rinaldi. *The Complete Idiot's Guide to Eating Raw.* Indianapolis, IN: Alpha Books, 2008.

————. *Vegan Fusion World Cuisine: Extraordinary Recipes and Timeless Wisdom from the Celebrated Blossoming Lotus Restaurants.* New York, NY: Beaufort Books, 2007.

Rinaldi, Bo. *The Complete Idiot's Guide to Green Smoothies.* Indianapolis, IN: Alpha Books, 2012.

Robbins, John. *Diet for a New America.* Tiburon, CA: HJ Kramer, 1987.

Organizations

American Dietetic Association

eatright.org

The American Dietetic Association (ADA) and the National Center for Nutrition and Dietetics provide nutrition information, resources, and access to registered dietitians. The website also provides a wealth of information on low-fat eating for heart health.

People for the Ethical Treatment of Animals

peta.org

People for the Ethical Treatment of Animals (PETA) is the largest animal rights organization in the world and is dedicated to establishing and protecting the rights of all animals.

Physicians Committee for Responsible Medicine

pcrm.org

The Physicians Committee for Responsible Medicine (PCRM) is a nonprofit organization that promotes preventive medicine, conducts clinical research, and encourages high standards for ethics and effectiveness in research. It promotes healthy living through low-fat, plant-based diets and regular exercise, as opposed to medications and surgery. Its website offers recipes, news, research, nutrition guides, and vegan/vegetarian starter kits.

The Vegan Society

vegansociety.com

The Vegan Society promotes ways of living free of animal products for the benefit of people, animals, and the environment.

The Vegetarian Resource Group

vrg.org

The Vegetarian Resource Group (VRG) is a nonprofit organization dedicated to educating the public on vegetarianism. VRG provides information on health, nutrition, ecology, ethics, and world hunger.

The Vegetarian Society
vegsoc.org
The Vegetarian Society is a registered charity committed to promoting the health, environmental, and animal-welfare benefits of a vegetarian diet.

The World Union of Vegetarian/Vegan Societies
ivu.org
The World Union of Vegetarian/Vegan Societies had been promoting vegetarianism worldwide since 1908.

Recipes

Compassionate Cooks
compassionatecooks.com
Compassionate Cooks offers vegetarian cooking classes, cooking videos, and recipes.

Vegan Fusion
veganfusion.com
My personal website offers monthly newsletters that include fresh, healthy recipes and focus on current events related to the plant-based lifestyle and veganism. Online and international classes are also available.

Vegan Meetup Groups
vegan.meetup.com
Meet up with other vegans in your town!

VegCooking
vegcooking.com
Hundreds of vegetarian and vegan recipes are featured on this website, with spotlights on vegetarian and vegan foods, products, menus, and restaurants.

VegSource
vegsource.com
This website features more than 10,000 vegetarian and vegan recipes, discussion boards, nutritionists, medical doctors, experts, authors, articles, a newsletter, and a vast vegetarian community.

VegWeb
vegweb.com
This vegetarian megasite offers recipes, photos, articles, an extensive online store, and much more.

Dining Out

Go Dairy Free
godairyfree.org
Go Dairy Free is a comprehensive website with information on how to cook, shop, and dine dairy free while still promoting a healthy lifestyle.

Happy Cow
happycow.net
Happy Cow is a wonderful, searchable guide to vegetarian and vegan dining, high-quality food stores, information on vegetarian nutrition, raw foods, and vegan recipes.

VegDining
vegdining.com
This vegetarian dining guide includes an international search option, a monthly veggie restaurant contest, and the opportunity to purchase a VegDining card for discounts at participating veggie restaurants.

Health and Nutrition

The Vegetarian Site
thevegetariansite.com
This website is an extensive online source for vegan and vegetarian living, providing health and nutrition info, animal-welfare info, vegetarian- and vegan-related news, and an online store.

VegFamily
vegfamily.com
This comprehensive resource supplies information on raising vegan children, including tips for pregnancy, vegan recipes, book reviews, product reviews, a message board, and more.

Doctors

Dr. McDougall's Health and Medical Center
drmcdougall.com
John A McDougall, MD, is a physician and nutrition expert who has been teaching better health through vegetarian cuisine for over 30 years. Dr. McDougall believes people should establish a proper diet and exercise regimen to look and feel great for a lifetime.

Michael Bluejay

michaelbluejay.com/veg/doctors.html

This website offers a comprehensive list of vegetarian doctors, who tend to be more sensitive to and less judgmental of the vegetarian lifestyle and its overwhelming benefits. The site is also a great place to learn more about the benefits of vegetarianism/veganism.

NutritionFacts.org

nutritionfacts.org

This comprehensive website, developed by Dr. Michael Greger, publishes the latest research on plant-based medicines and foods.

Prevent and Reverse Heart Disease

heartattackproof.com

This website is home base for Dr. Caldwell B. Esselstyn, an internationally known former surgeon, researcher, and clinician at the Cleveland Clinic. He is also the author of *Prevent and Reverse Heart Disease*, and is a leading proponent for the health benefits of a low-fat vegan diet.

Sustainable Health

vegandoctor.com.au

Dr. John Green is a vegan doctor who believes that peak energy and health are both possible through a vegan diet and proper nutrition further confirming the health benefits of a vegan diet.

T. Colin Campbell Foundation

tcolincampbell.org

T. Colin Campbell, celebrated author and China Study researcher, has established the T. Colin Campbell Foundation and its website as the definitive resource for a long, healthy, and strong life through a low-fat vegan lifestyle.

Juicers, Blenders, and Other Kitchen Devices

Cost Plus Juicers

costplusjuicers.com

This website carries more than juicers, including everything kitchen-related and a huge selection of books and articles.

Cutlery and More.com
cutleryandmore.com
A great "chopping" website full of useful tools for the kitchen, like knives, cutting boards, mandoline slicers, and no-cut gloves (which I highly recommend).

Discount Juicers.com
discountjuicers.com
This juicer website provides a great article about choosing your perfect juicer. A must-read before considering which type of juicer will best meet your needs. Discountjuicers.com is a massive distributor of raw and vegan food processing equipment, from dehydrators, to spiral slicers, to blenders.

Vitamix
vitamix.com
Find the latest Vitamix blenders on the official site, which even offers factory-reconditioned models that come with a seven-year warranty. For free shipping in the continental United States, enter code 06-002510.

Organic Vegan Products and Stores

Eco Products
ecoproducts.com
Eco Products is the premier site for biodegradable and compostable food service products and environmentally friendly household supplies.

Food Fight!
foodfightgrocery.com
Food Fight! grocery is an all-vegan convenience store located in Portland, Oregon. Its online market emphasizes vegan snack food, imports, and specialty items.

Green People
greenpeople.org
Green People provides a directory of eco-friendly products and services.

Live Superfoods
livesuperfoods.com
Live Superfoods has a great array of products for anyone interested in organic living and raw food creation.

Organic Spices

organicspices.com

This website is a clearinghouse for hard-to-find organic spices and organic spice mixes.

Natural Zing

naturalzing.com/catalog

This huge website offers tons of raw, organic, vegan products for sale at reasonable prices.

Pure Prescriptions Natural Health Solutions

pureprescriptions.com

Pure Prescriptions is an online superstore for high-quality nutritional products, complete with free consultations and a health library. This is the place for effective nutraceuticals.

The Raw Food World

rawfoodworld.com

The Raw Food World is the perfect place to find nearly any supplement, raw or transitional food, superfood powders like maqui berry and goji powders, or household gadget you could possibly find useful.

Sunfood

sunfood.com

David Wolfe's website provides the raw foodist with everything from food and supplements, to appliances, to books, to personals ads.

Media and Other Resources

Tasty and Meatless

tastyandmeatless.com

Tasty and Meatless is a weekly vegetarian television series on Time Warner Cable.

Veg TV

vegtv.com

The site for Veg TV video production company, it streams original content about vegetarian and vegan food, health, nutrition, and eco-travel.

Vegetarian Teen.com

vegetarianteen.com

This online magazine provides articles on the vegetarian teen lifestyle, activism, nutrition, social issues, and more.

VegNews

vegnews.com

This award-winning magazine focuses on a vegetarian lifestyle and features news, events, recipes, book reviews, the best veg products, travel tales, interviews, celebrity buzz, and more.

Wikipedia—List of Vegans

en.wikipedia.org/wiki/List_of_vegans

This is a list of vegans from around the world who eat an entirely plant-based diet. It's great for times when you feel alone in a world of unhealthy eaters.

Organic and Gardening Websites

International Federation of Organic Agriculture Movements

ifoam.org

International Federation of Organic Agriculture Movements (IFOAM) is the umbrella organization for hundreds of organic organizations worldwide.

Organic Consumers Association

organicconsumers.org

The Organic Consumers Association is an online, grassroots, nonprofit organization dealing with issues of food safety, industrial agriculture, genetic engineering, corporate accountability, and environmental sustainability.

Organic Trade Association

ota.com

The Organic Trade Association (OTA) website tells you anything you want to know about the term *organic*, from food to textiles to health-care products. The OTA's mission is to encourage global sustainability through the promotion, protection, and growth of the diverse organic trade.

Index

S

CHECK OUT THESE BEST-SELLERS

More than 450 titles available at booksellers and online retailers everywhere!

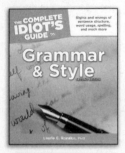

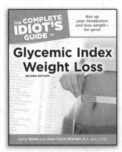
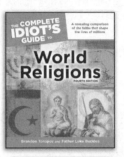

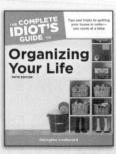

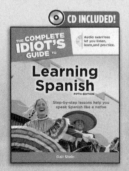

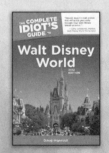